SMOKING
AND
POLITICS

REAL POLITICS IN AMERICA

Series Editor: Paul S. Herrnson, *University of Maryland*

The books in this series bridge the gap between academic scholarship and the popular demand for knowledge about politics. They illustrate empirically supported generalizations from the original research and academic literature using examples taken from the legislative process, executive branch decision making, court rulings, lobbying efforts, election campaigns, political movements, and other areas of American politics. The goal of the series is to convey the best contemporary political science research has to offer in ways that will engage individuals who want to know about real politics in America.

SMOKING
AND
POLITICS

Bureaucracy Centered Policymaking

SIXTH EDITION

A. Lee Fritschler
Catherine E. Rudder

School of Public Policy
George Mason University

PEARSON
Prentice
Hall

Upper Saddle River, New Jersey 07458

Library of Congress Cataloging-in-Publication Data

Fritschler, A. Lee.
  Smoking and politics : bureaucracy centered policymaking / A. Lee Fritschler,
Catherine E. Rudder. — 6th ed.
    p. cm. — (Real Politics in America)
  Includes index.
  ISBN-13: 978-0-13-179104-6
  ISBN-10: 0-13-179104-4
  1. Cigarettes—Labeling—Government policy—United States. 2. Advertising—Cigarettes—
United States. 3. Cigarettes—Labeling—Law and legislation—United States. 4. United States.
Federal Trade Commission.
  I. Rudder, Catherine E. II. Title. III. Series.
  HF6161.T6F75 2007
  659.19′679730973—dc22   2006010254

Editorial Director: Charlyce Jones Owen
Acquisitions Editor: Dickson Musslewhite
Editorial Assistant: Jennifer Murphy
Marketing Manager: Emily Cleary
Marketing Assistant: Jennifer Lang
Director of Production and Manufacturing:
  Barbara Kittle
Managing Editor (Production): Lisa
  Iarkowski
Production Liaison: Joe Scordato
Production Assistant: Marlene Gassler

Prepress and Manufacturing Manager: Nick
  Sklitsis
Prepress and Manufacturing Buyer: Mary
  Ann Gloriande
Cover Art Director: Jayne Conte
Cover Design: Kiwi Design
Cover Image: Jeff Greenberg
Composition/Full-Service Management:
  GGS Book Services/Chitra Ganesan
Printer/Binder: RR Donnelley & Sons, Inc.
Cover Printer: RR Donnelley & Sons, Inc.

This book was set in 10/12 Palatino
Real Politics in America
Series Editor: Paul S. Herrnson

Credits and acknowledgments borrowed from other sources and reproduced, with permission,
in this textbook appear on appropriate page within text.

Pearson Education LTD.
Pearson Education Singapore, Pte. Ltd
Pearson Education, Canada, Ltd
Pearson Education—Japan

Pearson Education Australia PTY, Limited
Pearson Education North Asia Ltd
Pearson Educacion de Mexico, S.A. de C.V.
Pearson Education Malaysia, Pte. Ltd

10 9 8 7 6 5 4 3 2 1
ISBN 0-13-179104-4

To Susan and Helen

CONTENTS

CHAPTER 4

THE LEGAL BASIS OF BUREAUCRACY CENTERED POLICYMAKING   45

CHAPTER 5

EFFECTIVE ENFORCEMENT AND STRATEGIES TO COMBAT IT: PROCEDURES USED IN ADMINISTRATIVE POLICYMAKING   59

CHAPTER 6

CONGRESSIONAL POWER AND AGENCY POLICYMAKING 80

CHAPTER 7

THE BUREAUCRACY, CONGRESS, AND THE PRESIDENT: BALANCING ACTS 99

CHAPTER 8

THE COURTS MOVE INTO THE SPOTLIGHT 117

PREFACE

The sixth edition of *Smoking and Politics* brings the extraordinary story of the smoking and health controversy up to date. It is as much an entirely new book as it is an updated edition. The subtitle, *Bureaucracy Centered Policymaking*, is an indication of the change.[1] We believe that it is impossible to understand the functioning of modern, democratic governments without recognizing the centrality of their bureaucracies in public policymaking. However, general treatments of U.S. government in American politics textbooks, as well as more advanced studies of policymaking in the United States, tend either to give short shrift to the fundamentals of policymaking within the bureaucracy or to omit it altogether.

One reason for this inattention may stem from the Constitution, which seems to overlook the possibility that bureaucracies may make policy. Another cause could be that bureaucracy centered policymaking is frequently complicated and administrative procedure can be intricate. Bureaucratic activity can seem dull and does not appear to warrant widespread media coverage.[2] Then, the technical complexity of modern society—a primary explanation for the ascendancy of agencies to power—ironically, may have discouraged students from concentrating on these important government functions. Except for aficionados, following the technical details of agency policymaking and the issues agencies tackle is hardly easy or compelling for most people. For example, the implications of accelerated depreciation accounting techniques for the electric power industry are tremendously important to both the industry and the public, but students of government

---

1. The subtitle was *Policy Making and the Federal Bureaucracy.*
2. James Mann, a longtime journalist for major U.S. papers, describes the important role of the bureaucracy in contemporary policymaking in a direct, attention-getting way. He writes that the public has been led to believe that policy is made by those who appear in the "Talk Show World" when in fact it is the bureaucracy, or the "Hidden World," that is driving policy arenas today. He writes, "It [the Hidden World] compromises bureaucracies and institutions through which the United States must operate day in and day out . . . Hidden World is by its very nature faceless, but also permanent. Administrations come and go; the big organizations remain." See "All the Bureaucracy's Men," *The Washington Post*, June 5, 2005, B1. While there are numerous studies of the bureaucracy, some particularly valuable readings for students interested in this subject are: H. George Frederickson , *The Spirit of Public Administration*, San Francisco: Jossey-Bass 1996; Charles T. Goddsell, *The Case for Bureaucracy: A Public Administration Polemic*, 4 th edition, Washington, DC: CA Press, 2003; Marissa Martino Golden, *What Motivates Bureaucrats?*, New York: Columbia University Press, 2000; James Q. Wilson, *Bureaucracy: What Government Agencies Do and Why They Do It*, Rev. Edition, New York: Basic Books, 2000.

should be forgiven if they find it difficult to give this complicated issue their concentrated attention.

With *Smoking and Politics*, we hope to put to rest the idea that bureaucratic policymaking is necessarily tedious or lacks much importance. To the contrary, public interests may be served by bureaucrats when other political actors are captured by a too narrow point of view or are held hostage by other forces representing only a slice of the American public. Sometimes public servants in the bureaucracy are deciding issues that can have life-and-death implications for an affected clientele. Government agencies offer an alternative venue to place issues on a government agenda, to shift the balance of forces on an issue, and to alter outcomes that have occurred or might occur in another government arena. Cast in this light, bureaucratic decision making is frequently exciting, an important element of political strategy, and potentially momentous in its results.

Not only do many people not realize the scope of the policymaking activities of the federal bureaucracy, they do not understand the procedures employed in making that policy and thus have little opportunity to participate meaningfully in bureaucratic policymaking. Instead, interest groups dominate the process, as they do the normal legislative process. Fortunately, however, not all interest groups are self-seeking economic ones, and consumer and public health groups may have a better chance to be heard in the bureaucracy than in the nation's elected assemblies. Certainly that has been the case in the saga of smoking and politics.

Because those who make policy in the bureaucracy are either civil servants or presidential appointees, the distance between the policy and the citizen can seem quite distant. Yet because bureaucrats must ultimately answer to all three branches of government—the courts, the president, and Congress—at different times and in different ways, they are far from free agents and ultimately accountable to the law as enacted by Congress, to the Constitution as interpreted by the courts, and to a considerable degree to the Office of the President through the chief executive's power of appointment and, for most, removal from office and presidential authority to review anticipated rules and regulations. Moreover, public participation in bureaucratic policymaking is explicitly required and prescribed under the Administrative Procedure Act. Nevertheless, the further away policy is made from the apparent reach of the voters, the more likely citizens are to feel, as Europeans sometimes do in the case of policy made by European Union institutions, a "democratic deficit." This neologism is applied to suggest that citizens do not feel that they have sufficient control over and say in their government. Surely the tobacco companies used this argument of representative alienation to good effect when fighting the decisions of the Federal Trade Commission (FTC) in the 1960s and the Food and Drug Administration (FDA) in the 1990s.

To prevent democratic lapses, perceived or real, successful oversight of the bureaucracy requires that the elected officials pay attention to what agencies are doing while avoiding micromanaging them. To perform its oversight role properly, Congress, for example, must order, read, and act on reports of the Government Accountability Office, a wholly congressional body, and those of the inspectors general within each agency.[3] Most difficult, members of Congress must be willing to review and act beyond their own parochial concerns, concerns usually dictated by their electoral coalition back home, by their campaign contributors, and by their future ambitions. Sadly, Congress can be more of the problem than the solution when it comes to effective governance. Too often, members seek to punish agencies that are trying to protect the public's health, as has been the case in the ongoing smoking and politics controversy, if those agencies interfere with jobs in their district and profits of companies with headquarters there.

For a half century, the medical community has known with an increasingly absolute certainty that cigarettes cause mortal injury to those who take up the habit. Since the 1950s, the steady drumbeat of bad medical news—from the diseases caused by smoking to the impact of secondhand smoke on nonsmokers to the highly addictive nature of the weed, akin to heroin—has crescendoed into a deafening noise that the public could not miss. That the cigarette corporations intentionally target children, teenagers, and members of vulnerable groups like minorities, women, and the poorly educated suggests an additional element of social injustice that cries out for attention. Now that the industry has transformed itself into a multinational enterprise, the focus of these corporations is on both developing countries and women, two potentially huge growth markets, fueled by population increases and a growing acceptability in traditional societies of smoking by women. The substantial damage caused by tobacco in the United States is almost entirely eclipsed by these current and future trends abroad, where almost half of all men and 12 percent of women smoke.

Under the circumstances, one might be compelled to ask whether our democratic institutions are failing to serve larger public interests whenever huge economic interests intrude. The brief answer is yes, but that response is highly misleading. We have developed democratic government because over time there is no better alternative. Occasionally, a nation might be lucky enough to have an enlightened autocrat to attend to the commons but not regularly. Nor would there be any guarantee that citizens would agree with the decisions of the dictator, enlightened or not. Leaders must gain legitimacy, and in the absence of the divine right of kings, there is no better source of that legitimacy than free, fair, regular, and competitive elections.

In short, there is no acceptable alternative to democracy, though our current system could stand for a number of improvements. Institutional and

---

3. Inspectors general have one foot in the bureaucracy and one in Congress by virtue of the inspectors general reporting mandate (to both the agency head and Congress), appointment process (by the president), term of office (explicit and not changeable by a disgruntled president), office location (within the agency), and budget (requested by the agency and appropriated by Congress).

electoral reform, however, is beyond the scope of this book. Instead, we seek to help the reader understand, on the one hand, why under our system of government tobacco is a legal and thriving industry despite the harms caused by using its products. On the other hand, we want to show how public interests are in fact attended to under our system of government, albeit incrementally and with abundant attention to powerful economic interests. Fighting for a public good frequently requires creating alliances across otherwise separated institutions, changing venues when the way is blocked, finding leaders in the right positions to help effect change and with an inner strength to push forward despite formidable obstacles, and having what sometimes seems like infinite patience. Indeed, some important progress has been made from the point of view of public health groups but surprisingly little given the devastation that smoking has caused and continues to cause.

Even though our focus is on bureaucracy, the story of smoking and politics takes us far beyond that single venue to Congress, the president, the courts, state governments and their attorneys general, and local governments. Personal injury attorneys not only interact with public officials but lead the charge against the tobacco industry on behalf of state governments. Nevertheless, our central purpose is to demonstrate the importance of agencies in public policymaking, to help the reader understand why they are important and how they operate, why they are an integral part of contemporary American democracy and modern democracies in general, and how they can work to attend to public interests, sometimes in concert with other parts of the government (including state governments) or with private entities like private plaintiffs' lawyers and sometimes alone.

Well-led agencies can bring attention to a public problem and can propose solutions. They can help set agendas. They enjoy a form of both legislative and judicial authority. And, as democratic theory would require, they can be and are checked by elected officials. We show how such actions actually occur in practice. We teach the reader the ways that agencies go about making policy and adjudicating complaints. Finally, our story takes us beyond the United States to other countries and another huge bureaucracy, the World Health Organization, and provides a glimpse into international policymaking and the creation of the world's first public health treaty, the awkwardly named Framework Convention for Tobacco Control, that took effect in 2005, but without U.S. ratification.

One aspect of the smoking and politics story may strike the reader: Why does the FTC raise its head in the 1960s and is hardly seen in the controversy two decades later? Why did not the FDA act much earlier and instead wait until the 1990s to get into the fight? What happened to the health advocates in Congress after the 1994 election and especially since 2000? The explicit and implicit answers to these questions can be found herein. For now, suffice it to say that serendipity, the unpredictability of the emergence of leaders in the cause of public health, opportunity for action, and elections all have a part in the explanation.

We complete this study with an enhanced respect for the men and women who have given their lives to serve the public in government agencies. The word "bureaucrat" has a most positive connotation for us. Despite popular belief, a bureaucrat need not be inflexible, inattentive to citizens, or clock-watchers. Instead, the bureaucrat is someone who is committed to the public interest, to fair play, and to vigorous public service without favor or bias. Bureaucrats provide the expertise, the continuity of service, the institutional memory, and the commitment to serving everyone, not just the powerful, that are indispensable in complex, modern democracies. Without the bureaucracy and bureaucratic policymaking, public interests would be considerably less well served.

ACKNOWLEDGMENTS

The School of Public Policy at George Mason University is a wonderful place to teach and write. Our Dean Kingsley E. Haynes and Senior Associate Dean James H. Finkelstein have been supportive throughout this project. Our faculty colleagues, Susan J. Tolchin and James Pfiffner, have advised and led us to ideas that we would not have found without their guidance. Thys van Schaik and Desmond Dinan, our suite mates, have provided good-natured encouragement along the way.

We are grateful to Professor James M. Hoefler of Dickinson College who coauthored the fifth edition of the book. He will recognize his words and wisdom in several places in the text. A group of talented graduate students enrolled in the doctoral program in the School of Public Policy at George Mason contributed to the manuscript in numerous ways. Paul F. Weissburg was our principal research assistant. He helped with some of the original research and made several fine editorial contributions. Nicola A. V. Virgill, Phillip W. Magness, and Kanishka S. Balasuriya brought order to footnote chaos and helped merge new materials with the text of the fifth edition and assisted in ferreting out information in a number of areas. James Lawrence did much of the research and writing of the first draft of our new chapter on the courts. Joel Yohalem, retired attorney and active friend, helped us understand some of the court decisions. James A. Thurber of American University has provided sage advice over the years, and Cornelius M. Kerwin, now acting president of American, helped guide us through some of the mysteries of rule-making processes.

We owe a special debt of gratitude to Series Editor Paul S. Herrnson for his supervision and assistance throughout this project.

Our partners, Susan T. Fritschler and Helen C. Gibson, were active contributors and commentators. We are deeply grateful for their support and dedicate this book to them. Alas, none of these folks can be held responsible for any mistakes in fact or interpretation that might have found their way into the book. We take exclusive ownership of those shortcomings.

Over the years, *Smoking and Politics* has been used in a variety of academic settings, from introductory courses on American government to intermediate-level courses on public policy, public administration, and administrative law. Students in graduate-level seminars on policymaking, public law, business–government relations, science and government, and public ethics have also found the book useful. We hope they continue to find this book instructive. We look forward to hearing from many of them as they consider what we have written.

A. Lee Fritschler and Catherine E. Rudder
School of Public Policy, George Mason University
Arlington, Virginia

ABOUT THE AUTHORS

A. Lee Fritschler is Professor, School of Public Policy, George Mason University. He was Vice-President of the Brookings Institution, Assistant Secretary for Post Secondary Education in the Clinton Administration and President of Dickinson College. He holds an undergraduate degree from Union College and a doctorate from the Maxwell School of Syracuse University.

Catherine E. Rudder is Professor and Associate Dean for Academic Affairs of the School of Public Policy, George Mason University. She was Executive Director of the American Political Science Association and Chief of Staff for Congressman Wyche Fowler, Jr., of Georgia. She is a member and Senator of Phi Beta Kappa. She earned her undergraduate degree at Emory University and her doctorate in political science at Ohio State University.

1

INTRODUCTION TO POLICYMAKING
IN THE BUREAUCRACY

Tobacco is a dirty weed.
I like it.
It satisfies no normal need.
I like it.
It makes you thin, it makes you lean.
It takes the hair right off your bean.
It's the worse darn thing I've ever seen.
I like it.

—"Unrepentant," by G. L. Hemminger

Traditionally, students of American national government have been taught that policy is made in Congress, by the president, and perhaps by the federal courts. That view has been confirmed and steadily reinforced by nearly all American government textbooks. The role of government agencies, it is said, is to implement policy and not to create it. More recent expositions acknowledge that implementation of laws may entail policymaking at the margins, and the sharp distinction between making and administering policy is recognized as having been overblown. However, the degree of bureaucratic policymaking is typically understated. The ways bureaucracies actually make policy are similarly neglected.[1]

Contemporary policymaking in the United States is far more complex, confusing, and different from the apparent prescriptions of the Constitution, where the policymaking role of the bureaucracy, as opposed to that of the president, is not anticipated. Democracies have come to rely on bureaucracies to make policy decisions that in less complicated times were made predominantly by elected executives, legislators, and, more controversially, judges. Bureaucracies have moved to the center of the policymaking process. Elected officials often find themselves *reacting to* more than *acting to shape* policy developments occurring within the permanent bureaucracy. As the number of policy issues multiplies and becomes intricately intertwined, officials increasingly

1

are dependent on decisions made by administrative agencies.[2] Confirming this shift are interest groups and journalists who have found it necessary to expand their activities to include nonlegislative institutions in order to be effective in their roles of influencing and covering government policymaking.

Once Congress passes a law authorizing and outlining a new policy, the agency responsible for implementing that policy determines how the law is to be *interpreted* as well as *implemented*. Subsequent policy is then formed through the steady accumulation of small (and sometimes large) changes in program implementation. Even when Congress uses ambiguous legislative language in its delegation of power to the bureaucracy, the courts have consistently ruled that deputation to agencies is intentional and legal. This delegated power of bureaucracies creates major challenges to political accountability and for democratic processes. Keeping the strictures and the spirit of the Constitution alive is a growing challenge in the modern state, a matter addressed explicitly and implicitly throughout this book.

The tools bureaucrats use in policymaking are numerous and range from informal to formal and traditional. Often policy change begins with a discussion among subject-matter professionals deep within the bureaucracy. For example, these experts have an idea: Policy X should be changed in the following ways. They develop the idea and then discuss it with the political leadership in the agency, assistant or deputy secretaries, or the secretary of the department. They or their superiors, in turn, are likely to raise the matter with the White House staff and perhaps the president if the issue is deemed to be of sufficient political importance. If there is agreement to move ahead, a decision is made on how best to proceed. Could the proposal be implemented through an executive order, which is issued by the president, would it be possible to utilize the rule-making powers of the bureaucracy, or is legislation needed? All of these avenues are examined. Often, the rule-making function of the bureaucracy is found to be the most expedient and appropriate choice.

There are many areas of public policy in which the bureaucracy has been the central operator. Two particularly striking examples are telecommunications and agricultural policies. Telecommunications policymaking was delegated to an administrative agency in 1934. Despite enormous changes in this field, Congress enacted no further significant legislation in that area until the mid-1990s. All the policy developed to deal with new and changing telecommunications, including television and wireless, were created and implemented without benefit of legislation. (With the collapse of the natural monopoly of AT&T, the courts, not Congress, after sixty years of permitting the agency to create policies on its own, finally forced the deregulation of the industry in 1982.) Similarly, agricultural policy initiated by Congress in the 1930s was left virtually untouched by the legislative hand for fifty years. Policies created during the Great Depression reflected the problems of an economy quite different from today's. Nonetheless, the development and adaptation of programs to fit the radically changed agricultural environment were left to a large degree to administrative agencies.[3]

THE SURPRISING REACH OF ADMINISTRATIVE POLICYMAKING

Recognizing the inherent limitations of writing practicable legislation and the difficulty of anticipating difficulties and new conditions that might arise in implementing legislation, Congress has increasingly left it to the agencies to initiate policies and promulgate rules and regulations to implement the broad programs created by legislation. The power that agencies have been delegated over the past several decades has made them an important force in the public policy process; some knowledgeable observers have even called them a fourth branch of government. Agency regulations have the effect of law—no different from the end product of the congressional legislative process or the decisions of courts of law—and the volume of these rules is much larger than laws. In fact, agency policy, made in the form of rules, regulations, and interpretations of the way a law is to be applied, accounts for most of the policy output of government today. The legislative output by administrative agencies of policies that directly affect and govern people and property may be thirty times greater than the number of laws passed by Congress itself, according to a leading scholar of administrative rule making.[4]

The reason for this fecundity stems from several sources. Over the years, Congress has found it necessary to grant or delegate policymaking powers to administrative agencies in part because insurmountable obstacles face Congress in writing legislation with sufficient detail and foresight to meet all the situations that might arise under that legislation. Frequently, Congress gives only the sketchiest guidelines to the bureaucracy, often requiring an agency to run a program in "the public interest" or in "the public interest, convenience, and necessity." These guidelines give agencies considerable freedom in administrative rule making.

A second, related explanation comes from the often highly technical nature of the subject matter under the purview of policymakers today that requires expertise that can be found in the bureaucracy. Giandomenico Majone provides a third, important reason. In policy space, which he visualizes as all current policies contained in one space bumping up against one another, a change in one policy increasingly impinges on many other policies, again requiring adjustments in those policies.[5] An example is the Medicare legislation providing prescription drug coverage for all participating recipients over sixty-five years of age. This program is paid for entirely by the federal government. Another program, Medicaid, had already been providing such coverage for the poor elderly, but the cost of Medicaid, unlike Medicare, is jointly shared between the federal government and the states. The immediate question in a budget-conscious world was one of whether the states should "pay back" the federal government the amount of money equivalent to that which the states had been spending for prescription drugs for the poor elderly and which they no longer needed to expend because the feds would be picking up the tab. Not surprisingly, the feds have pushed for reimbursement or, as it is sometimes called, "a clawback"—under the directive of agency rules. The budgetary impact on the states is huge in most cases, but the battle is being fought first in the bureaucracy and not in Congress, though Congress may be drawn into the battle to resolve the matter.[6]

Agencies are fully capable of adopting regulations under delegated authority that Congress itself might not have adopted. Again, such action is understandable from the point of view of those who desire a change in existing policy. Sometimes strong lobbies prevent elected members of legislatures from responding to public demands or to public interests as interpreted by a particular agency. For example, while Congress was struggling to strengthen gun control legislation in the wake of the murder of Senator Robert F. Kennedy, the Post Office Department used its delegated authority to discourage the shipment of all guns through the mails. The National Rifle Association had succeeded for years in keeping Congress inactive, but it was taken by surprise by the swift action of the postmaster general.

A shift in venue—in this case from Congress to the bureaucracy—is a common tactic in the pantheon of American pluralism. When their way is blocked in one venue, politicians and interest groups try to maneuver having their concerns considered in another venue. When Congress will not act or when it does but in an undesirable direction from the perspective of the losers, the rule-making process offers one alternative route and the courts another. Presidents, facing opposition or inaction on an issue, frequently avail themselves of their nonlegislative policymaking powers by issuing executive orders, encouraging and approving new agency regulations, or bringing issues to the federal courts.[7]

When the courts, like agencies, act to create seemingly new policy, Congress's legislative prerogatives are not necessarily undercut, as it must have created the basis in law for the decision in the first place. In addition, if a legislative majority does not agree with the court's interpretation of a law, a subsequent enactment, presuming it is constitutional, by Congress can overturn the court's action. Equally, Congress can overturn bureaucratic policymaking. The rub, of course, is that creating a legislative majority in normal times is mightily more difficult than blocking proposed legislation.

The point here is that when one of the branches of government does not act in a situation of perceived need to create new policy, other parts of the policymaking system are frequently activated. In the health and smoking arena, the surgeon general sounded the alarm bell in 1964 and every year thereafter on the dangers of tobacco use. Action by Congress to protect the public's health was highly unlikely given the array of tobacco forces there. If action were to occur, it would have to come not only outside Congress but outside the entire tobacco subsystem, and it did thanks to the seriousness with which the professional staff and appointed commissioners of the Federal Trade Commission (FTC) took their mandate to prevent deceptive advertising. Using its congressionally delegated power, the FTC intruded itself into the tobacco issue and proposed a rule requiring a health warning. Because the FTC existed outside the orbit of tobacco interests, it had no brief to protect them. The issuance of a requirement that there be a health warning in cigarette advertising and on packages was example of an administrative agency propelling change in the face of anticipated congressional inaction. Later, the FTC was to feel the full wrath of congressional disapproval, as congressional members of the pro-tobacco coalition greatly resented the FTC's intrusion into their bailiwick.

Clearly, Congress, under the thumb of tobacco interests, would not have done what the commission did. Nevertheless, the FTC's action forced the issue onto the congressional agenda, and the reluctant Congress subsequently acted. It legislated first half and then the entire FTC ruling. In that legislation, there was a severe rebuke that removed some of the FTC's power temporarily. Congress seemed to have tossed in the reproach for good measure. It was a demonstration of *ultimate* power as spelled out in the Constitution just in case anyone forgot where final authority to legislate really lies. But the fact of the matter is that the agency led Congress to the change by defining the issue, expanding the scope of conflict, and making the first move. It is only fair to note, however, that Congress eventually acted favorably on the issue, from the standpoint of the health advocates, only after the cigarette companies realized that a health warning might provide protective covering for them should a smoker decide to bring a personal injury lawsuit against one of them for manufacturing a product that damaged that person's health. In this determination, the corporations proved prescient.

SMOKING AND HEALTH: HOW AN ISSUE MUTATES OVER TIME

The labeling issue, however, constituted only one battle in the long and continuing war over regulation of tobacco use. Overall, the smoking and health issue demonstrates the twists and turns that can characterize issues with a long half-life: shifting venues within the bureaucracy and the federal government and then across levels of government, the reframing of issues to give them new life, the alliances between individuals and groups in different parts of the government and the larger policy system, the expansion of the perception of a problem, and the mobilization of advocates beyond national borders. Having begun as a scientific finding, the link between smoking and reduced longevity was for many years viewed as an unfortunate outcome of smoking, which was seen as an individual choice. Other than, perhaps, issuing a warning from the surgeon general, government action to proscribe or discourage smoking did not sit easily with an American culture that deemed individuals free to act as long as such action did not hurt other people. When Washington moved to limit cigarette consumption, it was ridiculed by many as attempting to become the "national nanny."[8] That attitude, however, began to undergo a transformation less charitable to the freedom to smoke, if not to smokers.

What changed? New scientific findings, reinforced by numerous subsequent studies, asserted that cigarette smokers were inflicting harm on others when nonsmokers breathed smokers' cigarette smoke. Children were found to be especially at risk, as were those, such as flight attendants, office workers, restaurant patrons, and waitstaff, trapped in enclosed spaces with smokers. Health policy entrepreneurs were quick to exploit the possibilities laid open by the scientific findings.

The phenomenon of secondhand smoke changed the ethical dimension of the smoking controversy. Once a matter of individual choice, smoking came to be an aggressive act infringing on the rights of innocent people to healthy air. This shift from free choice of individuals to a matter of the commons or a public good was furthered by another development: the rapidly escalating cost of health care.[9] To the degree that such costs were seen as borne by the society at large rather than by the individuals who chose to smoke, the nature of the issue changed dramatically. These changes in the definition of the issue expanded the scope of conflict and significantly increased the numbers of people who saw their interests and society's interests at stake.[10] It also shifted the fortunes of plaintiffs filing against tobacco companies in court.

Yet another factor helped move the issue away from individual choice. Evidence was uncovered in 1994 that the tobacco companies were well aware of the highly addictive nature of nicotine—a fact to which Surgeon General C. Everett Koop had alerted the public years earlier—and had for decades been perfecting methods to manipulate nicotine levels in cigarettes to addict smokers. Confidential papers stolen from Brown and Williamson Tobacco Company and a few key informants not only confirmed this information but also showed that the corporations were intentionally targeting minors. "Addiction is not freedom," asserted Dr. David Kessler, the anti-smoking commissioner of the Food and Drug Administration (FDA). Instead, he said, what we have is a man made "pediatric epidemic" entirely controllable if the political will to do so existed.[11] This shift in the issue was afforded by the power of information and its effective use by health policy entrepreneurs, a central feature of modern politics and a theme in this case study.

Consider this highly abbreviated policy history of the smoking issue. For well over a century, scientists have known that cigarette smoking is a danger to health. It took more than half a century, however, for the evidence to amass and the issue to transition from the laboratories of science to the halls of government. The matter was studied by the surgeon general and a regulatory agency, the Federal Trade Commission (FTC). A policy was then developed and put in place and implemented by that same agency under its authority afforded by an implied delegation of responsibility from Congress. Subsequently, Congress and the president caught up with the agencies' actions and briefly regained control by limiting the FTC's policymaking power in this area for four years. The courts then weighed in to extend the work begun by the agencies and amended by political leadership by upholding Congress's ultimate authority. Two and a half decades later, state attorneys general, led by the innovative chief counsel for the State of Mississippi, Michael Moore, demonstrated state interests in the sale of cigarettes to their citizens. At the same time, the FDA, like Rip van Winkle, emerged from its somnolence on the smoking issue and boldly asserted regulatory authority over tobacco use and its sale to minors. Private plaintiffs' or personal injury lawyers representing smokers mortally wounded by their smoking habits were working closely with the state attorneys general and sharing information with the FDA and friendly members of Congress. Through their efforts, the attorneys general and their allies among the personal injury lawyers made *de facto* national policy, a remarkable fact little commented on.[12] Concurrently, as tobacco became a global enterprise, transnational policy networks had entered the scene and were making the cigarette and health issue one of international importance.

It took nearly a half century, but a major change has occurred in society, if not in law: today, for the first time in history, *former* smokers outnumber *current* smokers in America. Whether a parallel outcome will occur internationally is yet to be determined.

DILUTED RESPONSE TO THE IMPACT OF SMOKING: WHY?

From the perspective of public health officials and health-focused interest groups, progress has been made but not nearly enough. They see smoking as the largest cause of death from a single, identifiable and controllable source. That source—cigarettes and other such tobacco products—is a legal product available in the marketplace with only a few restrictions. Although the number of smokers in the United States has been cut in half since cigarette health warning labels appeared in the 1960s, more than 1,200 people still die of smoking-related diseases daily in the United States. It is remarkable that this issue fades into the background at any time. One would think it would never weaken given the large death rate attributable to smoking.

The numbers who die each day in the United States alone is the equivalent of three fully booked jumbo jets crashing each day of the year without a single survivor. On a global basis, a similar number is twenty-five jumbos crashing each day.[13] In the aviation industry, that would be an unspeakable catastrophe. If an aircraft tragedy of such proportions were actually to happen, public attention would be riveted on the issue and immediate change demanded. That level of awareness and those sorts of demands for change have not occurred in the cigarette and health arena. Such is the force of visible, concentrated disasters that attract media attention and that befall innocent people who have every right to expect safe transport.

Unlike victims of airline crashes, however, smokers and users of smokeless tobacco become ill and die one by one. The distance between cause—picking up that first cigarette—and effect—sickness and dying—is great, usually decades apart. Importantly, smokers are portrayed as implicated in their own tragedy. That this last aspect—that smokers have a hand in their demise—is relevant is a characteristic of American culture. Policy, for example, to address poverty in the United States has historically been predicated more on who "deserves" help than on who simply needs it.[14] As a result, war widows and children whose destitution is beyond their own control stand first in line for deserving aid. In contrast, European public policy offers a much broader social safety net for everyone in need. In the case of cigarette use in the United States, smokers, having been informed of the health consequences, are seen to have chosen to smoke.

However, empirical medical and social science research and its widespread dissemination have demonstrated that this apparent choice is typically made not by adults but by minors, manipulated by the manufacturers' marketing and advertising. Smokers remain addicted in large part because those companies adjust nicotine levels to ensure continued addiction. Even so, the predominant attitude in the United States is that smokers choose to smoke.

However smoking is viewed, its consequences are disastrous. The Centers for Disease Prevention and Control (CDC), the U.S. government agency responsible for tracking and finding ways to ameliorate diseases that threaten public health, summed up the depth and breadth of the cigarette smoking threat in the following succinct and alarming sentence:

> Each year in the United States, approximately 440,000 persons die of cigarette smoking-attributable illness, resulting in 5.6 million years of potential life lost, $75 billion in direct medical costs, and $82 billion in lost productivity.[15]

Deciding who is to blame and who should suffer the consequences is a central feature not only of the smoking issue but of public policymaking in general.[16]

BUREAUCRACY CENTERED POLICYMAKING

As a matter of public policy formation, the smoking and health issue follows the paths laid out by John W. Kingdon in his widely read work *Agendas, Alternatives, and Public Policies*. He writes that policymaking is best understood as a set of roughly four processes:

(1) Setting the agenda
(2) Specifying alternatives from which a choice is to be made
(3) Choosing by an authority among those specified alternatives, as in a legislative vote or a presidential decision
(4) Implementing the decision[17]

Although Kingdon's third step should be amended by including the rule-making powers of the bureaucracy as a central component in decision making, his process definitions are useful tools for analysis. The process is dynamic. Policy agendas often shift from one venue to another, and issues expand to include more participants and more arenas—some of them quite unexpected by those who have watched an issue from the beginning. This dynamism is borne out by the history of smoking as a public health issue.

Not only do policies pertaining to tobacco use illustrate the key elements of policymaking, but the original cigarette and health controversy was a harbinger of things to come in the broader policymaking environment. The debate was one of the first major events in a movement that made consumerism an important political force.[18] Furthermore, the methods used by health advocates were for a time employed first by well-organized, highly skilled groups representing consumer interests. Citizen advocates at all levels of government discovered that change can be brought about by participating in the processes agencies follow to write rules. The use of agency powers has been a cornerstone of the success of these groups.

Other kinds of interest groups, especially business and free-market advocates, have come to understand and use these levers of power as well, overpowering consumer groups and those focusing on broader public interests. This development is again well illustrated by the rule making emanating from the 2003 Medicare legislation to extend a drug benefit to the elderly and disabled. Billions of dollars were in the offing with each adjustment to the rules, fueling what one reporter called an "explosive growth" in lobbying by the health care industry and crowding out other interests. "To keep track of the new rules and to decipher their meaning is a full-time job for hundreds of lawyers and lobbyists, who regularly seek changes advantageous to their clients," the *Washington Post* reported.[19] Similarly, when the FDA decided to assert regulatory authority over tobacco marketing and use, health interests were far outnumbered among the hundreds of thousands of comments responding to FDA's proposed rule. Frequently, then, lobbying aimed at bureaucratic decisions is as intense as that experienced by Congress, and it is less likely to be dominated by consumer interests than it was at the start of the smoking and health controversy.

In the case of tobacco, savvy political actors have understood the importance of bureaucracy centered policymaking from the beginning. Health advocates, facing a brick wall in Congress, took advantage of the multiple points of access characteristic of American politics. They looked to the bureaucracy to educate the public on the harms of smoking and to make policy reining in the practices of the tobacco corporations. The companies, in turn, continued to work through Congress to limit the actions of the agencies but also quickly recognized that exclusive reliance on the legislative branch to achieve their policy goals would be a mistake. Unfortunately for the tobacco interests, while they could use their congressional influence to constrain agencies' regulation of their product, they could not alter the steady drumbeat of damaging research findings funded by the federal government and disseminated by the surgeon general and the CDC year after year. Nevertheless, in the United States, the tobacco industry has managed to forestall much regulation of their products, maintain a price support system for tobacco farmers until 2005, and keep their products legal. This merchandise, when used as directed, injures and kills its customers and those nearby. How is it possible that such products remain legal and scarcely regulated?

NOTES

1. In a detailed study of eighteen American government textbooks, Cigler and Neiswender found that only 2 to 7 percent of the content of the textbooks focused on bureaucracy. Further, when they did, bureaucracy was not linked directly with policymaking. In only three of the eighteen texts were there linkages to "bureaucracy and discretion," only a small hint of the policy role bureaucracies now play. The most popular topics found in the texts under the subject of bureaucracy were "control," "oversight," "size," and "red tape." See Beverly A. Cigler and Heidi L. Neiswender, "'Bureaucracy' in the Introductory American Government Textbook," *Public Administration Review* 51, no. 5 (1991): 442–50. A separate project, the Institution of American Democracy, has produced five volumes on the central institutions of U.S. government, including one particularly impressive book on the executive branch, featuring essays by leading scholars in the field. The policymaking powers of government agencies, however, are hardly mentioned. See Joel D. Aberbach and Mark A. Peterson, eds., *The Executive Branch* (Oxford: Oxford University Press, 2005).
2. For a particularly helpful discussion of the concept of policy space, see Giandomenico Majone, *Evidence, Argument, and Persuasion in the Policy Process* (New Haven, Conn.: Yale University Press, 1989).
3. See Wayne D. Rasmussen, "The New Deal Farm Programs: What They Were and Why They Survived" (in Invited Papers Sessions; New Deal Farm Legislation after Fifty Years and Lessons for the Future), *American Journal of Agricultural Economics* 65, no. 5 (1983): 1158–62.
4. See Cornelius M. Kerwin, *Rulemaking: How Government Agencies Write Law and Make Policy*, 3rd ed. (Washington, D.C.: CQ Press, 2003), esp. chap. 1.
5. Majone, *Evidence, Argument, and Persuasion in the Policy Process*, 158–61. For an example of complex policy space, see Robert Pear, "Under New Medicare Prescription Drug Plan, Food Stamps May Be Reduced," *The New York Times*, May 8, 2005.
6. Andy Schneider, *The 'Clawback:' State Financing of Medicare Drug Coverage*, Kaiser Commission on Medicaid and the Uninsured, Henry J. Kaiser Family Foundation, June 2004.
7. The attempt to integrate labor unions in the late 1960s and the early 1970s provides a celebrated case of using the courts to effect change. Because forced desegregation was widely opposed by southern Democrats and by many of the labor unions themselves, the pressure applied by these two powerful interest groups left Congress deadlocked. The courts, however, were able to force unions to integrate. Just as the Supreme Court had ordered desegregation of the schools in 1954, the courts pressed labor unions to reform. As one study reported, "[J]udges rewrote key civil rights statutes, oversaw the implementation of their rulings, and used attorneys' fees and damage awards to impose significant financial costs on resistant unions" (Paul Frymer, "Acting When Elected Officials Won't: Federal Courts and Civil Rights Enforcement in U.S. Labor Unions, 1935–85," *American Political Science Review* 97, no. 3 [August 2003]: 483–99). President Richard Nixon's Justice Department then moved to enforce the rulings of the courts. For the courts to act, of course, the judges needed a ground—constitutional or statutory—on which to base their decisions.
8. Political parties were unlikely to take up this issue. If any regulation were likely, it would come from the party historically more likely to favor regulation of business, the Democratic Party. During most of the second half of the twentieth century, however, both Congress and the tobacco states were largely in the hands of Democrats. Smoking regulation would have been inimical to their interests. Presumably, the Republicans would have opposed such legislation on philosophical grounds.

9. There is a policy analogy on this point with the motorcycle helmet requirement laws. Cyclists object to this requirement on the basis that it is their life that is at risk and therefore the state should not interfere. However, there are health care costs associated with helmet-less riders who are involved in collisions just as there are with individual smokers. But when the secondhand smoke revelations were made, smoking policy took a different turn. Science demonstrated that one person's cigarette could affect another's health. Smoking became an issue that clearly affected the "common good," and the policy debate changed accordingly. For a useful discussion of the commons in the context of public policy, see Deborah A. Stone, *Policy Paradox: The Art of Political Decision Making*, rev. ed. (New York: Norton, 2002).

10. For the original exposition of this idea, see E. E. Schattschneider, *The Semisovereign People: A Realist's View of Democracy in America*, Seymour Martin Lipset Collection (New York: Holt, Rinehart and Winston, 1960).

11. David A. Kessler, *A Question of Intent: A Great American Battle with a Deadly Industry* (New York: Public Affairs, 2001), 291, 320.

12. For an enlightening exception, see Rorie L. Spill, Michael J. Licari, and Leonard Ray, "Taking on Tobacco: Policy Entrepreneurship and the Tobacco Litigation," *Political Research Quarterly* 54, no. 3 (2001): pp. 605–622.

13. This comparison has been made by several people. For a number of provoking insights into the cigarette industry, see Tara Parker-Pope, *Cigarettes: Anatomy of an Industry from Seed to Smoke* (New York: New Press, 2001; distributed by W. W. Norton & Co.).

14. See Theda Skocpol, *Protecting Soldiers and Mothers: The Political Origins of Social Policy in the United States* (Cambridge, Mass.: Belknap Press of Harvard University Press, 1992), and Gwendolyn Mink, *The Wages of Motherhood: Inequality in the Welfare State, 1917–1942* (Ithaca, N.Y.: Cornell University Press, 1995).

15. *Morbidity and Mortality Weekly Report* 52 (35, September 5, 2003): 842–44.

16. See comments on "Problems" (part 3) in Stone, *Policy Paradox*.

17. John W. Kingdon, *Agendas, Alternatives, and Public Policies*, 2nd ed. (New York: HarperCollins College Publishers, 1995), 2, 3.

18. For an excellent book on the shift of fundamental political attitudes giving impetus to the shifts in public policy beginning early in the twentieth century, see David Von Drehle, *Triangle: The Fire That Changed America* (New York: Atlantic Monthly Press, 2003).

19. Robert Pear, "Medicare Law Prompts a Rush for Lobbyists," *The New York Times*, August 23, 2005, A1.

2

THE GRIP OF TOBACCO INTERESTS ON POLICYMAKING

You ask me what we need to win this war. I answer tobacco as much as bullets.

—WORLD WAR I GENERAL JOHN J. PERSHING, U.S. ARMY

Tobacco has a long and colorful history. Cigarettes have a shorter history. And the idea that smoking cigarettes could cause major health problems has an even shorter history. Still, it took more than fifty years from the point when scientists first presented credible evidence that smoking was a health hazard to the time when the issue was placed into play in the policymaking arena. The issue resided in that policy warehouse—gathering interest within the policy community as scientific evidence grew and as smokers got sick and died—for all those years before it was rolled out into the policy world for attention.

Long in use by Native Americans, tobacco was subsequently made known to the larger world when a Frenchman, Jean Nicot, introduced the indigenous American plant to Europe four centuries ago. Nicot, the French ambassador to Portugal, wrote to a friend in 1560 that an American herb he had acquired had marvelous curative powers. Soon after, consumption of tobacco spread, and Nicot earned a place for himself in history. His name became the base for the scientific term for tobacco, nicotiana.

Not long after Nicot discovered the pleasures of smoking, skepticism of the marvelous curative powers of tobacco began to develop. Some condemned smoking as a foul, smelly habit that rendered social intercourse distasteful. More serious criticism developed in the 1850s when scientific evidence began to appear that supported the skeptics who questioned the medicinal value of cigarettes.

A British medical journal, *The Lancet*, published an article on March 14, 1857, that proved to have an element of timelessness about it. The scientists' indictment, which could well be the same today, read,

> Tobacco is said to act on the mind by producing inactivity thereof; inability
> to think, drowsiness; irritability . . . on the respiratory organs, it acts by
> causing consumption, haemoptysis, and inflammatory condition of the
> mucous membrane of the larynx, trachea, and bronchae, ulceration of the
> larynx, short irritable cough; hurried breathing. The circulating organs
> are affected by irritable heart circulation.[1]

These alarming charges against smoking received little public notice. The
worlds of science and government in those days were largely separate. Using
scientific discoveries as the basis for public policy was not yet common, nor
was national government as pervasive in people's everyday lives.[2]

There were relatively few smokers and chewers of tobacco in those days.
The medical or scientific disclosures were not received as a threat to the
larger public. During the nineteenth century, smoking was neither easy nor
feminine because one had to roll one's own or smoke a pipe or cigar. Not
until the introduction of the factory-rolled cigarette and the advertising that
accompanied it in the early 1900s were these barriers removed and did
cigarette smoking became both fashionable and more frequent in Europe
and in the Americas.

Spurred by advertising, which made smoking seem like good sense (and
even healthful), sales of cigarettes soared. Per capita annual consumption of
cigarettes for people over eighteen years old grew from forty-nine cigarettes
in 1900 to a high of 4,345 by 1963. This figure amounted to more than eleven
cigarettes per day for every American over the age of eighteen.[3]

THE PROHIBITION ERA: A SHORT-LIVED, STATE-LEVEL PHENOMENON

Smoking was not always legal or considered socially acceptable, however, in
all parts of the United States or Europe. By 1890, small groups of social
reformers had convinced legislators in twenty-six states to enact laws prohibiting the sale of cigarettes to minors. Then, when medical research began
to suggest a positive relationship between illness and smoking early in the
1900s, the puritanical movement against adult cigarette smoking moved
toward the center of the political arena in a number of states in the United
States. In concert with alcohol prohibitionists of the same era, an Anti-
Cigarette League formed and was becoming more organized and effective in
pushing for statewide bans on the sale of cigarettes to residents of all ages.
By 1909, fifteen states had done just that. Meanwhile, excise taxes were
raised high enough in two other states—Tennessee and West Virginia—that
Prohibition was the indirect result.

The successes of these grassroots prohibitionists were short lived. By
1918, cigarettes had become identified with the war effort as a symbol

of courage and dignity. Citizens' groups organized to send cigarettes to soldiers, and General John J. Pershing was quoted as saying, "You ask me what we need to win this war. I answer tobacco as much as bullets."[4]

Manufacturers and merchants organized to repeal existing prohibitions during the 1920s as the temperance movement declined and the political emancipation of women made smoking more socially acceptable for them. These developments spelled doom for the anti-cigarette movement, and by 1930 every single prohibitionist law enacted in the preceding decades had been repealed. Those interested in advancing the cause of cigarette smoking, including tobacco growers, cigarette manufacturers, retailers, advertisers, and even smokers themselves, enjoyed wide social acceptance and even encouragement by governments for the next quarter century. During this time, however, medical science was producing disturbing research findings that would challenge the industry in a more devastating fashion.

SCIENCE UNCOVERS A LARGER HEALTH HAZARD

In 1939, results of a major health study were released.[5] This research offered a greater degree of scientific precision and a more substantial set of data to support the findings of the harms of smoking than previous studies had. The results received little public attention and demanded even less credence because the study used medical records and had not directly examined human beings themselves. Hence, as frightening as the results of this and other earlier studies were, they failed to make the impact on the public that the post-1954 studies did. The degree to which health concerns associated with smoking were ignored is illustrated by the fact that during World War II, all U.S. servicemen were treated to cigarettes as a part of their rations.

In contrast with the earlier studies, the post-1954 analyses compared heath outcomes of smokers and nonsmokers, were conducted in laboratories and hospitals, and included autopsies. The results of the first of these studies, by E. Cuyler Hammond and Daniel Horn, concluded firmly that smoking causes lung cancer.[6] Later research discovered major and disturbing changes in the cellular structure of smokers' lungs. The statistics were startling; they revealed that 93.2 percent of smokers had abnormal lung cells, whereas only 1.2 percent of the lungs of nonsmokers contained evidence of abnormality. The Public Health Service analyzed seven population studies ten years after the first study was released. It was found that among 1,123,000 men, the mortality ratio of smokers to nonsmokers was 1.7 to 1, or nearly 70 percent higher for smokers than for nonsmokers. Drs. Hammond and Horn wrote that the death rate from all causes for male smokers between the ages of forty-five and sixty-four was twice as high as that for nonsmokers.[7]

This research gave public health groups the impetus to mobilize their educational and lobbying activities. The Public Health Cancer Association and the American Cancer Society adopted resolutions acknowledging support of the studies and agreeing that there is a positive relationship between smoking and lung cancer. A report issued simultaneously by the British Ministry of Health came to the same conclusion. Four public health groups in 1957 joined to examine the accumulating scientific evidence. The conclusion of their survey, released on March 6 of that year, stated,

> The sum of scientific evidence established beyond reasonable doubt that cigarette smoking is a causative factor in the rapidly increasing incidence of human epidermoid carcinoma of the lung. The evidence of a cause-effect relationship is adequate for the initiation of public health measures.[8]

Congress Rebuffs Health Proponents

One distinct advantage the pro-tobacco forces had throughout much of the twentieth century was that members of Congress from tobacco states held powerful positions in the two legislative chambers. After the 1911 revolt against Speaker Joe Cannon's centralized control over the House, institutional power flowed to the chairmen of committees. Once seniority became the sole criterion for a chairmanship, southerners needed only to reelect their representatives until they reached the pinnacle of power and then continue to reelect them. For most of the century, including the time of the labeling debate, the heads of committees were considered to be barons of their jurisdictional duchies. Nearly one-fourth of the committees in the Senate were chaired by senators from the six leading tobacco states. Of the twenty-one committees in the House, tobacco-state congressmen chaired seven.[9] The configuration of power in Congress allowed the members from these states to exert extraordinary influence on matters that would come before their committees and to horse-trade to achieve their goals on virtually any issue in which they took interest. As committee chairmen, they could demand the support of their colleagues in return for legislative favors covering the broad spectrum of congressional action, and they could refuse to act on pet projects of other members if they voiced opposition to tobacco. Given the inherently conservative nature of U.S. institutions limited by constitutional checks and balances, chairmen could deploy this power to delay indefinitely consideration of measures that might adversely affect their constituents. In short, the tobacco-state members skillfully used their positions to protect the tobacco industry.

Despite the political danger of opposing tobacco, some brave or perhaps foolhardy members of Congress challenged the tobacco subsystem's monopoly on tobacco policy by introducing legislation that would have either restricted the sale of cigarettes or conveyed health warnings to the public. More than fifteen bills were introduced in the House and Senate by various lawmakers between 1962 and 1964 alone. The opposition of the tobacco congressmen, combined with the absence of public support for these health measures, however, thwarted any serious consideration of such proposals.

The outcome of the first set of committee hearings on smoking and health, held in 1957, was indicative of just how potent the opposition of tobacco-state congressmen could be. The hearings, conducted by John A. Blatnik (D-Minn.), chairman of the Legal and Monetary Affairs Subcommittee of the House Government Operations Committee, were intended to define or redefine the responsibility of the Federal Trade Commission for enforcing standards of truthfulness in advertising claims relating to the effectiveness of cigarette filters. The subcommittee found that smokers were not safer if they used filter-tip cigarettes. Filters were not as effective as the manufacturers claimed; furthermore, lower-grade tobacco can be used in filter cigarettes, and lower-grade leaves contain more tars and nicotine. The committee report concluded, "The cigarette manufacturers have deceived the American public through their advertising of cigarettes."[10] Shortly after the report was issued, however, Blatnik's subcommittee was dissolved, and he lost his chairmanship. The subcommittee was revived, but without Blatnik as a member. His loss was attributed to the power of the tobacco lobby.

BIRTH OF A POWERFUL, SEEMINGLY INVINCIBLE LOBBY

Beginning in the early 1950s, the tobacco supporters found it expedient to go on the offense, combine forces, and attempt to counter the increasing amount of data running against their product. The first visible sign of significant change was the creation of the Tobacco Industry Research Committee (later called the Council for Tobacco Research—U.S.A.). Its ostensible purpose was to distribute funds for scientific research for studies on the use of tobacco and its effect on health. In its first twenty-five years of operation, it awarded 744 grants totaling $64 million to 413 scientists at 258 hospitals, laboratories, research organizations, and medical schools. By the mid-1970s, 1,882 reports had been published acknowledging council support.[11]

The creation of this research organization was an indication that there would be intensified opposition from the tobacco interests on the health issue. Whenever criticism of smoking grew, the tobacco interests responded with more research or more public relations expenditures. They firmly and repeatedly denied the causal link between smoking and cancer. Formation of the Tobacco Institute, Inc., a lobbying and public relations group formed in 1958, was a further indication of the industry's will to contain the possible adverse political effects of the health studies. In 1964, cigarette producers set up still another organization called the Cigarette Advertising Code, Inc. This entity called itself a self-policing organization that would ensure fairness and accuracy in competitive advertising, thus obviating the need for government regulation.

The most important of these organizations was the Tobacco Institute, formed by the fourteen major tobacco producers at the time. The chief executive officers of these companies sat on its board. The institute was financed by contributions from these large corporations, which contributed according to their market share.

In its promotional literature, the institute noted that it is concerned with the historical role of tobacco, its place in the economy, and public understanding of the tobacco industry. To these ends, it published a monthly tabloid, *The Tobacco Observer*. The real genius of the institute rested with the executives it hired, like Earle C. Clements.

A former U.S. senator well versed in the tobacco cause, Clements was president of the institute during the labeling battle and for more than a decade thereafter. Before joining the Tobacco Institute, he had lobbied for the six major cigarette companies. Clements brought a very impressive set of credentials to the institute, including a public service record of long standing and a political background that few could equal. Previously, he had been Kentucky's governor and had represented the Blue Grass State in the House before his election to the Senate.[12] Politically, Clements had a direct line to the White House. His daughter, Bess Abell, served as Lady Bird Johnson's social secretary. As a Johnson confidante and colleague of the best-known law partner of the firm of Arnold, Fortas and Porter, Abe Fortas—another Johnson intimate and later Supreme Court justice and one-time nominee for the chief justice position—Clements helped plan and execute a careful and forceful campaign to save the tobacco industry from any government action that might be harmful to its sales.

The government action that the cigarette manufacturers anticipated as early as 1954 did not begin to materialize until the mid-1960s. The slowness of the government's response to the smoking studies the previous decade was due, in part, to the successful efforts of the Tobacco Institute and, in part, to the relative weakness of the public health interest groups and hence slight organized public sentiment against tobacco. The institute had enough economic and political influence to make certain that government activity would be unproductive. The size and economic strength of the tobacco industry was bolstered politically by the size and strength of the advertising industry. In 1967 alone, advertisers received $312 million a year in tobacco advertising revenues. Cigarette promotions earned 8 percent of the total advertising revenue for television, 2.7 percent for radio, 2.3 percent for newspapers, and 3.3 percent for magazines. These figures show the importance of cigarettes to the business ledgers of the mass media.

The disorganized array of health groups did not have the leadership, the financial means, or the national organization to coalesce into an effective lobbying organization. They were overwhelmed by the giant tobacco industry and its supporters from the early 1950s until the 1990s when the political winds shifted and their own strength was considerably more muscular.

THE TOBACCO POLICY SUBSYSTEM

What had come to be the normal relationship among the institutions of national government was typified by traditional, or pre-1964, tobacco politics. Policy was made in a spirit of friendly and quiet cooperation between small segments of Congress, the bureaucracy, and the interest group community. The coalition of these fragments is referred to in social science literature as a subsystem.[13] The term "subsystem" describes a structure dependent on a larger political entity but one that functions with a high degree of autonomy. A committee of Congress could be called a subsystem of the larger legislative system, just as an agency might be referred to as a subsystem of the bureaucracy. The tobacco policy subsystem was different from these in that it was more encompassing. It cut across institutional lines and included within it all groups and individuals who were making and influencing government decisions concerning cigarettes and tobacco.

The tobacco subsystem included the paid representatives of tobacco growers, marketing organizations, and cigarette manufacturers; members of Congress representing tobacco constituencies; the leading members of four subcommittees in Congress—two appropriations subcommittees and two substantive legislative committees in each house—that handled tobacco legislation and related appropriations; and certain officials within the Department of Agriculture who were involved with the various tobacco programs of that department. This was a small group of people well known to each other and knowledgeable about all aspects of the tobacco industry and its relationship with the government.

As long as no one with political clout objected too loudly, the important and complex tobacco programs, like price supports and export promotion, were conducted without interference from those not included in this subsystem. There are hundreds of similar subsystems and looser, less consensual policy networks functioning in Washington that quietly and efficiently bridge the gap created by the constitutional separation of powers.

Tight policy subsystems, increasingly rare in modern American politics, functioned to contain conflict and maintain a veto, if not a monopoly, on policy in the areas of concern, like tobacco. These systems managed conflict by concentrating economic and political power in the hands of a few individuals who have overlapping interests in an issue. However, the world does not stand still. New, competing interests arise and with them dissidents interested in altering the status quo. Challenging existing policy requires that the scope of conflict is broadened beyond the subsystem, thereby breaking the hold that established interests have on a policy set.[14]

Those who seek to change a policy controlled by a subsystem often use the policymaking powers of one institution of government to provoke a response and further action from another. A different committee of Congress or an agency of the bureaucracy, outside of a subsystem, might be persuaded to concern itself with the issue that heretofore had been tightly held within the guarded domain of the subsystem. Perhaps an interest group or a power-ful individual encourages other groups to use their political powers to challenge those who in the past had succeeded in keeping the conflict within manageable bounds. One agency of the bureaucracy might challenge the jurisdiction of another. All these actions could receive further impetus by direct appeals to public opinion. Conflict is thus created and expanded as more and different actors are induced to challenge the decision makers in the subsystem. The quiet ways of the tobacco subsystem ensured that there would be no major disruptions to the status quo for a long time. Not until the late 1970s did the participants in the tobacco subsystem begin to lose its grip, and then only slowly and never completely.

THE TRANSFORMATION OF TOBACCO POLITICS: THE COLLAPSE OF A POLICY MONOPOLY

The groups that made up the tobacco subsystem before 1964 were few in comparison to the cast of characters involved in tobacco politics today, when conflict over tobacco policy is anything but contained. One of the chief additions to the forces effecting this change is, of course, health-related organi-zations. Groups like the American Cancer Society, Campaign for Tobacco Free Kids, and the American Medical Association now lobby for a total ban on ciga-rette advertising. For years, citizens' lobbying groups fought the tobacco price support system, which supported and stabilized prices for tobacco farmers and was terminated with the $10 billion tobacco farmer buyout provisions of the American Jobs Creation Act of 2004. By the late 1980s, state and municipal governments also were added to the fold of anti-tobacco advocates, through litigation aimed directly at the tobacco industry as well as through their suc-cessful efforts to pass local antismoking ordinances in public places.

In addition to the increased number and influence of private pressure groups and the actions of subnational governments, the smoking issue began appearing as early as the 1980s on the agendas of nonregulatory fed-eral agencies with no jurisdiction over tobacco per se but with authority over activities within their purview (and thus their congressional oversight com-mittees). With the damning research findings on environmental tobacco smoke or secondhand smoking, these bodies came to understand that the health of both citizens and personnel for whom they had responsibility required action against smoking. It became the business of the Federal Aviation Administration to decide if citizens could smoke on airplanes, while the Interstate Commerce Commission did the same for the nation's commercial buses and trains. The General Services Administration banned smoking in all 6,800 federal buildings in 1986, and in 1994 the Department of Defense banned smoking in all the thousands of common work areas it controls worldwide, though full implementation of those rules awaited the turn of the century to actually occur. Other agencies that have became involved in the tobacco issue include the Veterans Administration, which prohibited smoking in its hospitals, and even the U.S. Fire Administration, which got into the act by calling for development of a self-extinguishing cigarette, citing statistics that in one year alone, home fires started by cigarettes killed or injured over 5,000 people and cost $305 million in damages.

The Food and Drug Administration (FDA), meanwhile, in a novel application of its authority, pursued regulation of both the sale and the distribution of tobacco. A suit was immediately brought against the FDA by the tobacco industry with the charge that the agency was overstepping its delegated authority. In 2000, the Supreme Court ruled that the FDA did not have the requisite authority, although the decision was split, five to four, indicating the controversial nature of the issue. The question of FDA involvement did not end there, however. In March 2005, a few members of Congress sponsored legislation to authorize the FDA to regulate tobacco. In an indication of the vast change in tobacco politics by the first years of the twenty-first century, Atria, parent company of the Phillip Morris Tobacco Company, did an about-face and supported the FDA's regulation of its product.

The collapse of the tobacco subsystem, the rupture of the coalition of tobacco corporations and the U.S. tobacco farmers (which had previously been inseparable allies), the divisions among the companies themselves, the globalization of the tobacco industry, and the rise of powerful anti-tobacco forces signaled the collapse of the tightly controlled tobacco subsystem but not the extinction of pro-tobacco forces by any means. Control of tobacco policy was no longer in any single interest's—or group of allied interests'—hands. Instead, a broader, larger, more inclusive, contentious, and sometimes international policy network developed, perhaps best seen in the battle over content of the first international treaty on public health, the Framework Convention for Tobacco Control. No longer does a narrowly defined set of interested parties privately broker policy for their own selfish ends in the domain of tobacco.

This development is consistent with Hugh Heclo's observations on emergence of issue networks. Heclo writes,

> The iron triangle [a term sometimes used instead of "subsystem"] concept is not so much wrong as it is disastrously incomplete. . . . The notion of iron triangles and subgovernments presumes small circles of participants who have succeeded in becoming largely autonomous. Issue networks, on the other hand, comprise large numbers of participants . . . and include individuals and organizations with intellectual, professional, and emotional interests that serve to broaden the basis for conflict with the more narrowly focused economic and electoral interests held by members of the more traditional issue subsystem.[15]

When it comes to the regulatory realities of tobacco politics and policymaking today, the concept of an issue network clearly seems more descriptive than one of a policy subsystem. The dissident individuals, groups, and institutions—along with the myriad policymaking actors at the state, local, national (outside the United States), and international levels where a great deal of the regulatory action has taken place in recent years—have altered the policymaking process by breaking the monopoly held by the old subsystem, expanding it, and creating something very different in its place, a more open, penetrable tobacco network in the United States and abroad.

With health groups becoming increasingly powerful and with agencies becoming bolder and more effective in challenging vested tobacco interests, it seems highly unlikely that a smaller, insular subsystem—one in form similar to the tobacco subsystem of the 1960s—will reemerge anytime soon. Despite the current tobacco- and business-friendly Bush administration, this issue will not die, specifically because worldwide 10 million people a year *will* die from the effects of smoking unless action to curtail smoking is undertaken successfully.[16] Still, the substantial interests involved in the health of the industry, ideological as well as economic, have complicated efforts to regulate its products.

BEYOND THE SUBSYSTEM: TOBACCO INTERESTS AND THEIR ALLIES

Any challenge to the old tobacco subsystem was fraught at the outset with serious difficulties. Long before the requirement of a health warning label was threatened by the Federal Trade Commission, tobacco power had established itself as an important force in American politics. With revenues of $48 billion a year, tobacco companies were big economic players in state and local economies in the 1960s and 1970s. In addition to their own financial clout, these companies accounted—either directly or indirectly—for millions of dollars more in advertising and other related economic activity. Tobacco companies employed nearly 47,000 workers and provided $2.8 billion in crop income for over 100,000 farmers in sixteen states, most of which is, however, produced in just two states: North Carolina and Kentucky. The industry as a whole accounted for nearly 2 percent of the nation's gross national product and raised over $12 billion in taxes for federal, state, and local treasuries every year. The philanthropy of the corporations was—and still is—legend, with the result that recipient groups that normally would be uninterested or even negative in the battles over tobacco would either become tobacco supporters or at least be neutralized and stay out of the fight. Further, the tobacco coalition was supported, at least presumably, by a clientele of the tens of millions in the United States who smoked.

The beneficiaries of this multi-billion-dollar industry included manufacturers and their employees, advertising agencies, farmers, shopkeepers, tax collectors, politicians whose campaign coffers were filled by tobacco contributions, and the general public through tobacco taxes used to support government activities. The stakeholders worked hard to discourage any government activity that might in turn dampen smoking. And smokers themselves disliked being told, particularly by politicians, that their pleasures could be injurious to their health. Consequently, even health-oriented politicians had a strong incentive to devote their time to more popular activities.[17]

The beneficiaries of tobacco also included the entertainment and news media, from which Americans receive much of their information about smoking and health. The Federal Trade Commission reported that in 1983, tobacco companies spent $2.6 billion on advertising. In the nation's twenty largest magazines, tobacco ads made up 10 to 20 percent of all advertising income. This fact caused antismoking advocates to question whether newspapers and magazines could be unbiased in their reporting of the smoking and health issue. In a study cited in the *New England Journal of Medicine*, magazines accepting tobacco ads ran from twelve to sixty-three times as many stories on health issues like stress and nutrition than on smoking, although smoking was generally considered the nation's number one behavioral health problem.

Tobacco interests also found support in American traditions. Tobacco was an early American crop and was so important to the early economy that it was used for a time as currency. Furthermore, attempts to regulate business enterprise are generally received by most Americans without enthusiasm and frequently with considerable derision. Smoking bans reminded some of the failure of Prohibition and the disruptive era that it ushered in. Smokers could see no reason for government to be shaking its finger in the face of the pleasures and sophistication of a lighted cigarette.

THE SCHIZOPHRENIA OF BUSINESS TOWARD GOVERNMENT REGULATION

In many public policy arenas, support for regulation comes from industry itself. In those cases, regulation is seen as an advantage and in its own best interest. For example, support for much of the state and national economic regulation is rooted in business. Fair competition guarantees, antitrust laws, banking and currency regulations, and airline, trucking, banking, and financial market regulations have all been supported over the years by business and its representatives. There is little reason for business opposition to these regulations when they support business generally. Dominant businesses in an industry often champion regulations that advantage them at the expense of other segments of the industry or of society. Banking and currency regulations organize the marketplace, antitrust rule making tends to pit big business against small, and airline and trucking rate regulation (before those two were eliminated altogether) were supported by the large, established carriers and opposed by the smaller ones and potential entrants into the market. On these matters, influential businesses generally favor government intervention.[18]

Regulation of environmental or health matters or regulation of advertising for public health reasons is another matter altogether, as such supervision can cut into autonomy and profits. The cigarette industry and its allies were hostile to regulation and supported it only when what was proposed seemed to generate specific benefits for them. Once it became apparent that warning labels could be used to protect cigarette producers from legal liability, for example, resistance to such warnings dwindled.

In the past, there had been occasional moves by government to regulate the entire tobacco industry in a comprehensive, across-the-board fashion. No part of the tobacco industry could see any advantage in such initiatives, nor could other, unrelated corporations. When such a comprehensive policy change is proposed, the business community typically finds common ground in opposing large-scale government regulation of any industry whether or not a rule touches directly on them. In addition, opposition often elicits the broader citizenry in the battle, as such government regulatory actions are deemed to be imposing "big government" and excessive regulation of free enterprise, contrary to basic American cultural values.

The business schizophrenia toward government regulation is nowhere more clearly seen than in the smoking and health area. From 1933 to 2005, tobacco producers profited from federal regulation through the U.S. Department of Agriculture's price support program and marketing quota rules, which carried with them mandatory limits on production. Although the costs of these activities to government were relatively small, the regulations benefited the industry by keeping prices up and supply down. The beneficiaries of the multi-billion-dollar tobacco industry endeavored to encourage such tobacco regulatory programs that aid the industry while arguing forcefully against big government and government intervention in the economy. They fought consumer health regulations on the grounds that government regulation is unwarranted interference by Big Brother and that such regulation is inherently bad for the economy. This view, however, was not to prevail.

NOTES

1. Quoted by Franklin B. Dryden, assistant to the president, Tobacco Institute, before the 21st Tobacco Workers Conference, January, 1967, Williamsburg, Virginia.
2. Sanitation regulations at the turn of the century and the Food and Drugs Act of 1906 are examples of policymaking arising from scientific findings. The classic book on the subject of the two separate spheres of science and government is C. P. Snow, *The Two Cultures and the Scientific Revolution* (Cambridge: Cambridge University Press, 1959). Since that seminal work was published, a large and useful literature on the culture and philosophy of science has emerged.
3. M. W. Schooley, G. A. Giovino, B. P. Zhu, J. H. Chrisman, S. L. Tomar, J. P. Peddicord, R. K. Merritt, C. G. Husten, and M. P. Eriksen, "Surveillance for Selected Tobacco-Use

Behaviors—United States, 1900–1994" (Atlanta: Office on Smoking and Health, Centers for Disease Control and Prevention, 1994).

4. Paul Verkuil, *A Leadership Case Study of Tobacco and Its Regulation* (Penn National Commission on Society, Culture and Community, 1998), available at http://www.upenn.edu/pnc/ptverkuil.html.

5. M. Ochsner and M. DeBakey, "Symposium on Cancer. Primary Pulmonary Malignancy. Treatment by Total Pneumonectomy: Analyses of 79 Collected Cases and Presentation of 7 Personal Cases." *Surgical Gynecology and Obstetrics* 68 (1939): 435–51.

6. E. Cuyler Hammond and Daniel Horn, "The Relationship between Human Smoking Habits and Death Rates: A Follow-up Study of 187,766 Men," *Journal of the American Medical Association* (August 7, 1954), vol. 155, no. 15, pp. 1316–28.

7. U.S. Surgeon General, "Smoking and Health: Report of the Advisory Committee to the Surgeon General of the Public Health Service, Public Health Service Document No. 1103" (Washington, D.C.: U.S. Department of Health, Education, and Welfare, 1964).

8. The four groups were the American Cancer Society, the National Cancer Institute, the American Heart Association, and the National Heart Institute.

9. The words "congressmen" and "chairmen" are used in this text in an attempt to lend verisimilitude and historical accuracy to the text. Today, "members of Congress" or "representatives" are generally preferred to "congressmen," and "chairs" is sometimes substituted for "chairmen" in order to avoid the implication that these people are exclusively male and that the positions are held exclusively by men.

10. Subcommittee of the Committee on Government Operations, *False and Misleading Advertising (Filter-Tip Cigarettes)*, House of Representatives (Washington, D.C.), 1st sess., July 18–26, 1957.

11. In addition to the $64 million expended by the council, the six major cigarette producers contributed $15 million between 1964 and 1973 to the American Medical Association Education and Research Foundation to support a comprehensive program of research on tobacco and health. The initial award came at the time the Federal Trade Commission announced that it was considering a health warning requirement. The American Medical Association did not actively support the commission's proposal.

12. As an alumnus of Congress, he still had floor privileges, though he was never known to have used them during the debates on the labeling bill.

13. For discussions of the subsystem idea, see J. Lieper Freedman, *The Political Process: Executive Bureau-Legislative Committee Relations* (New York: Random House, 1965), and E. E. Schattschneider, *The Semi-Sovereign People* (New York: Holt, Rinehart and Winston, 1960).

14. For more on broadening the scope of conflict, see Schattschneider, *The Semi-Sovereign People*; Georg Simmel, *Conflict and the Web of Group Affiliations* (New York: Free Press, 1955); and Lewis Coser, *The Functions of Social Conflict* (New York: Free Press, 1956).

15. The term *issue network* comes from Hugh Heclo, "Issue Networks and the Executive Establishment," in *Public Administration: Concepts and Cases*, 4th ed., ed. Richard J. Stillman (Boston: Houghton Mifflin, 1988).

16. A well-respected student of administrative politics, Thomas Vocino, writes, "In sum, with a now well-accepted role for the President in the regulatory process, the near future outcome of this struggle suggests a decided edge in the process for the conservative, business interests with significant White House access" ("American Regulatory Policy: Factors Affecting Trends over the Past Century," *Policy Studies Journal* 31, no. 3 [2003]: 441).

17. In some countries, cigarette manufacturing is a government monopoly. In those places, programs to reduce consumption are particularly difficult to generate and support. As the ill effects of smoking have become better known, those countries face a difficult dilemma. Luckily, the United States was not placed in this awkward position.

18. For another example of the selective desire for government regulation in the area of global warning, see "Regulate Us, Please," *The Economist*, October 8, 2005, p. 69.

3

SMOKING AND HEALTH MOVE
TO THE PUBLIC AGENDA

THE SURGEON GENERAL REPORTS
AND THE FTC ACTS

*If tobacco were spinach the government would have outlawed it years ago,
and no one would have given a damn.*

—THE NATION, NOVEMBER 30, 1963

In 1964, the Federal Trade Commission (FTC) stepped forward and proposed that a health warning be announced in all cigarette advertising as well as on cigarette packages. Two years later, a mandatory health warning began to be printed on all cigarette packages sold in the United States. The original admonition read, "Caution: Cigarette Smoking May Be Hazardous to Your Health." In 1970, legislation was passed to make the caution more emphatic. Initially appearing only in small print on the side panel of cigarette packages, in 1972 it also began appearing in all billboard, newspaper, and magazine advertising in the United States. In 1985, the surgeon general's warning became a series of statements, rotating every three months: "Smoking Causes Lung Cancer, Heart Disease, Emphysema, and May Complicate Pregnancy"; "Smoking by Pregnant Women May Result in Fetal Injury, Premature Birth, and Low Birth Weight"; "Cigarette Smoke Contains Carbon Monoxide"; and "Quitting Smoking Now Greatly Reduces Serious Risks to Your Health."

To read this rendition of increasingly serious health warnings over a twenty-year period as steady, easy progress for the health advocates would be a mistake. Prior to the initial FTC proposal, much groundwork had been laid by the FTC and by the surgeon general. After issuing the proposal, the FTC was called to task by Congress, which overruled and punished the agency and enacted its own diluted legislation that precluded any FTC activity on smoking and health for a five-year period. Every gain by the anti-smoking proponents was hard fought and then only partial.

REGULATION ON THE BASIS OF FALSE ADVERTISING

While professionals in the FTC were undoubtedly concerned with cigarette health questions, it was the commission's jurisdiction over unfair and deceptive trade practices that brought about its regulation of the advertising claims of cigarette manufacturers. Since the early 1930s, the commission had brought approximately twenty actions against cigarette companies for false or misleading advertising. Many of these actions involved what the commission considered misleading health claims. The manufacturers of Chesterfields were prohibited, for example, from claiming that their product had "no adverse effect upon the nose, throat or accessory organs."[1] Another producer was proscribed from claiming that Kools would keep one's head clear in the winter or any other time, give extra protection, or provide an excellent safeguard during cold months.[2]

The commission broadened its attack on cigarette advertising in September 1955 when it adopted some advertising guides.[3] It prohibited, among other things, stating or implying in advertising that there is medical approval of cigarette smoking in general or smoking any brand of cigarette in particular.

After the guides were issued, the FTC attempted to monitor cigarette advertising in order to ensure compliance. Monitoring ads and moving to prohibit some of them did not satisfy the commission's goals, however. In light of the increasing scientific data that questioned the healthfulness of cigarette consumption, the actions of the commission looked puny and insignificant. The commission knew that consumption of cigarettes was increasing rapidly, particularly among younger age-groups. It attributed this increase to advertising that portrayed smoking in an attractive way, particularly on television. Advertisements associated smoking with individuals or groups worthy of emulation, especially with the young. Smoking was portrayed as being fun, romantic, and even sexy.

To the FTC's consternation, these advertisements did not violate any law. They did not even violate the intent of the 1955 advertising guidelines. It became clear to the commission that a positive health warning was needed; otherwise, any health message could be overcome by the subtleties of modern advertising. To adopt a new policy requiring a warning not only would necessitate overcoming the tobacco interests in and out of Congress but also could be expected to involve doing battle in the courts, where the right of the FTC to take such bold policymaking steps would surely be questioned by the tobacco industry. Opposition from other agencies in the bureaucracy that were sympathetic to tobacco interests could be expected as well.

But the warning labels on cigarettes, which were the initial focus of antismoking efforts, were only the beginning. Today, a worldwide antismoking movement involving agencies of international government as well as a large number of nongovernmental organizations has flowered. In the United States, smoking has been banned from most buildings by local authorities. Office buildings in the private sector are mainly nonsmoking facilities, and businesses have even begun to discriminate in hiring against smokers.[4] The Food and Drug Administration (FDA) can claim credit for moving to end the marketing of cigarettes to children and teenagers in the United States and closing down cigarette vending machines. The courts have presided over negotiations leading to awards in the hundreds of billions of dollars to organizations created to reduce the consumption of cigarettes, to states, and to individuals.

These changes did not occur in a vacuum, nor did they occur in an automatic way. Like most major changes in policy, they were the result of countless individual efforts. The issue had to be placed on governments' agendas. Support had to be earned. Political actors, many without experience, gradually gathered political clout and learned where to apply pressure within the policymaking process. Many efforts failed at first. Through persistence and a creative use of policymaking tools, changes were eventually pushed through despite tremendous pressure by the tobacco industry to maintain the status quo of minimal government regulation and laws that favored tobacco farmers. In this, as in a growing number of other cases, health advocates realized that using the bureaucracy's policymaking tools would be an effective means by which to move the issue forward.

The politics of cigarette labeling and subsequent broader proposed regulation demonstrate how institutions with separate responsibilities in the framework of the Constitution cooperate, conflict, and form temporary alliances to achieve policy goals. Further, such controversies illustrate the central role of the bureaucracy as policy initiator and policymaker in modern society. While policymaking powers are shared among the three constitutional divisions of government—the legislative, the executive, and the judicial—one of these institutions is usually more able to initiate a change in policy than the others, depending on the nature of the issue and the historical era. Frequently, when the issue involves matters of technical complexity and powerful special interest opposition, the bureaucracy can play the leading role, but there is no fixed rule in this regard. And even though one institution might play a leading role, it is clear that the policy process cannot function with much in the way of dispatch or efficiency when one of the institutions encounters concentrated opposition from another. Both the FTC and the FDA discovered the truth of this statement when they encountered a Congress hostile to their proposals for cigarette health warnings and then for regulation of tobacco use and marketing two decades later.

WHERE DO ISSUES COME FROM? WHERE DO THEY GO? WHY?

Identifying the time and place of the birth of an issue is a virtually impossible task. Policy ideas are discussed both informally and formally in a large number of places, among experts in policy shops and among ordinary citizens encountering problems that can be addressed only collectively. Public courses of action are discussed, for example, in the media and on talk radio, in academe and think tanks, and in the institutions of government and the commercial sector. Policy designs might be conceptualized figuratively as goods generated in policy idea space and stored in a great metaphorical warehouse.[5] These ideas—sometimes inchoate, sometimes more fully developed and waiting for a problem to emerge,[6] and often evolving over time as they are propelled by research findings and discussion— may sit on a shelf for years before someone or something comes along to move one into a position where it can be activated. Prior to action, the policy idea may be reshaped to fit the current context and particular need at hand.

Most policy ideas, however, do not advance at all. The chances of a particular issue gaining official consideration are severely circumscribed by the fact that the public and policymakers can pay attention to only a limited number of issues at one time. Policy science has not developed (and may never develop) sufficiently to discover an exact formula that accurately specifies the necessary and sufficient conditions that lead to the selection of issues to address and then to particular policy outcomes. In a democracy, for a problem to be recognized as a public problem that ought to be addressed by some unit of government requires a fortuitous convergence of precipitating events, alliances among interests, strategic leaders, public awareness, and appropriate venues and solutions.[7] This simultaneity of elements is sometimes called a "window of opportunity."[8]

In the United States, this window may open less frequently than in other democracies because of its extensive system of checks and balances that puts an additional thumb on the scale of inaction. Conversely, the multiple venues afforded exactly by these checks and balances and by the federalist structure, offering multiple levels of government for policymaking, may increase the chances of a policy idea being considered and possibly adopted in one of these arenas.

In the case of tobacco, scientists and physicians were well aware of the health consequences of smoking decades before the issue was on any policy agenda of Congress, of any agency of the bureaucracy, or of the public. Until the New Deal era, inaugurated with the election of Franklin D. Roosevelt in 1932, it would not have occurred to anyone that the federal government should be interfering with people's decision to smoke. After the public came to accept a more muscular role for national government in protecting its citizens and in limiting corporate practices, much time would pass before the public's health would have equal standing in government arenas with that of the tobacco companies. Some health advocates today would argue that such equal standing does not yet exist and that, if anything, forward motion has been reversed in the early years of the twenty-first century, a reminder that policy development is rarely linear.

A Challenge to the Old Subsystem

Those who opposed a warning were able to keep the issue off the congressional agenda until the mid-1960s. Because the tobacco interests were successful in keeping control of the issue within the confines of a few agencies and within the offices and committee rooms of a few key congressmen, those who favored a cigarette health warning had to devise some method to involve other agencies and different members of Congress and to interest them in working for the adoption of legislation that would limit cigarette consumption despite the consequent risks to their careers.

The strategy of the cigarette interests was to play off various agencies against each other or against Congress to prevent the smoking and health controversy from expanding. This style of tobacco politics resulted in little government regulation of tobacco advertising or sales. The approach was successful as long as there was little public support for a government policy to reduce cigarette consumption. As scientific evidence began to document the link between smoking and death, pressure for regulation grew, but the tobacco subsystem proved impenetrable. Tobacco was more firmly entrenched and more richly supported than most other consumer products. One journalist succinctly described the dilemma of the health groups: "If tobacco were spinach the government would have outlawed it years ago, and no one would have given a damn."[9] There were many people—ranging from addicted smokers to tobacco farmers to the tobacco industry to the participants in the tobacco subsystem and many others whose livelihoods and profits depended on tobacco—who cared about the fate of this product, unlike spinach.

The normal difficulties of transferring matters of scientific importance to the lay public were exacerbated by the successful efforts of the cigarette manufacturers to allay any smokers' fears by pretending that the medical evidence was uncertain and that reasonable people disagreed on the effects of smoking on the human body. When unfavorable research findings were released, the manufacturers found ways to discredit and obliterate them in the public consciousness through more glamorous advertisements, intensified lobbying, and their own "scientific" studies. Each major medical discovery and government response was followed by a reaction of the manufacturers, their agents (such as the Tobacco Institute), or their advertisers. Because the tobacco interests exerted considerable influence within the traditional legislative system through congressmen serving on committees or subcommittees immediately involved in tobacco politics, there was little hope for the successful initiation of new policy within Congress. To effect a change in public policy, other avenues of policymaking had to be used. Through the collaboration of a few members of Congress and two agencies of the bureaucracy that were not part of the tobacco subsystem, a new coalition was formed to combat the tobacco interests. Congress was generally unfriendly to consumer legislation since consumers rarely generated pressures or did favors on a scale to match the organized interest groups. As consumer groups organized in the late 1960s, congressional resistance to consumer legislation lessened. When the labeling controversy began, however, the fate of the cigarette health warning, like other consumer measures, depended on the power of administrative agencies to make public policy.

The initial effect of the FTC's proposal to require a health warning was to broaden the opposition to the FTC's plan. The American Newspaper Publishers Association, the Advertising Federation of America, the Association of National Advertisers, the Radio Advertising Bureau, and the National Association of Broadcasters, all fearing that advertising restrictions would mean a loss of revenues, aligned themselves with the tobacco interests. This coalition strengthened the position of those who supported business as usual within tobacco-government decision-making structure. Nor could the FTC count on sister agencies within the federal government to counter opposition to requiring a health warning.

A BUREAUCRACY DIVIDED: THE GOVERNMENT DOES NOT SPEAK WITH ONE VOICE

A large, complex operation, the federal bureaucracy employs about two and a half million people in thirty or so large (depending on one's definition of "large") and hundreds of smaller agencies. One agency or another has had some interest in cigarettes since the beginning of the twentieth century. Until recent years, however, there has been little agreement among them on what the government position was—or what it should be—concerning smoking and health. The cigarette issue divided the bureaucracy rather sharply, pointing out the inescapable fact that although the bureaucracy is large, it is anything but monolithic in its views. On cigarettes, agencies were on both ends of the policy spectrum. Some, like the U.S. Department of Agriculture (USDA), were attempting to boost cigarette and tobacco sales, while others—the FTC, the Federal Communications Commission (FCC), and the FDA, for example—were at various times planning programs designed to reduce cigarette consumption.

The challenge for the health interests was how to place the cigarette and health issue on an agenda where some authoritative action could and would be taken. How might these interests focus their strength to move the issue forward?

The USDA, a loyal part of the tobacco subsystem, certainly did not offer a promising venue. Its interest was to protect tobacco farmers and to promote their products. The department administered price support programs for tobacco and endeavored to promote the sales of U.S. tobacco abroad with assistance and encouragement from the office of the U.S. trade representative.[10] At the height of the cigarette warning controversy, the USDA was distributing an expensive sales promotion film that it had paid to have produced. The film stressed the virtues of cigarette smoking, and it was available at no charge to any nation that wanted to consider importing U.S. tobacco products. Former Secretary of Agriculture Orville Freeman found himself in a tight spot when reporters questioned him about the continuation of tobacco price supports in view of recent smoking and health revelations. In what could be a political classic, the secretary responded that the government could in good conscience continue price supports and, indeed, must continue the price support program for tobacco. If the program were discontinued, he argued, tobacco prices would fall and cigarettes would cost less. The price reduction would then result in more people smoking, and this, after all, would be contrary to the spirit of the health studies.

Later the USDA took an official position against the inclusion of a health warning on packages or in advertising. Acting to protect its constituent tobacco producers, the department wrote, "Much more explicit identifications of the constituents of tobacco smoke and more complete understanding of their role as related to health must be sought and achieved."[11] Science had provided a basis for action, but apparently health science research produced by other government agencies and by independent scientists did not resonate in the USDA. Again, the bureaucracy is not monolithic. That is arguably one of its positive attributes in a policymaking culture that values competing ideas and competing sources of power, but dissonance among agencies can send a confusing signal to citizens and to other nations.

One of the bureaucracies opposing the health warning idea was, surprisingly, the large Department of Health, Education and Welfare (HEW; after 1980, the Department of Health and Human Services [HHS]), the parent organization for both the FDA and the Public Health Service [PHS]). Just as siblings frequently are quite different from each other and from their parents, even the agencies *within* HEW have held remarkably divergent views. From the top, then Secretary Anthony Celebrezze indicated that he thought the government should play no significant role in advising the public of the supposed hazards of cigarette smoking. In mid-1964, Celebrezze wrote to the chairman of the House Interstate and Foreign Commerce Committee that the department advised rejection of all those cigarette control bills then pending. He argued that the bills might be helpful in developing legislation that the department would submit, but they were, for reasons not explained, unacceptable to the department. HEW never submitted any legislation on cigarettes and health. Senator Maurine Neuberger (D-Ore.), a staunch congressional advocate of the antismoking position, referred to the action of that department in straightforward terms: "It's fair to infer that they [members of HEW] don't want anything at all."[12]

The hesitancy displayed in the secretary's office was not an accurate index of the feelings on the smoking and health issue *within* his department, however. The PHS had undertaken some research in 1957 and since that time showed some desire to act. After the head of the PHS, Surgeon General Luther L. Terry, had publicly adopted a position that favored a health warning, he was sent to Congress to testify on the labeling requirement bill.

He was obliged to state the position of the secretary of HEW, however, and consequently made it appear that the PHS did not strongly favor the bill. This unnecessary opposition helped to split the bureaucracy at a crucial time; it also helped to ensure that meaningful antismoking action would either not be taken or at least be substantially delayed. Later, when the PHS was prodded to move by President Johnson in 1964, the agency's quick response was an indication of the extent to which its leadership was anxious to take some action.[13]

The FDA, the agency that the surgeon general suggested as the proper regulator of warning requirements, had evinced even less interest in the smoking and health issue than its sister agency, the PHS. The FDA's reluctance was due, according to Senator Neuberger's book *Smoke Screen: Tobacco and the Public Welfare*, to a late-Victorian episode in congressional politics.[14] The item "tobacco" appeared in the 1890 edition of the U.S. Pharmacopoeia, an official listing of drugs published by the government. It did not appear in the 1905 or later editions, according to the senator, because the removal of tobacco from the Pharmacopoeia was the price that had to be paid to get the support of tobacco-state legislators for the Food and Drug Act of 1906. The elimination of the word "tobacco" automatically removed the leaf from FDA supervision in the view of FDA leadership at the time.

The FDA was given what appeared to be another opportunity to concern itself with cigarette smoking when the Hazardous Substances Labeling Act was passed in 1960. It empowered the FDA to control the sale of substances that, among other things, had the capacity to produce illness through inhalation. Secretary Celebrezze suggested in a letter to the Senate that the act could be interpreted to cover cigarettes as "hazardous substances." In what had become characteristic behavior of HEW, however, the secretary went on to argue that it would be better to wait and let Congress amend the act to make it more explicit and thereby avoid controversy. Subsequently, Congress rejected the amendment. When sued in federal court for its unwarranted timidity in interpreting the 1960 act, the FDA won its case and sat out the smoking and health battle for the next thirty-five years.[15]

The reluctance of the FDA could be traced to still other factors, such as its identification with the business community and apparent sensitivity to their interests over that of the public. During the early 1960s, the agency suffered through some devastating investigations conducted by the late Senator Estes Kefauver (D-Tenn.). The hearings dealt with the pricing practices, safety, and monopolistic elements of the drug industry. One of the alarming revelations to emerge from the hearings was the extent to which the FDA was dominated and supported by that sector of the business community that it was supposed to regulate: drug manufacturers and distributors. Instead of using the opportunity to show its commitment to public health over business profits, the FDA found it easier to keep quiet and follow Secretary Celebrezze's lead in order to continue to protect its good standing in the business community. In a corresponding fashion, the leadership of the FDA found it expedient to try ignore the cigarette health issue even though scientific indictments mounted in the early 1960s and other agencies began to step forward.

The disparity of views and the bickering among agencies existed up to and through the congressional hearings on requiring a health warning in 1965. President Johnson made no attempt to coordinate agency programs, although he had the administrative mechanism to do so. One of the functions of the Bureau of the Budget (now called the Office of Management and Budget) was to make certain that all agency programs were consistent with the president's program. All agency letters sent to Congress, whether favoring or opposing the health warning idea, had to have been cleared by the bureau. The final paragraph of each letter contained these words (or a slight variation of them): "The Bureau of the Budget has advised us it has no objection to the submission of this report from the standpoint of the administration's program." With the White House publicly silent, the bureaucracy divided among itself, and Congress in the grip of inaction, there appeared to be very little hope for enacting the requirement of a health warning.

Public support might have been favorable toward the health groups in the early 1960s, but it was not well organized or forcefully articulated, a classic case of widely dispersed public interests pitted against intense, concentrated economic interests. Surveys taken by the government in 1964 and 1966 showed between 70 and 75 percent of the public agreeing with the statement "Cigarette smoking is enough of a health hazard for something to be done about it."[16] A newspaper poll in 1967, two years after the passage of the first cigarette act, revealed that members of Congress favored, two to one, a stronger health warning on packages and a requirement that the warning appear in all advertising. More than majority support is sometimes necessary to overcome the power of strongly entrenched interests, however. One of the members surveyed commented, "Let's face it. . . . When you combine the money and power of the tobacco and liquor interests with advertising agencies, newspapers, radio, and television . . . there is too much political muscle involved to expect much accomplishment."[17] Certainly, Congress was unwilling to take this issue on, but two agencies in the bureaucracy, the office of the surgeon general and the FTC, used their wits and their authority to confront the status quo.

AN ADVISORY COMMITTEE SETS A NEW POLICY DIRECTION IN MOTION

Organizing sufficient public support to overcome the resistance built into policy subsystems or networks is difficult. At certain times in consumer history, a dramatic event or the work of a single individual has provided the impetus necessary to stimulate a change in policy. Examples of this phenomenon are Upton Sinclair's book *The Jungle*, on the stenches of the meatpacking industry at the turn of the twentieth century[18]; Rachael Carson's *Silent Spring*, which is credited with inaugurating the modern environmental movement in the United States[19]; Ralph Nader's forceful volume *Unsafe at Any Speed*, accusing the automobile industry of irresponsibility in the safety field[20]; and the shirtwaist factory fire in New York in 1911, which is documented in David Von Drehle's *Triangle: The Fire That Changed America*.[21] In 1962, drug control legislation proposed by Senator Kefauver was floundering until Frances Kelsey, a medical officer of the FDA, shook the government's conscience with data demonstrating that a sleep-inducing drug called thalidomide, when taken by pregnant women, caused severe, ghastly deformities in babies. Air travel safety systems were expanded and improved after 1986 when a small plane and a sightseeing helicopter collided in midair over the Grand Canyon, killing all the passengers.

Unlike these cases, however, no single catalyzing event placed cigarettes on the policy agenda. Nor was there a champion clearly identified as leading the charge against tobacco. Although the smoking issue was to have its highly visible public advocate, John F. Banzhaf and his group called ASH (Action on Smoking and Health), Banzhaf did not appear until after the first major policy breakthrough for the health interests. The cigarette issue first came to the government's agenda without the backing of organized public opinion.

Moving an issue from obscurity to the top of the government's agenda can be a hit-and-miss affair; there are no guidebooks describing best approaches to success. Change in policy comes with hard work, careful strategy, and large portions of luck. In consumer affairs, the obstacles to change are very large; they range from the potent inertia of tradition to forceful opposition from important individuals and groups who see some challenge to their fortunes in whatever policy change is contemplated. Those who oppose government action to protect consumers are historically better organized and financed than consumer groups.

Admittedly, in the end it could be argued that the cigarette warning legislation that was passed by Congress in 1965, trumping the FTC, was of dubious value to the public; it contained a mild health warning requirement for packages but prohibited government agencies from imposing other health rules on cigarette advertising or labeling. However, the substance of the initial legislation was arguably of secondary importance; the true significance of what had occurred was that the FTC's action forced congressional consideration of the labeling issue and that these changes compelled future policymaking on smoking to include new interests and participants broader than the subsystem that had traditionally controlled smoking and health politics. Once the characteristics of the policy subsystem began to change, the possibilities for significant alteration in those policies increased dramatically.

Support for a Health Warning:
Serendipity and Allies

The events that led to action on the labeling issue were characteristic of the manner in which bureaucrats and members of Congress draw on each other's assets to bring an issue into public view. Although developing support for a health warning was not easy, the success of the supporters of the warning is an indication of the political power latent within the bureaucracy. When this power is skillfully marshaled, change can be initiated.

Three serially related occurrences set the policymaking process in motion. The first of these was Senate Joint Resolution (SJR) 174 introduced by Senator Neuberger in March 1962, calling for the establishment of a presidential commission on tobacco and health. Congressional reaction was predictable; there was no interest in the resolution. There were no hearings, there was little discussion, and SJR 174 seemed to face certain death. Senator Neuberger knew from experience that Congress would do little on the smoking issue because of the support the tobacco industry had. Furthermore, if the resolution had passed, it would have only encouraged, not required, the president to establish a study commission. The use of this tactic suggests that the senator was seeking a wider audience than Congress. Her resolution provided health interests with an opportunity to rally and take the idea to the president or directly to the public. The resolution lay dormant for two months after Senator Neuberger had introduced it. Had it not been for the efforts of an enterprising reporter, the resolution might have simply died from lack of legislative interest due to other, more pressing, more politically rewarding issues crowding it out.

In the second occurrence, a reporter was spurred by the suggestion in the resolution of a presidential commission. At one of President Kennedy's major televised press conferences, he asked the president what he intended to do about the question of smoking and health. Such live televised news conferences put the president under considerable pressure to appear calm, knowledgeable, and confident. President Kennedy had earned the reputation of handling questions at these conferences with skill and poise. Witty and thoroughly briefed by his staff on what questions the press might be expected to raise, he was seldom embarrassed.

Lengthy briefing sessions preceded each press conference, but the preparation for the conference in May 1962 must not have included the smoking and health issue. When the president was asked whether he or his advisers agreed with the findings of an increasing number of studies that linked smoking and ill health, there was an embarrassing pause. Then the response came awkwardly:

> The—that matter is sensitive enough and the stock market is in sufficient difficulty without my giving you an answer which is not based on complete information, which I don't have, and therefore perhaps we could—I'd be glad to respond to that question in more detail next week.[22]

As a result of the press conference, the issue was moved from Congress to the desk of the president. He was now publicly committed to initiating some action within the bureaucracy and within one week. The pressure of public opinion, combined with pressure from those bureaucrats who saw an opening they had been waiting for, guaranteed a speedy presidential response. Soon after the press conference, President Kennedy asked the PHS to report on what it had been doing in the field of smoking and health, the third impetus to action. The agency had done a considerable amount, although its activities were not well known or, in Washington parlance, had taken place "beneath the radar."

Officials of the PHS not only were knowledgeable about the smoking studies undertaken by medical scientists but had even carried out some investigations of their own. In 1957, the PHS had published the report of a study group that assessed smoking and health data available at the time. The report concluded that "excessive" smoking was one of the causal factors in lung cancer. Soon after its release, the report was officially endorsed by the PHS.[23]

When the Kennedy White House expressed interest in the research of the PHS in terms that indicated that the research findings might be implemented, it was not surprising that the PHS responded enthusiastically. Only two weeks after the press conference, Surgeon General Luther Terry announced that he would establish a high-level advisory committee to study the impact of smoking on health. The appointment of the committee was the culmination of the events that gave the health warning the momentum it needed to eventually receive serious consideration as national policy.

ADVISORY COMMITTEES AS LEGITIMIZING AGENTS: THE IMPORTANCE OF NEUTRAL EXPERTISE

Advisory committees have been used by the bureaucracy for a long time in order to bring outside views into their policymaking, usually at the outset of policy development. Some advisory committees are composed entirely of experts who provide an agency with special kinds of information it could not expect to get from its own staff. Others, called representative advisory committees, are comprised of people representing special interests. Representative committees serve at least two useful functions for the agency they advise: they inject some new, outside ideas that might not otherwise find their way into agency policy, and they serve as sounding boards for testing agency proposals.

Both the representative and the expert advisory committees can be used for political purposes. The Surgeon General's Advisory Committee on Smoking and Health was an expert committee. Its purposes, however, were as much political as scientific. The report of a high-level committee of well-known, respected experts was bound to have a significant impact on the public.

The forcefulness of that impact could be heightened if selection of committee members, reports of their meetings, and announcement of their findings were handled with political skill and an understanding of the dynamics of the formation of public opinion. The Surgeon General's Advisory Committee and its recommendations could give the PHS the support it needed to pursue programs designed to reduce the health threat posed by the mass consumption of cigarettes. The events that followed the announcement that a committee would be created proved that at least some physicians and bureaucrats knew the politics of policymaking very well.

The first clues to the political dimensions of the surgeon general's committee appeared early. For example, the committee's mandate was to assess the value of existing studies and their conclusions and not to perform a new scientific study. This task had already been completed on a small scale by private health groups and earlier by the PHS itself. However, it was important to the PHS to have a new, outside group review the results of the existing studies. The Advisory Committee was well suited to giving the existing studies new currency in the public eye.

Another indication of the political nature of the committee was the manner in which the twelve (later ten) members were nominated and selected. The surgeon general stated publicly that the group was to include scientific, professional persons concerned with all aspects of smoking and health. The tobacco industry, health groups, professional associations, and federal agencies were called on to participate in selecting individuals who might serve on the committee.[24]

The names of 150 scientists were presented to those groups involved in the nomination process. These groups were to eliminate from consideration individuals for any reason they saw fit and return the list to the surgeon general. One "blackball" or veto apparently could have eliminated any name from consideration for appointment. Only then did the surgeon general choose the members of the Advisory Committee on Smoking and Health from the approved lists.

The selection process underscores the great pains to which the surgeon general went to make certain that the report of the committee would not be attacked on the grounds that the membership was stacked against any particular interest. To further protect the committee from such an attack, anyone who had made any public statements on the smoking and health controversy was ineligible to serve. The first executive director of the panel was removed shortly after he was appointed. Learning of the appointment, reporters from his hometown newspaper asked for a comment. The response they received was that recent studies definitely suggested that tobacco is a health hazard.[25] With this challenge to the neutrality of the committee thus challenged, the executive director was replaced.

Those appointed to the Advisory Committee, all professors from academic research centers, were among the most distinguished members of their professions. Eight were M.D.s with specializations in internal medicine, epidemiology, and pharmacology. The nonphysicians included a chemist and an epidemiologist or statistician. The panel's staff director, Dr. Eugene H. Guthrie, was a twelve-year veteran of the PHS. Despite their health credentials, this committee was not composed of rabid antismokers. In fact, three members of the group were cigarette smokers themselves, and two smoked pipes and cigars on occasion.[26]

The newly formed Advisory Committee on Smoking and Health met for the first time on November 9, 1962. At this meeting, the committee agreed on its operating procedures. First, it would review the scientific literature on all aspects of the use of tobacco and smoking habits. Then it would consider other possible contributing factors to ill health, such as air pollution, industrial exposure, radiation, and alcohol.

The full committee held nine meetings of two to four days' duration during 1963 in addition to several meetings of subcommittees. The witnesses who appeared were consultants hired by the committee and representatives of special interest groups, including the tobacco industry. A transcript was kept but not made public. In fact, a great degree of secrecy surrounded all activities of the Advisory Committee. The extraordinary precautions taken to ensure that there would be no leaks were so far out of character for the PHS that the secrecy added to the apprehension of those who already entertained substantial fears about the content of the committee's report. These precautions helped limit the leaks of fragmentary—and hence potentially misleading—information to the public and allowed frank exchange of ideas. The secrecy served another function. It provided some suspense, and by the time the committee was ready to release the report, all the major news agencies of the nation focused their attention on the Advisory Committee's findings.[27]

In Washington, even the most tightly sealed conferences emit some information to the press. There was substantial speculation about the committee's meetings taking place deep within the confines of PHS headquarters in Washington's fashionable suburb of Bethesda, Maryland. Virtually none of the speculation gave any comfort to those whose fortunes were dependent on the sale of tobacco and tobacco products.

IMPACT OF THE ADVISORY COMMITTEE'S REPORT: STAGING AND CONTENT

On Saturday, January 11, 1964, the world discovered what had made the tobacco interests uneasy. In a well-prepared, carefully staged news conference, the surgeon general announced the results of the Advisory Committee's study.[28] The conference was held behind locked doors in the State Department auditorium, the same room used by President Kennedy for his meetings with the press. With the reporters seated and the television cameras in place, the surgeon general and his committee took seats on the stage. The large No Smoking signs affixed to the walls on both sides of the raised platform were unintentional indices of the tone of the conference that was to follow. The reporters were given ninety minutes to ask questions and scan the published 387-page report. At the end of ninety minutes, the doors were opened, the reporters were released, and the results of the study were telegraphed around the country and the world.

Selecting a Saturday for the day of the press conference had some significance. It signaled that the report might adversely affect the price of tobacco shares on the nation's stock exchanges when they reopened from the weekend break on Monday.[29] Scheduling the press conference on a Saturday, normally a slow news day, increased the chances that the report's findings would make headline news in the Sunday morning papers. Politically, this was a savvy move to make, considering the fact that bureaucrats, the orchestrators of this event, tend to operate outside the media limelight. Media neophytes or not, the tack paid off, for Sunday's papers were splashed with headlines about the commission's report. The news for the tobacco subsystem was not good, as their territory was being invaded.[30]

The report included detailed summaries of the studies that the committee had considered. These studies established a positive relationship between cigarette smoking and a host of other diseases. There was scant encouragement in the report for those who smoked cigars and pipes. Although the evidence of the ill effects from these tobacco products was not as devastating as for cigarettes, there was indication that their consumption was related to high mortality ratios for "cancers of the mouth, esophagus, larynx and lung, and for stomach and duodenal ulcers."[31]

At the press conference, the surgeon general noted that the precise way that smoking caused chronic diseases was not established by the studies. The Advisory Committee agreed, however, that it was more prudent from the public health viewpoint to accept the cause-and-effect relationship that the data indicated than to wait until the exact relationship had been determined. In short, the members of the committee concluded unanimously that "cigarette smoking is a health hazard of sufficient importance in the United States to warrant appropriate remedial action."[32]

The selection techniques employed by the surgeon general and the reputation of the Advisory Committee's members ensured that there would be little *ad hominem* criticism of the committee itself. The surgeon general held his committee in high esteem, and he worked closely with it. He officially accepted the committee's report within sixteen days of its completion, although HEW, the parent of the PHS, was less than enthusiastic about the report and its political implications.

A measure of the political success of the Advisory Committee on Smoking and Health was the speed with which the FTC rallied to the antismoking cause. One week after the Advisory Committee's report was issued, the commission announced that it would issue rules governing the advertising and labeling of cigarettes. The announcement was accompanied by a draft of the proposed rules and an invitation for all interested parties to submit their views to the commission. Hearings were held on the new rule within a month, and six months later an FTC rule requiring package and advertisement warnings was published in the *Federal Register*.[33] Soon thereafter, the FCC decided that it had a role to play in this issue.

Ultimately, the impact of the surgeon general's report was just what the antismoking interests had hoped for: it opened a window of opportunity and even issued an implicit mandate, for the FTC and, later, the FCC, to act. The Advisory Committee, by bringing the severity of the health impact of smoking into focus and by entering the previously exclusive province of the tobacco subsystem, gave that subsystem a blow that proved to become a mortal wound, like a slow leak in a heart valve. The bureaucracy was given the backing it needed to spring into action if it so chose, but before the FTC could succeed in implementing its policy, congressional resistance had to be overcome.

Congress was to make it clear that it still had a great deal to say about what policy would be made and how it would be made. As it turned out, the cigarette labeling rule first floated by the FTC in 1964 did not stand, for tobacco interests successfully convinced Congress to enact a watered-down version of the FTC rule the following year. Still, it would be hard to imagine any policy being made at all had it not been for the surgeon general's skillful maneuvering in both framing and highlighting the issue. This pattern of a threat to the tobacco interests, followed by a fierce response and then a repositioning to accommodate some objections, was to repeat itself over the next four decades.

BUREAUCRATS AND MEMBERS OF CONGRESS: A SYSTEM OF MUTUAL DEPENDENCIES

Despite the tobacco industry's general success in maintaining this balancing act of supporting regulation in its own interests and forestalling regulation harmful to its interests, the grip of the tobacco subsystem was loosened slightly when the FTC proposed the rule in 1964 to require that a health warning label be printed on all packages of cigarettes. The FTC was accused of acting unconstitutionally, in isolation from any checks generated by a system of constitutionally separated powers and hence unaccountable for its actions. During the course of the affair, however, it became clear that the FTC was not acting in isolation. On the contrary, there were checks on the commission's powers through its interaction and conflict with other agencies, the public, interest groups, the courts, and eventually Congress. Indeed, the cigarette labeling episode demonstrates for those concerned about the potential abuses of unchecked power in bureaucratic agencies that limits to agency power exist in a pluralistic system of separated, partially overlapping, and shared powers. In the labeling fight, as in other areas of domestic policymaking, the bureaucracy found it difficult to start anything without at least the acquiescence and usually the outright support of some members of Congress and portions of the interested public. Congressmen, bureaucrats, and pressure groups each have at least one political resource the other needs. The bureaucracy has expertise and knowledge derived from continued experience. Congressmen control the money and have the political power that bureaucrats lack. Pressure groups often are the catalytic agents and possess the power to unite congressmen and bureaucrats for action.

These fundamental relationships are often overlooked by those who argue that bureaucratic policymaking power is excessive. For example, an idea for new policy (or at least its impetus) comes from within the halls of Congress. A member of Congress finds it easy to give voice to a new idea. Getting traction on a legislative idea sufficient to enact it, however, is considerably more difficult. A member's status (stemming from seniority, expertise, and membership in the majority party), the popularity of the idea among party leaders, and the congruence of the proposal with the current tenor of the times and the legislative agenda affect the support the member might receive in Congress, as does the member's being in a position to move the legislation (by, for example, serving on the committee of jurisdiction). The eager member faced with little prospect of success inside the institution must look outside Congress for help to enact a bill. The member has the option of turning to the bureaucracy for expertise and, perhaps, presidential support and to a pressure group for necessary public support.

The bureaucrats' problems, on the other hand, are nearly the opposite of those experienced by members of Congress. Most bureaucrats find it difficult to initiate change, particularly if that change is substantial and unwanted by the leaders of a powerful subsystem or by vocal parts of an issue network. Bureaucrats may also find it difficult to access a public forum for advancing their views. Their ideas have to be cleared by committees and officials inside and outside their respective agencies before they are advanced in public. For example, typically the Office of Management and Budget's Office of Information and Regulatory Affairs has to clear all new policies to make certain that they conform to the president's program. All of this is complicated; it takes time, and issues may die because of the barriers that these difficult procedures create. In contrast, a member of Congress has access to the public, the White House, and the cabinet. Drawing on these assets, he or she can assist the agency by shortening the bureaucrats' clearance process and by removing some opposition. A system of mutual dependencies even at the stage of policy initiation is operating across the branches, and these dependencies are observable right through the implementation stage of policy development.

Tobacco politics would have continued as it had for years if those favoring change had relied solely on Congress or solely on the bureaucracy to initiate that change. Instead, members of Congress and bureaucrats in league with some interest groups called on each other for help. The bureaucracy had a long, although mixed, history of concern with the content of cigarette advertising and the dangers of smoking to health. In its employ were scientists, doctors, and economists who had devoted a large portion of their professional careers to these issues. At least one agency in the bureaucracy, the FTC, had been ready to implement a health warning for several years but lacked the power or support to do so. To realize their goals, bureaucrats had to act in concert with other bureaucrats, friendly members of Congress, the White House, and representatives of special interests, just as the tobacco policy subsystem did. Once the coalition of tobacco dissidents was formed and active, they were able to challenge the policymaking monopoly that the traditional tobacco subsystem enjoyed.

NOTES

1. *Liggett and Myers Tobacco Co.*, 55 Federal Trade Commission 354 (1958).
2. *Brown and Williamson Tobacco Corporation*, 34 Federal Trade Commission 1689 (1942).
3. *Guides* is the official term for these rules and can be thought of authoritative guidelines.
4. Shirleen Holt, "Companies Increasingly Saying Smokers Need Not Apply," *Seattle Times*, October 10, 2004.
5. For an insightful discussion of policy ideas and policy space, see Giandomenico Majone, *Evidence, Argument, and Persuasion in the Policy Process*. (New Haven, Conn.: Yale University Press, 1989).
6. Deborah A. Stone, *Policy Paradox: The Art of Political Decision Making*, rev. ed. (New York: Norton, 2002), explains how policy solutions may precede policy problems that the solutions address.
7. Majone, in *Evidence, Argument, and Persuasion in the Policy Process*, suggests that the following factors influence whether a particular proposed solution is actually picked up in the political arena: the solution is available (i.e., it is sitting on the shelf of the warehouse); the solution is persuasively communicated to policymakers and the public; the proposed solution is seen to meet the demands of the political environment; a professional consensus underlies the solution; it is consistent with the prevailing ideology, such as that of free enterprise; the theory underlying the proposed solution can be shown to have actually worked in practice; and the solution is related to broader public concerns (like jobs, inflation, consumer protection, and disaffection with big government).
8. For an enlightening discussion of this phenomenon, see John W. Kingdon, *Agendas, Alternatives, and Public Policies*, 3rd ed. (Reading, Mass.: Addison-Wesley, 2003). Also, for the classic statement on the fortuitous convergence of forces that leads to policy outcomes, see M. D. Cohen, J. G. March, and J. P. Olsen, "A Garbage Can Model of Organizational Choice," *Administrative Science Quarterly* 17, no. 1 (1972): 1–25.
9. "If Tobacco Were Spinach," *The Nation*, November 30, 1963.
10. One signal that the tobacco industry was losing its congressional support in the 1990s was the curtailment by Congress of promoting the sale of tobacco products abroad. The General Accounting Office, however, found that the Foreign Agricultural Service was poorly implementing its mandate (U.S. General Accounting Office, "USDA's Foreign Agricultural Service Lacks Specific Guidance for Congressional Restrictions on Promoting Tobacco," GAO-03-618, May 2003). The General Accounting Office is now the Government Accountability Office.
11. Letter to Senator Warren G. Magnuson, printed in U.S. Senate Committee on Commerce, *Cigarette Labeling and Advertising: Hearings before the Committee on Commerce*, 89th Cong., 1st sess., 1965, 28.
12. Dan Cordtz, "Congress Likely to Vote a Mild Law Requiring Warnings on Packages," *Wall Street Journal*, March 22, 1965, 1.

13. This kind of disagreement between the political appointees and the career professionals (who, like the surgeon general, may be appointed but who tend to identify with their professional duties and ethics more than with the administration that appointed them) is a long-running and continuing theme in modern American politics.

14. Maurine B. Neuberger, *Smoke Screen: Tobacco and the Public Welfare* (Englewood Cliffs, N.J.: Prentice Hall, 1963).

15. *Action on Smoking & Health V. Harris*, 655 F.2d 236, 239 (1980).

16. U.S. Department of Health and Human Services, Public Health Service, Office on Smoking and Health, *Use of Tobacco* (available at the Technical Information Service, Office on Smoking and Health, Rockville, Md.), July 1969, 431–32. A discussion of one of these public health surveys can be found in *Reports of the United States Senate Report of Proceedings Held before Committee on Commerce S. 559 and S. 547 Bills to Regulate Labeling of Cigarettes, and for Other Purposes*, March 22, 1963, 7.

17. *Christian Science Monitor*, October 20, 1967. Similarly, Senator Robert Kennedy was once heard to have said, "Cigarettes would have been banned years ago were it not for the tremendous economic power of their producers." Cited in Kenneth Michael Friedman, *Public Policy and the Smoking-Health Controversy: A Comparative Study* (Lexington, Mass.: Lexington Books, 1975), 1.

18. Upton Sinclair, *The Jungle* (New York: New American Library, 1960).

19. Rachel Carson, *Silent Spring* 40th Anniversary Edition (Boston: Houghton Mifflin, 1994).

20. Ralph Nader, *Unsafe at Any Speed: The Designed-In Dangers of the American Automobile* (New York: Grossman, 1965).

21. David von Drehle, *Triangle: The Fire That Changed America* (New York: Atlantic Monthly Press, 2004).

22. *The New York Times*, May 24, 1962, 16.

23. On June 12, 1957, Surgeon General Leroy E. Burney declared it the official position of the PHS that the evidence pointed to a causal relationship between smoking and lung cancer.

24. Those groups asked to suggest people for the committee were the American Cancer Society; the American Medical Association; the Tobacco Institute, Inc.; the FDA; the National Tuberculosis Association; the FTC; and the U.S. Office of Science and Technology.

25. Neuberger, *Smoke Screen*.

26. Members of the Advisory Committee were Dr. Eugene H. Guthrie, PHS, the committee's staff director; Dr. Stanhope Bayne-Jones, Walter Reed Army Institute of Research; Dr. Walter J. Burdette, University of Utah; William G. Cochran, Harvard University; Dr. Emmanuel Farber, University of Pittsburgh; Dr. Louis F. Fieser, Harvard University; Dr. Jacob Furth, Columbia University; Dr. John B. Hickman, Indiana University; Dr. Charles A. LeMaistre, University of Texas; Dr. Leonard M. Schuman, University of Minnesota; and Dr. Maurice H. Seevers, University of Michigan.

27. In 1972, Congress enacted two laws that would have made the procedures used by the surgeon general's committee improper. These were the Federal Advisory Committee Act (5 U.S.C., App. I) and the Government in the Sunshine Act (5 U.S.C. 552b). Under these laws, meetings must be in the open, and transcripts must be available to the public. Although certain advisory groups and some meetings are exempted, the smoking and health committee would almost certainly not be exempt were it to meet today. Secrecy and the drama it generated were important to the political strategy of the Surgeon General's Advisory Committee. The outcome of its work (or at least the timing of its implementation) would be different under the new requirements. The Advisory Committee's impact would surely have been less significant.

28. U.S. Department of Health, Education and Welfare, *Smoking and Health: Report of the Advisory Committee to the Surgeon General of the Public Health Service*, Public Health Service Document No. 1103 (Washington, D.C.: U.S. Government Printing Office, 1964).

29. When the smoking and health issue was first raised in 1954, there were pronounced adverse effects on tobacco shares, and the new report was even more directly critical of smoking than the earlier study. The bold-faced summaries of the committee's work were forceful enough for reasonable people to anticipate an unfavorable reaction in the stock market and in certain other quarters. The summaries read, "Cigarette smoking is causally related to lung cancer in men; the magnitude of the effect of cigarette smoking far outweighs all other factors. The data for women, though less extensive, point in the same direction" (U.S. Department of Health, Education and Welfare, *Smoking and Health*, 37).

30. Ronald J. Troyer and Gerald E. Markle, *Cigarettes: The Battle over Smoking* (New Brunswick, N.J.: Rutgers University Press, 1983), 77.
31. U.S. Department of Health, Education and Welfare, *Smoking and Health*.
32. U.S. Department of Health, Education and Welfare, *Smoking and Health*.
33. The notice was published in the *Federal Register* on January 22, 1964, four days after the FTC made the announcement (*Federal Register* 29 [1964]: 530–32).

4

THE LEGAL BASIS OF BUREAUCRACY
CENTERED POLICYMAKING

*It may clarify the proper administrative function . . . to think
of [congressional] legislation as unfinished law.*

—SUPREME COURT JUSTICE ROBERT JACKSON

The Federal Trade Commission's (FTC's) announcement of its intention to require a health warning was a reminder to everyone that agencies have the power to make policy. The cigarette interests were not pleased by the announcement, although they had every reason to expect it after the release of the surgeon general's report.

A commonly held notion in American public life is that regulatory agencies are the captives of those they regulate. The commission's action demonstrated that capture is not the only rule governing agency behavior. Those who were to be regulated knew that FTC policymaking would be different in both procedure and outcome from congressional policymaking because agency personnel were much less sympathetic to the tobacco position than were members of Congress. Lobbyists make it their business to know where they are likely to receive the most favorable decisions, and those representing business and industry have come to view Congress as being more responsive to them than the bureaucracy in many cases.

The strategy of the tobacco supporters was to question FTC authority to make policy involving a cigarette health warning and thereby ensure that the final policy decision would be made by Congress, not the FTC. Consequently, in their argument against the commission's announcement of its intention to require a health warning, the tobacco interests raised with skill and eloquence some of the most basic questions that have stalked the growth of agency policymaking powers. For example, they asked, How, in a democratic form of government, could nonelected bureaucrats be permitted to exercise powers of government that are constitutionally allocated to elected representatives of the people? How could so important a matter, one affecting a large industry and thousands (perhaps millions) of people, be decided by bureaucrats?

How were those associated with the tobacco interests to participate in the policy process when the policymakers were not subject to popular control through elections? And how might they hold the administrative decision makers accountable for their decisions when they had no electoral process to resort to? These questions were then and are now fundamentally important to any system of representative government.

CONGRESSIONAL DELEGATION OF AUTHORITY

The basis of the complaints of the cigarette interests rested in the clear language of article 1 of the Constitution, "All legislative powers herein granted shall be vested in a Congress of the United States." There is nothing in other sections of the document to indicate that legislative or policymaking powers should reside in the bureaucracy. Yet the accumulation of all policy powers in the legislature has never worked well, and from the beginning, Congress has been obliged to find ways to share its powers.

Although legislative bodies theoretically could write and enact all the rules that govern society, it is seldom practical for them to do so. For a time, Congress and state legislatures tried it. They grappled with many complex policy issues that experience has now taught them to entrust to administrative agencies. Railroad rates and other matters of a regulatory nature, for example, were once written by legislatures. Yet, from the time the Constitution was adopted, Congress recognized that it could not effectively handle the intricacies of policymaking. In 1789, the first Congress delegated to Alexander Hamilton's newly organized Department of the Treasury the authority to set benefits and establish reimbursement policies for disabled Revolutionary War veterans. Even in those early years, it was recognized that there are natural limitations on legislatures that make them incapable of acting as effective policymakers under conditions where details are complex and unclear.

These conditions arise especially when policy decisions involving technical knowledge are deemed necessary. Congress does not have sufficient expertise or the necessary time to devote to the details of much modern policymaking. It is very nearly impossible to foresee all the individual cases and circumstances that are bound to arise in a given area of policy in a dynamic environment. Under these circumstances, policy is usually made incrementally, over extended periods of time, in the legislature and in the bureaucracy. Career experts in the bureaucracy are in a better position to devote continued attention to a particular problem and develop policy standards and guidelines than are members of Congress. If Congress were to enact all the specific rules and regulations necessary for the administration of programs, one of two equally undesirable results would occur: The rules would be too general to serve as effective guidelines for administrators, or they would be too rigid and inflexible, rendering them foolish in short order. In delegating policymaking powers to agencies, Congress relieves itself of the burden of detailed work and frees itself to devote time to issues of basic policy.

Under delegated authority, agencies shape, mold, and even change policies set down by Congress in legislation. When Congress authorizes the creation of an agency or a new program, there is usually little reference to the intricacies of implementing the program. Instead of writing an operations manual that would guide the agency through all situations, Congress usually states simply that a program should be carried out in a "just" or "reasonable" manner. A phrase that sometimes appears in legislation is the mandate that an agency perform "in the public interest, convenience, and necessity." The vagueness of such instructions or guidelines allows an agency considerable latitude in making policy as it sees fit.

The policymaking process might be thought of as taking place in three consecutive stages. The first (begging the question of where the idea for change originated, for the moment) is legislative, involving Congress and the president, that is, congressional passage and presidential approval of a bill. A major, new policy begins in that process. The remaining two stages are administrative. The second has been alluded to by the late Supreme Court Justice Robert Jackson: "It may clarify the proper administrative function . . . to think of [congressional] legislation as unfinished law which the administrative body must complete before it is ready for application."[1] In this stage, the agencies clarify legislation by writing specific regulations or rules. The third stage occurs when a program is being administered. At that point, policy is made and altered to account for changing conditions. There is sometimes a fourth stage, review by Congress or the courts. Congress, through its oversight procedures, can change the handiwork of an agency as it changed the FTC policy in the cigarette controversy. By writing new legislation, changing appropriations, or simply threatening to take such actions, Congress can make its influence felt. And whether or not Congress acts, judicial review of agency policymaking might reverse or substantially alter what an agency has done.

As the problems of society become more complex, Congress tends to rely increasingly on agencies for policymaking. American society has already reached a point where administrative agencies are producing more policy than the other two branches of the government combined. One observer, former Commissioner Lee Loevinger of the Federal Communications Commission, has compared the frequency of agency policymaking with that of Congress and the courts:

> While the courts handle thousands of cases each year and Congress produces hundreds of laws each year, the administrative agencies handle hundreds of thousands of matters annually. The administrative agencies are engaged in the mass production of law, in contrast to the courts, which are engaged in the handicraft production of law.[2]

One cannot quantify and measure amounts of policymaking with precision. Yet there are some reasonable statistical indicators. Cornelius Kerwin makes the case by using a variety of them. He notes that the number of agency rules reviewed by the Office of Management and Budget is well over 2,500 per year for the past two or three decades. And the number of proposed rules published in the *Federal Register* is around 15,000 per year.[3] The number of laws passed by Congress in comparable years is between 300 and 400. Using these data alone, it is not unreasonable to assert that in terms of policy decisions that directly affect persons and property, administrative agencies are today central to the processes of policymaking.[4]

Production of law by agencies could be dangerous for representative government. If there were no way for elected officials or an independent judiciary to control administrative decisions, policymaking by an independent bureaucracy would contradict traditional theories of representation on which democratic systems are built. As indicated earlier, such traditional theories imply that means should be available for citizens to both participate in policymaking and hold government accountable for the decisions it makes. The effectiveness of democratic controls on agency policymaking has been questioned for many years, as the history of the FTC and other agencies shows. The protestations of the tobacco lobbyists over placing a health warning on cigarette packages were a modern revival of all the most difficult questions about agency policymaking that had been raised in the past. Yet the actions of the FTC in the cigarette labeling controversy show that in some circumstances bureaucratic policymaking can enhance the representational qualities of government.

Although there are serious theoretical and practical obstacles to the delegation of policymaking authority, agencies have been operating under the umbrella of delegated authority for many years. If the court determines that Congress has been ambiguous in authorizing an agency to act, court precedents mandate that judges defer to the agency's view. The Supreme Court has held congressional delegations to be unconstitutional in only a handful of cases and then on grounds that the delegated power has been overly broad in scope or that Congress has explicitly denied that a particular delegation should occur.[5] Consequently, many claim there is little question about the legal ability of Congress to delegate. The law on this point seems so firm to Kenneth Culp Davis, an authority on administrative law, that he advised, "Lawyers who try to win cases by arguing that congressional delegations are unconstitutional almost invariably do more harm than good to their clients' interests."[6] Nevertheless, this constitutional issue, as any other, remains within the discretion of a court guided by precedent—a practice known as *stare decisis*—but not entirely bound by it.

Congressional delegation has two aspects, however. Even if it is rarely possible to argue today that Congress has transgressed constitutional limits in delegating its powers to an agency, it is still feasible to argue in a practical instance that some specific action by the agency has exceeded the limits of the power delegated to it. The basic delegation, in other words, may be constitutionally proper, but the agency's particular action may exceed the delegated powers.

An argument like this was made in 1972, when one industrial group, the National Petroleum Refiners Association, persuaded a U.S. district court that the FTC lacked the statutory authority to issue trade regulation rules. The immediate issue concerned whether the commission could issue a rule requiring octane ratings on gasoline pumps. The U.S. court of appeals reversed the district court on June 27, 1973, and upheld the commission's authority to make binding rules. Neither court was asked to say whether Congress could or could not delegate the power to make these rules without violating the Constitution. The issue was simply whether Congress had delegated that power; the district court thought it had not, but the appellate court disagreed.[7]

The tobacco interests' strategy against the FTC's action to require a warning on cigarette packages and advertising was based in part on the claim that Congress had stopped short of providing authority to the commission to issue a so-called regulation rule—essentially the same kind of argument made a few years later by the National Petroleum Refiners Association. The Tobacco Institute's position in regard to the FTC is summarized in the following words:

> [I]n terms of policy and discretion, whatever substantive regulation may be believed to be necessary in this area of smoking and health, Congress alone should enact it. . . we respectfully submit that in these proposed Trade Regulation Rules the Commission is not exercising the authority conferred upon it by Congress in the Federal Trade Commission Act. It is plainly legislating.[8]

The tobacco interests must have recognized that their argument contained some elements of risk in view of the Supreme Court's long-standing position on congressional delegation. If it were thought that they were arguing that any delegation of power to make the rules in question was unconstitutional, their argument might be dismissed in the way asserted previously by Davis. This case never reached the Supreme Court. Nonetheless, the Tobacco Institute's approach could be viewed as astute in more than one respect. Important segments of public opinion could be expected to rally to the cry that faceless administrators were performing a role that should be—and indeed was—reserved to the elected representatives of the people. Industrial and commercial entities, not desirous of being future targets of bureaucratic zealots, could be expected to be sympathetic to that view. Furthermore, by arguing the delegation issue, they were able to gain the attention of Congress and thus increase the possibility that the controversy would be transferred, eventually, from the commission to Congress.

Questioning the power of Congress to delegate and examining closely the limits of its delegations challenge the concept of administrative policy-making and, indeed, the nature of policy process in which powers are shared by several institutions of government. The challenge is obvious when it is argued that a particular delegation is unconstitutional. It is more subtle (but no less real) when the focus is on whether the agency has exceeded the limits of a delegation that is conceded to be proper in itself. A narrowly legalistic reading of the delegation can go far to cripple the agency's policymaking efforts, while a broader construction, tending toward the conclusion that any powers reasonably needed to achieve the law's objectives are implicitly given to the agency, can greatly facilitate them.

Since the legality and limits of delegation are so important to the administrative system in general, one profits from a closer examination of the causes that have prompted Congress to delegate authority and the basis for judicial approval of such action. The history of the FTC and its early responsibilities in the antitrust field are relevant to an understanding of these subjects.

REGULATORY AUTHORITY DELEGATED TO THE FTC

In the latter part of the nineteenth century, the nation experienced the growth of large industrial enterprises that cornered large shares of the market for various commodities. The notion that one or a few companies should control a market ran counter to the laissez-faire ideal of vigorous competition. State regulation proved to be largely ineffective in breaking up or preventing the creation of large monopolies, partially because many of them were national in scope. The federal government inaugurated so-called trust-busting with the passage of the Sherman Act in 1890. The Sherman Act used vague legislative language, thus leaving government agencies without adequate guidance or mechanisms to implement policy consistent with the hazy statute. The act created no administrative agency; no policymaking authority was delegated by Congress. The statements of major purpose in the first two sections alert the reader to the problems of enforcement that were to develop:

> **Section 1:** Every contract, combination in the form of trust. . . or conspiracy in restraint of trade or commerce. . . is hereby declared to be illegal. . . .
>
> **Section 2:** Every person who shall monopolize, or combine or conspire with any other person or persons, to monopolize. . . shall be deemed guilty of a misdemeanor . . .

The language of these sections required further definition. Who was to define what constituted "a conspiracy in restraint of trade," for example? There was no answer to this question in the Sherman Act, although by implication the burden fell on the federal courts.[9]

Thirteen years after passage of the act, the Antitrust Division was established within the Department of Justice to investigate and initiate prosecution of those corporations and individuals who violated the Sherman Act. Almost immediately, the division encountered serious difficulty. The wording of the act provided very few guidelines for prosecution, and the division had to develop workable definitions or guidelines from the act's general language. Without delegated policymaking powers from Congress, the division found its job exceedingly difficult and, eventually, close to impossible.

The only technique available for developing standards was the case-by-case method. Alleged violators of the act had to be taken to court. The judges, on the basis of the information presented, decided whether the challenged action violated the Sherman Act. This method proved to be unsatisfactory in developing standards. Not only slow, awkward, and unpredictable, it relied on judges who might or might not have been fully aware of the intricacies of corporate finance and economics. The courts were confronted with a wide range of cases; judges could not afford to specialize in these vastly complicated matters. The results were that no hard or firm standards emerged under the Sherman Act. Nearly all questions that could conceivably arise under the act had to be tested in the courts. At the same time, precedent proved to be of little use because cases differed sufficiently enough from one another to make the formulation of rules of general applicability virtually impossible.

Inevitably, reliance on the courts for interpretation bred uncertainty. Neither the government nor the corporate giants knew what might violate the Sherman Act. The pinnacle of uncertainty was reached in 1911 with two Supreme Court decisions, one involving the Standard Oil Company and the other the American Tobacco Company.[10] In these cases, the Court wrote what came to be called the "rule of reason." Basically, the Court said that only unreasonable restraints of trade or monopolies were in violation of the Sherman Act. These decisions underscored the frustration of the Court in dealing with antitrust policy. Nothing was clarified; in fact, the situation was made even more difficult because there was another term that begged for definition. What constituted an "unreasonable" restraint of trade? Where would the courts draw the line between what was "reasonable" and what was "unreasonable"?[11]

The experience of the government with the Sherman Act dramatized the need for Congress explicitly to delegate policymaking power to the agency administering the act. It was clear that reliance on the courts for policymaking would result in an inadequate body of law, unpredictable and difficult to enforce. The antitrust situation grew increasingly problematic and even came to the attention of the president. Expressing the fears of many parties familiar with the morass, President Taft stated that judicial involvement in antitrust policymaking "might involve our whole judicial system in disaster."[12]

Concerned members of Congress realized that the Sherman Act had to be modified. Some members thought that the modification ought to be in the direction of making the act more explicit. They wanted to spell out in detailed legislation the corporate actions that violated the Sherman Act. This delineation would have eliminated or reduced reliance on the courts for the development of enforcement standards, according to those who favored this approach. Others disagreed. They argued that Congress was not well equipped to write the detailed legislation necessary; furthermore, Senator Francis G. Newlands (D-Ariz.) argued that it would be unwise to attempt to write detailed legislation to clarify the Sherman Act. He said on the floor of the Senate, "If there were 20 bad trade practices today and you were to name them in law and condemn them, there would be others established tomorrow."[13]

Continuity and expertise were needed to enforce antitrust policy. The senator supported the creation of an administrative board that would have both enforcement and policymaking powers. The Interstate Commerce Commission, established in 1887, served as Senator Newlands's model. A panel of this sort, he reasoned, could develop precedents, traditions, and a continuous policy based on orderly experience in enforcement and in the refinement of guidelines. The views of Senator Newlands prevailed, and the FTC was established by Congress in 1914.

That same year, Congress passed the Clayton Antitrust Act. Passage of this act showed that Congress was not yet willing to give up its prerogative of writing detailed regulations for an agency such as the FTC. In an attempt to refine the Sherman Act by legislating regulations, the Clayton Act detailed those actions of corporations or individuals that were prohibited. Thus, for example, the Clayton Act prohibits price discrimination if the purpose of such discrimination is to lessen competition or create a monopoly. This congressional attempt to be more explicit did not withstand the tests of time and experience, however. The provisions of the Clayton Act were still too broad and ill defined to provide enlightened guidance for effective enforcement. The courts would have remained the principal policymaker in the antitrust field had Congress not created the FTC, for neither the Clayton Act nor the Sherman Act ended the need for interpretation by the courts. It eventually fell, at least in part, to the FTC to interpret and enforce the provisions of the Clayton Act, thereby reducing some of the burden on the courts.

The process of experimentation with antitrust policymaking at the turn of the twentieth century has been repeated in other areas of public policy. Whenever standards have had to be developed for the administration of new and continuing programs, Congress has increasingly found it practical to empower bureaucratic agencies to do the task. Since agencies are better equipped to carry out the task of filling out congressionally enacted skeletal programs—with sometimes contradictory and vague provisions necessitated by the need to gather sufficient support to pass the legislation in the first place—they have, over the years, required and received increased policymaking responsibilities in order to carry out the apparent will of Congress and the president.

THE SUPREME COURT ON DELEGATION

Even from the earliest days of our constitutional history, Congress has found it necessary to delegate certain of its powers to bureaucratic agencies. Yet the Supreme Court held unconstitutional delegations in only the two cases previously cited, both of which were decided in 1935. It could be argued that the decisions in these cases were guided more by the Court's skepticism of New Deal programs than by genuine concern about violation of the doctrine of separation of powers. For years prior to 1935, the Court had upheld delegation after delegation. While doing so, the justices inserted into their opinions statements on the inviolability of the separation thesis. In one of the earliest cases involving this question, the Court wrote a reaffirmation of the separation principle while upholding the delegation itself:

> [I]t is essential to the successful working of this system that the persons entrusted with power in any one of these branches (executive, legislative and judicial) shall not be permitted to encroach upon the powers confided to the others, but that each by the law of its creation be limited to the exercise of the powers appropriate to its own department and no other.[14]

A few years later, in 1892, the Court upheld powers delegated to the president to change import duties. In doing so, the majority declared, "That Congress cannot delegate legislative power to the President is a principle universally recognized as vital to the integrity and maintenance of the system of government ordained by the Constitution."[15] Having made this point, the Court satisfied itself that the power to change import duties was not a legislative power.

The doctrine of separation came into conflict with the demands of modern policymaking long ago. The Court, through semantic flights of fancy, seemed content to satisfy itself with strong statements about the theoretical impossibility of delegation while in the same decisions upholding the impossible. The Court began to take a less ambiguous approach in the 1930s when it held that, under certain circumstances, Congress might find it necessary to delegate authority. Still, these powers were to be limited by congressional standards. "Congress cannot delegate any part of its legislative power except under the limitation of a prescribed standard," wrote the justices in 1931.[16]

The question of standards did not erect any important barriers to delegation. Acceptable standards were as vague and ill defined as such statements as "the public interest" and "fair and equitable allocation." Within a few years, the Court came very close to admitting that, in certain circumstances, no standard at all was necessary. In a 1947 decision, the Court wrote that it might have been desirable to have written explicit standards in the Home Owners Act of 1933 but acknowledged that the existence of standards in this field perhaps was not crucial. In such a highly developed and professionalized field as corporate management, the Court reasoned, "experience and many precedents have crystallized into well-known and generally acceptable standards."[17] Therefore, Congress did not have to write standards into the legislation in this case.

At various times, certain portions of the Federal Trade Commission Act were tested on the grounds that they were unconstitutional delegations. A court of appeals held that similar delegations had been upheld in the past and found no reason to hold these unconstitutional.[18]

The policymaking powers of regulatory commissions such as the FTC have caused some special problems of control. Congress, anxious to keep the regulatory commissions under surveillance, was reluctant to give the president as much influence over them as he had over the executive departments. Consequently, the commissions were assigned to a kind of no-man's-land between the executive agencies and Congress. Their unusual status led to the use of the term "independent" in describing their relationship to both Congress and the chief executive.

The history of the commissions has been one of debate and political struggle between those who argue that the president should have more power over commissions and those who wish to strengthen congressional control. The presidential backers argue that the president is responsible for seeing that the law is faithfully executed and that independent commissions, specifically because of their relative autonomy, make this responsibility difficult, if not impossible, to carry out. Others cite the broad, delegated powers enjoyed by the commissions and argue that Congress, as the source of these powers, should keep close watch over their use. Over the past fifty years, the presidential power advocates have won a number of victories, including establishing regulatory agencies like the Environmental Protection Agency and the Occupational Safety and Health Administration clearly within the executive branch (following the mold of the Food and Drug Administration) with their heads serving at the pleasure of the president rather than serving a specific term of years.

The institutional location of the independent commissions does result in differences in the way they are managed as well as differences in the way policy issues and goals are selected and decided. Often, disagreement over policies leads to calls for organizational reform that would put a commission more clearly within the orbit of either the president or Congress. However, throughout U.S. history, the independents seem to relate more closely to Congress than the president. One would surmise this to be true because those agencies are doing the work Congress once did and because Congress holds the power of the purse.[19]

Not everyone agrees with this assessment. William L. Cary, former chairman of the Securities and Exchange Commission, for example, claims there is little difference between an executive agency and a regulatory commission in its relationship to the president or Congress. He argues that some executive agencies, like the Army Corps of Engineers, are closer to Congress than to the president even though scrutiny of an organization chart would seem to reveal the opposite. However, influence over the commissions depends to a considerable extent on personalities within the congressional interest groups–executive branch subsystem and the nature of the issue involved. Cary reflects that the frustration of those caught between Congress and the president in this observation:

> Government regulatory commissions are often referred to as "independent" agencies, but this cannot be taken at face value by anyone who has ever had any experience in Washington. In fact, government regulatory agencies are stepchildren whose custody is contested by both Congress and the Executive, but without very much affection from either one.[20]

CHANGE IN EMPHASIS AT THE FTC

That the Supreme Court supported delegation in the area of antitrust did not immediately provide the FTC with an entirely free hand to engage in policymaking. Immediately after its establishment, the FTC encountered difficulties in enforcing laws within its jurisdiction because of the Court's narrow interpretation of the FTC's enabling legislation. A member and one-time chairman of the commission wrote that in the first ten years, the Court eviscerated the commission's powers.[21] Although the commission had made serious and thoughtful attempts to determine what it could and should prevent, the courts were not impressed, and the FTC's powers were seriously limited in four cases decided soon after it had been established by Congress.[22]

The Supreme Court also narrowly defined the FTC's jurisdiction over unfair trade practices. When the commission acted to prevent misleading advertising for an obesity cure called Marvola, the Court objected. The FTC directed the producers of this substance to include in their advertising the statement that Marvola could not be safely taken without the supervision of a competent physician. After reviewing medical testimony, the Court held that the question of safety was one of opinion and not one of fact. The Court said that since the advertisers testified that they honestly believed their product to be safe, the FTC would have to prove with scientific evidence that the product was harmful before it could act. Any question about the safety of a product, therefore, was resolved in favor of the producer. In an earlier case, the Court had weakened even more substantially the powers of the commission. According to the Court, the FTC's jurisdiction over unfair trade practices was limited to instances where a party injured or impaired the business of a competitor.[23] This interpretation of the law left the commission without the power to move against a company that injured consumers through harmful or deceptive practices. Consumer protection was wrested, almost in its entirety, from the FTC by this decision; the consumer had no grounds on which he could bring a complaint.

By 1938, however, sufficient momentum had been generated in Congress to expand the jurisdiction of the FTC to include consumer protection. The Wheeler-Lea Act of that year specifically empowered the commission to deal with "unfair or deceptive acts or practices in commerce." It contained provisions extending the commission's powers to dealing with false advertising of foods, drugs, devices, and cosmetics. With this law, the FTC began to devote most of its energies to the elimination of deception, particularly deception in advertising. At the same time, its antitrust activity subsided precipitously.

By the time that the surgeon general's report on the hazards of smoking appeared in 1964, the FTC had a substantial amount of experience with misleading advertising, including cigarette advertising. It had refined its regulatory techniques considerably over the years. A court decision had even upheld the commission's right to demand positive disclosure of information where the effect of nondisclosure was to deceive a substantial segment of the purchasing public.[24]

Yet even with this experience and the necessary legal authority, all was not well with the FTC and its regulation of cigarette advertising. The commission had succeeded in issuing a ban on cigarette advertisements that made or implied claims about the supposed health benefits of smoking in 1955. And in 1960, the FTC banned advertising claims regarding the relative health benefits of smoking filtered cigarettes. All the while, cigarette consumption was rising rapidly. Policing advertisements had apparently not resulted in conveying to the public the health dangers involved in cigarette smoking. The commission was coming around to the view that in the face of all the adverse health reports, it was cigarette advertising alone that accounted for the rise in sales. Some of the commissioners had concluded that the public was being deceived into thinking that the consequences of smoking were social acceptability and popularity rather than ill health. They felt that FTC actions against cigarette ads were not productive and, at the same time, that the commission should be able to use its powers over deceptive trade practices to stop whatever parts of advertisements were misleading the public.

Ironically, the root of the FTC's problem was substantially the same as the government's under the Sherman Act over half a century earlier. The commission was attempting to regulate cigarette advertising on a case-by-case basis. Each time the commission ruled a particular advertisement deceptive, the industry came up with a variation that could squeak by under the rule of the previous case. This cat-and-mouse game was proving to be an endless and fruitless process. The commission needed to write general regulations for the whole industry; the case method, whether employed by an agency or by the courts, had proved to be too cumbersome a method of developing regulatory policy.

In 1963, the commission moved to solve its problems by incorporating in its rules a procedure that could be used to write enforceable regulations for a whole category of industries. The chairman of the FTC saw the adoption of rule-making procedures as the only way to make the commission an effective regulator. The surgeon general's report gave the commission both the substantive information and the impetus it needed to use its new rule-making procedure in the field of cigarette advertising. This new procedure was set into motion only one week after the surgeon general released his report on smoking and health.[25]

NOTES

1. *Federal Trade Commission v. Ruberoid*, 343 U.S. 470 (1952).
2. Lee Loevinger, "The Administrative Agency as a Paradigm of Government—A Survey of the Administrative Process," *Indiana Law Journal* 40, no. 3 (spring 1965): 305. Justice Jackson noted the rise of administrative powers in a now famous dissent, "The rise of administrative bodies probably has been the most significant legal trend of the last century and perhaps more values today are affected by their decisions than by those of all the courts. . . . They also have begun to have important consequences on personal rights. They have become a veritable fourth branch of Government, which has deranged our three branch legal theories much as the concept of a fourth dimension unsettles our three-dimensional thinking" (*Federal Trade Commission v. Ruberoid*).
3. Cornelius M. Kerwin, *Rulemaking: How Government Agencies Write Law and Make Policy*, 3rd ed. (Washington, D.C.: CQ Press, 2003).
4. The Administrative Conference of the United States claims that there are more than thirty departments and agencies that have power to make decisions affecting individual rights. Each year the conference develops recommendations to Congress and the president for improvements in agency procedures that affect the rights of private persons and business interests through administrative investigation, adjudication, licensing, rule making, rate making, claims determination, and other proceedings.
5. The two classic cases in this area are *Panama Refining Company v. Ryan*, 293 U.S. 388 (1935), and *Schechter Poultry Corporation v. United States*, 295 U.S. 495 (1935).
6. Kenneth Culp Davis, *Administrative Law and Government* (St. Paul, Minn.: West, 1960), 55.
7. *National Petroleum Refiners Association v. FTC*, 482 F.2d 672 (D.C. Cir. 1973).
8. From the statement on behalf of the Tobacco Institute, Inc., submitted to the FTC, 6 (mimeograph).
9. *Standard Oil Co. v. United States*, 221 U.S. 1, 66–70 (1911).
10. *Standard Oil Co. v. United States*, and *American Tobacco Company v. United States*, 221 U.S. 106 (1911).
11. For a thoughtful discussion of the enforcement problem, see Gerard C. Henderson, *The FTC: A Study in Administrative Law and Procedure* (New Haven, Conn.: Yale University Press, 1924).
12. *Congressional Record*, 61st Cong., 2nd sess., 382, quoted in Henderson, *The FTC*, 16.
13. *Congressional Record*, Senate, 63rd Cong., 2nd sess., June 13, 1914, 11084.
14. *Kilbourne v. Thompson*, 103 U.S. 168 (1881).
15. *Field v. Clark*, 143 U.S. 649 (1892).
16. *United States v. Chicago, Minneapolis and St. Paul Railroad Company*, 282 U.S. 311, 324 (1931).
17. *Fahey v. Mallonee*, 332 U.S. 245, 250 (1947).
18. *Sears, Roebuck and Company v. Federal Trade Commission*, 258 Fed. 307 (CCA 7 1918).
19. For a discussion of management and goal setting in independent regulatory commissions, see Robert A. Katzmann, *Regulatory Bureaucracy: The Federal Trade Commission and Antitrust Policy* (Cambridge, Mass.: MIT Press, 1980).
20. William L. Cary, *Politics and the Regulatory Agencies* (New York: McGraw-Hill, 1967), 4.
21. Nelson B. Gaskell, *The Regulation of Competition* (New York: Harper and Brothers, 1936).
22. *Federal Trade Commission v. Warren, Jones and Gratz*, 253 U.S. 421 (1920); *Federal Trade Commission v. Curtis Publishing Company*, 260 U.S. 568 (1923); *Federal Trade Commission v. Klesner*, 230 U.S. 19 (1929); *Federal Trade Commission v. Raladam*, 233 U.S. 643 (1931).

23. *Silver v. Federal Trade Commission*, 292 F. 752 (1923).
24. *P. Lorillard Company v. Federal Trade Commission*, 136 F.2d 52.58 (4th Cir. 1950).
25. According to the FTC's manual, which was amended in 1962 to include this new rule-making procedure, trade regulation rules may "cover all applications of a particular statutory provision, may be nationwide in effect, or may be limited to particular areas or industries or to particular products or geographical areas." Trade regulation rules give the FTC the capability of issuing formal rules or guides to govern the conduct of large categories of producers. Further, it was stipulated that once the rules were issued, any violation of them could be used to initiate adjudicatory proceedings.

5

EFFECTIVE ENFORCEMENT
AND STRATEGIES TO COMBAT IT

PROCEDURES USED IN ADMINISTRATIVE
POLICYMAKING

Or has Congress allowed us an alternative method of proceeding?

—FTC CHAIRMAN PHILIP ELMAN IN THE CIGARETTE LABELING HEARING

Although the agencies of government are pictured in organizational charts as arms of the executive, they derive their power from acts of Congress. To enable regulatory agencies to implement and enforce the laws, two types of authority are granted by Congress: rule making and adjudicatory. These powers are often indistinguishable because they functionally overlap and mutually support one another. Adjudicatory authority is quasi-judicial in nature, while rule making is quasi-legislative or sublegislative. As a practical method of distinguishing these powers from each other, one may think of adjudicatory actions as being used to perform judicial or court-like activities, while rule-making activities serve to develop policies in a manner comparable to that used by legislatures.[1] They are powers and processes parallel to those in judicial and legislative institutions both in the sense that each is seen as a separate function and in the sense that in practice they are not separable from the other.

One thinks of a judicial action as a court applying law to a specific situation. Did person X or company Y violate a specific law? However, inevitably courts develop policy in the course of making judicial decisions in individual cases. Hence, judicial decisions frequently have the same effect as legislative acts, making it difficult to distinguish between rule-making and adjudicatory powers wherever they might be exercised. Courts might engage in rule making and adjudication simultaneously, as Supreme Court decisions in school desegregation illustrated. For example, applying a constitutional provision against the actions of *one* school district, the one named in the case, resulted in a major policy change for *all* school districts in the United States.

Yet legislative and judicial policymaking are conceptually and practically distinct. Rule making, which corresponds to legislating, is characterized by its general applicability. Rules formulated by agencies uniformly affect all within a given category, such as all cigarette producers. In contrast, adjudicatory action, which corresponds to judicial decision making, is based on a specific case involving an individual, a partnership, or a corporation. The end result of an adjudicatory proceeding is a determination of whether those named in the suit have violated a law or rule or perhaps whether the parties in question qualify for a license of some kind. Once the adjudicatory decision is made, a precedent is established that may apply to others similarly situated.

Procedurally, the two methods of exercising power differ. When an agency acts in its adjudicatory capacity, it must use procedures that are more formal than those employed under its rule-making functions. Rule-making procedures, on the other hand, are less formal, parallel to procedures used in legislative hearings. The different degree of formality of the procedures varies and is determined largely by the expected impact of the rule under consideration. At times they are similar to the procedures (or absence of procedures) used by moderators of roundtable discussions. In agency rule making, it is incumbent on the agency itself to determine which issues require formal rule-making procedures and which do not. The more formal procedures require that the public be notified and given the opportunity to be heard. They are patterned after those used when congressional committees hold public hearings and call witnesses to testify. In contrast, the procedures used in adjudicatory proceedings are parallel to procedures used in courts of law. Witnesses are sworn in before they testify, transcripts of the proceedings (and supporting documents) are made, all parties and the public have access to the transcript of the proceedings, and the agency's decision is made only on the basis of that transcript.

ADJUDICATION AND RULE MAKING AT THE FEDERAL TRADE COMMISSION

The Federal Trade Commission (FTC) uses both adjudicatory and rule-making powers to enforce and implement the laws within its jurisdiction, although for many years it used rule-making powers only in certain very narrowly defined areas. The commission had historically relied primarily on *informal* agreements for enforcement purposes. The characteristics of both formal and informal policymaking processes are shown in Figure 5.1. In the cigarette and health controversy, the FTC used its formal rule-making authority for the first time. This move sent a signal to the tobacco industry of the seriousness with which it approached cigarettes and health. Smoking gave the FTC the impetus to assert its power, although the tools it was to use were untested.

The adjudicatory procedure may be initiated through a complaint filed by those who consider themselves aggrieved by a violation of one of the laws within the commission's jurisdiction. The complaint is followed by a formal

FIGURE 5.1 FEDERAL TRADE COMMISSION POWERS

I. Formal Powers

Procedurally cumbersome but relatively easy to enforce

A. Adjudicatory (quasi-judicial)

1. What: independent administrative law judges preside over court-like proceedings
2. Benefits: regular, predictable procedures with many protections; ability to appeal
3. Drawbacks: case-by-case, court-of-law–like decision-making process; fine for specific cases but hard to regulate general behavior
4. Example: 1942 cease-and-desist order regarding Penn Tobacco Company's claim that its Julep brand of cigarettes was a remedy for coughs

B. Rule Making (quasi-legislative)

1. What: commissioners and staffers preside over proceedings (very much like congressional hearing; quite informal compared to adjudicatory procedures)
2. Benefits: easier to control industry with class-based decisions
3. Drawbacks: concern for arbitrary use of agency powers

II. Informal Powers

Less costly and complex but difficult to enforce

A. Advisory Opinion

1. What: commissioners make a nonbinding ruling on a hypothetical case
2. Benefits: popular: gives industry chance to meet agency standards before the fact
3. Drawbacks: decisions are nonbinding on government; industry may be misled
4. Example: FTC's 1993 advisory opinion that gasohol should be considered automotive gasoline for purposes of octane-posting requirements

B. Trade Practices Conference

1. What: broad-based arbitration of voluntary codes or trade practice rules between agency and parties from affected industry
2. Benefits: builds a consensus that both the agency and the industry can live with
3. Drawbacks: bargaining required of both sides to the conflict
4. Example: FTC's 1955 advertising guidelines prohibiting claims about the tar and nicotine content of various brands (ending the tar derby)

continued

C. Consent Order

1. What: mutual agreement between agency and industry: no admission of guilt
2. Benefits: may be the most expeditious course; in lieu of adjudicatory proceeding
3. Drawbacks: no official record of malfeasance
4. Example: 1972; six cigarette companies agree (at behest of FTC) to include clear and conspicuous health warnings on all cigarette advertisements

---

hearing, usually before an administrative law judge, designed to assure the accused party of many of the same protections provided for defendants in court. If the examiner decides there has been a violation, he or she can recommend that a cease-and-desist order be issued. The defendant then has the opportunity to appeal to the commissioners themselves. Should that attempt fail, defendants are permitted to make an appeal to a U.S. court of appeals, which may render a decision that can then be appealed to the Supreme Court. As a result of its ruling, the commission has the power to levy substantial fines if the offense continues.

Although adjudicatory and rule-making procedures are the most powerful devices at the command of the commission, rule making was utilized very sparingly until the commission rewrote its own operating procedures in 1963, and adjudicatory proceedings are initiated in cases of blatant industrial violations, and then only when everything else has failed. Most of the FTC's efforts over the years have been directed toward gaining voluntary compliance or informal agreement. This practice is comparable to settling matters out of court and has the same virtues (expediency, less complexity, and lower costs), but it is also fraught with disadvantages. No formal record is made to guide others, and neither party in the dispute is protected by the rights and practices of legal proceedings.

The FTC uses three techniques to secure voluntary compliance with the law. One device is the advisory opinion. In the federal judicial system, unlike those of other countries and some of the states, the courts will not tell an inquiring party hypothetically whether something it plans to do might be illegal. Courts will decide only actual cases and controversies at law. However, the bureaucracy is not so limited. Given the complexities of modern government and of modern business planning, it is fortunate that the bureaucracy is free to tell an interested party how it might view some proposed action. Industry frequently requests opinions from the FTC, and the commissioners respond but note that their opinions are only advisory and not binding on the government. The advisory opinion is a useful device and accounts for a large part of the growth of quasi-judicial functions of agencies.

When the FTC wants to reach a broad spectrum of the corporate world, it resorts to another informal device called the trade practices conference. The commission invites industry to these conferences to discuss with the commissioners their regulatory problems, and, it is hoped, all leave the conference with their problems solved. Occasionally, voluntary codes or voluntary trade practice rules come out of these meetings.

The third kind of informal procedure leads to what are known as consent orders. These are voluntary agreements reached by the commission and a party about to enter (or in the course of entering) an adjudicatory proceeding. In the case of the consent order, the FTC has some leverage to exert over an accused business or corporation. By signing a consent order, the parties involved in the proceeding agree to stop whatever they are doing that the commission thought suspect, and the commission agrees to drop the proceedings. Signing the consent order is not an admission of guilt. The pressure that the commission can apply to sign an order—especially on a small company that might find it could ill afford the time or cash required to fight the commission or the publicity that would result—has made the consent order procedure one that has received much criticism over the years.

The informal procedures and adjudicatory procedures are tantamount to a relatively flaccid regulatory stick for the commission compared to general rule making, which is, in many ways, a much more potent device. Predictably, strong pressures have been placed on the commission not to use this procedure. And, of course, there was some question—articulated by industrial groups such as the cigarette producers during the labeling controversy—as to whether the legal authority to exercise general rule-making powers had been legally delegated to the FTC at all.

THE FTC'S EXPERIENCE WITH CIGARETTE REGULATION

The limited effectiveness of the commission's policymaking procedures was evident in the FTC's record on cigarette advertising regulation. The commission had invoked its adjudicatory powers in individual cases of deceptive advertising involving cigarette producers approximately twenty-five times between 1938 and 1968. But each of these decisions applied only to the parties cited in the particular case. Others who might have been engaged in the same deceptive act (or one closely related act) were not immediately affected by the commission's decision involving their less fortunate brethren. It is possible for those not named as a party to the case to continue the illegal practice until the FTC moves against them. Such action can take months or even years. Furthermore, only activities or practices complained of in the suit can be prohibited by the decision; slight variations from that practice even by the same parties must be dealt with by separate decisions. These same kinds of deficiencies that the FTC had found with its use of adjudicatory powers could be seen four decades later when the state attorneys general settled out of court with four major cigarette companies. In absence of a law or a rule covering all parties in a class or industry and enforceable by imposing significant penalties on wrongdoers, the public is left unprotected from fraudulent, deceptive, harmful, and predatory practices in a free-enterprise world that otherwise rewards and encourages such behavior.

In the case of cigarette advertising, the commission found itself putting out brushfires of deception while the inferno raged on. There was no way for the commission to state authoritatively a general policy of what constituted deception in cigarette ads for all advertisers. The procedures employed in adjudicatory actions narrowly define the scope of admissible evidence. Discussion of the ramifications of an industry-wide problem is difficult under such circumstances. Then too, the commission's action against cigarette producers provided requirements only about what could not be done, not about what had to be done. That is, the FTC could not require that a health warning appear on all packages through its adjudicatory procedures. Without rule making, the only way it could have approached this requirement would involve convening a trade practice conference in which a voluntary agreement to this effect was hammered out. Failing that, the FTC would have to deal with cigarette companies one at a time. In each instance, the FTC would have had to prove that such a positive disclosure was necessary.

One of the early cases involving cigarette advertising points up the problems with the commission's adjudicatory procedures. The manufacturers of a now extinct brand called Julep cigarettes claimed in their advertisements that their product was a remedy for coughs. Even in the early 1940s, this strained the credulity of the commission, and the Julep makers were forced to stop making the claim.[2] Yet within a short period, other makers advertised similar health claims. One producer proclaimed that there was not a cough in a carload of their cigarettes. That same manufacturer later announced that more doctors smoked their cigarettes than any other brand. Other manufacturers still use subtle techniques to achieve the same purpose, as when they imply that a filter protects the smoker or that light brands are less harmful than others.

Since it was impossible to fight the health inferences and subtleties in cigarette ads through adjudicatory procedures, the best way to eliminate deception according to the FTC was to require that a positive health warning statement appear in each advertisement. Rule-making authority was necessary before that requirement could be made. Commissioner Philip Elman summed up the FTC's frustration with adjudicatory procedures in the field of cigarette advertising and defended the effectiveness of rule-making procedures. When the tobacco interests challenged the commission's authority to use rule-making procedures, Commissioner Elman responded,

> Suppose there is a product in general use throughout the United States. . . .
> And suppose scientific research should conclusively establish that product
> induced sterility. Would you say that under the Federal Trade Commission

Act the only way in which this Commission could proceed to carry out its responsibilities of preventing deception . . . is to issue a complaint and a cease and desist order against each of the thousands and thousands of manufacturers? Or has Congress allowed us an alternative method of proceeding?[3]

The FTC did not rely on adjudicatory procedures alone but also attempted, without success, to deal with misleading cigarette advertising by informal means. In 1955 as a result of a trade practices conference, the commission issued a set of cigarette advertising guidelines. These were used in an attempt to have cigarette manufacturers voluntarily refrain from advertising the levels of tar and nicotine contained in their cigarettes. The guidelines did bring an end to the tar derby when the manufacturers agreed to discontinue advertisements containing confusing and ambiguous claims about the tar and nicotine content of their products.[4] But other parts of the voluntary guidelines were unsuccessful because the FTC was powerless to enforce them.

Ultimately, it would become clear to individuals, both inside the FTC and outside, that case-by-case quasi-judicial rulings and voluntary trade practice agreements, while helpful in specific instances, would be inadequate to the broader task of effectively warning the public of the health hazards of smoking. To accomplish that end, quasi-legislative rule-making procedures would have to be developed and adopted for commission use. These rule-making powers are not always granted to agencies by Congress in any specific, formal way. Instead, agencies often must nurture these procedures into existence themselves. So it was with the FTC.

THE FTC ADOPTS RULE-MAKING PROCEDURES

In April 1962, Senator Maurine Neuberger (D-Ore.)—unable to move a cigarette health warning through a Congress dominated by the tobacco subsystem— wrote a letter to Paul Rand Dixon, the newly appointed chairman of the FTC, suggesting that any cigarette advertisement that failed to carry a health warning was inherently deceptive. She asked why the FTC could not adopt this position officially and subsequently require that all cigarette advertising carry a health warning. The answer to Senator Neuberger's inquiry was that the commission had never adopted the necessary rule-making procedures to do what she suggested. None of the informal or adjudicatory procedures that the FTC had been using could have accomplished what the senator was suggesting.

Senator Neuberger's letter found a responsive ear within the commission, however. When Chairman Dixon came to the FTC in 1961, he began almost immediately to push for the use of general rule-making powers. He saw the incorporation of rule making as an important means to strengthen what was a rather ineffective regulatory process. Plans for the adoption of rule-making procedures were already in the works when the chairman answered Senator Neuberger's letter. His response hinted openly that the only major obstacle to the adoption of the Neuberger suggestion was the gathering of substantial evidence establishing a direct relationship between smoking and ill health:

> If the Commission is able to secure competent probative scientific evidence including that furnished by the Public Health Service, that a causal relationship exists between cigarette smoking and lung cancer, heart ailments, etc., it is likely that an order of the Commission, based on such evidence, which required an affirmative disclosure of the possible hazards to health from smoking cigarettes, would be upheld in the appellate courts.[5]

One might have guessed, as the cigarette people did, that the FTC was preparing itself for the report of the Surgeon General's Advisory Committee. The FTC announced the adoption of general rule-making procedures in June 1962, at about the same time the surgeon general set up his Advisory Committee.

Although the adoption of rule-making procedures was probably coincidental to the cigarette controversy, the commission busied itself issuing trade regulation rules (the official name given to the end product of the new rule-making procedure) for uncontroversial products almost as if it might have been practicing for its cigarette rule. The first rule was issued in mid-1963 while the surgeon general's committee was preparing its report. It concerned the standards for size of sleeping bags. A few months later, another rule was issued concerning the use of the term "leak proof" or "guaranteed leak proof" in advertising dry-cell batteries. Another prohibited misbranding leather belts. None of the three trade regulation rules stirred much controversy; they were promulgated with little popular reaction. The fourth rule-making attempt was, however, destined to stir more public reaction than the FTC had anticipated or desired.

The FTC followed the progress of the Surgeon General's Advisory Committee by appointing a liaison who attended most of the open meetings of the committee. Several months before the surgeon general was to issue the reports, the FTC organized within its staff a special task force on cigarettes, consisting of physicians, economists, and attorneys. When the report was issued, the commission was ready to move. Within one week, the FTC issued a notice that it planned to begin a rule-making proceeding that would lead to the issuing of a requirement that cigarette ads and packages carry a warning label describing the health hazards of smoking.

The cigarette makers, committed at the time to resisting such a requirement, were determined to prove that the FTC had no authority to write such rules. If they had succeeded, they would have had a double victory: the cigarette rule would have been quashed, and the commission would have remained a weakened watchdog of its view of the public interest, confined to either its informal or its case method of regulation.

THE RULE-MAKING HEARINGS

Witnesses and spectators at FTC hearings sit in a large, impressive, wood-paneled room that resembles both a congressional hearing room and a courtroom. The focal point of the chamber is a raised bench, behind which are velvet drapes that serve as a backdrop for the elegantly upholstered swivel chairs of the five commissioners. There are counsel tables in front of the bench, a small table for the official recorder, and a lectern on which witnesses may rest their notes and elbows. A railing separates the hard wooden spectator pews from the seats of the staff and those who are participating in the hearing.

Ordinarily, the commissioners rely on the commission staff to write the draft rule and arrange for and conduct preliminary hearings in this venerable setting. Typically, after the record has been made, the commissioners examine it and decide either to vote on the proposed rule or to call a second round of hearings over which they may preside, either individually or as a group. The cigarette labeling rule was no ordinary rule, however. The commissioners decided to handle this matter themselves, and they prepared for it carefully.

On March 16, 1964, the commissioners took their seats in front of the long, blue velvet drapes to begin three consecutive days of hearings on the cigarette labeling and advertising rule. The proposed rule, which had been circulated well in advance of the hearing, contained two major sections. The first was the requirement that a health warning appear in all advertising and on cigarette packages. Drafts of two warning statements, either of which would have satisfied the FTC, were also in the first section:

(1) **Caution—Cigarette Smoking Is a Health Hazard:** The Surgeon General's Advisory Committee has found that cigarette smoking contributes to mortality from specific diseases and to the overall death rate.

(2) **Caution:** Cigarette smoking is dangerous to health. It may cause death from cancer and other diseases.

A second section of the rule attempted to reach the more subtle implications of cigarette advertising by banning words, pictures, symbols, sounds, devices or demonstrations, or any combination thereof that would lead the public to believe that cigarette smoking promotes good health or physical well-being.

The FTC was to find itself overruled by Congress on half of its proposal. The label was to be required only on packages, not in advertising. The ban on radio and television ads came later, and when it came, it was by an act of Congress, not the FTC or the Federal Communications Commission. The requirement for inclusion of the health warning in all printed advertising also came later. It was the result of a voluntary agreement between the commission and the manufacturers, the result of a consent order arrived at in

1972 when a congressional ban on commission action against forcing such a requirement was expiring.

CIGARETTE HEARINGS AT THE FTC

Hearings themselves serve some useful and important purposes. However, one of these purposes does not seem to change the viewpoints of any of the participants. The hearings do provide an opportunity to make a public record on the issue and to communicate views among those involved in a controversy. Such a hearing is likely to facilitate subsequent enforcement and public acceptance of the agency action. In some highly complex, technical matters, agency hearings provide useful, factual information that the staff has not been able to find elsewhere. With the considerable amount of time that went into the preparation of the cigarette labeling case, however, there was little factual information that the commissioners did not have at their disposal. Backed by the scientific evidence of the surgeon general's report and the detailed legal work of their counsel's office, the commissioners seemed fairly certain as to what the outcome of the hearings would be. Chairman Paul Rand Dixon had some doubts about the wisdom of confronting the powerful cigarette industry, while the FTC's new rule-making procedures might be vulnerable. He was anxious to expand the use of the rule-making device in commission activities, but as an experienced chief investigator for a congressional committee during the Kefauver drug investigation, he was sensitive to the political pitfalls of consumer regulation.

Three commissioners—John Reilly, Mary Gardiner Jones, and Philip Elman—were in favor of the rule as the FTC had drafted it. Commissioner Reilly took no part in the questioning at the hearings, but the active participation of Commissioner Elman apparently strengthened his support of the FTC's proposed rule. The tobacco interests' challenge to the commission's power to issue the ruling irked Elman. His interest in establishing the authority of the commission to act in the cigarette case seemed to grow stronger with the intensity of the tobacco interests' challenge.

Commissioner Everett A. MacIntyre, who had been with the FTC about twenty-five years, was not a strong supporter of the rule, yet he was not active in opposition to it. Regarded as the commission's expert on administrative law, he was cautious about infringing on the powers of other agencies, particularly the FCC and its jurisdiction over radio and television advertising. Commissioner MacIntyre was more reluctant than the others to undertake any action that could have proved injurious to the tobacco economy, and after the other commissioners had adopted the proposed rule, he issued a separate statement of disagreement. (Some attributed this reluctance to the fact that he was a native of North Carolina, which was the leading tobacco-producing state in the country.) He wrote that the wording of the health warning both in advertising and on packages should be left to negotiations that would follow further developments in the smoking and health field. He also suggested delaying the effective date by six months to give all parties more adequate opportunity to work out an effective solution. Indeed, Commissioner MacIntyre opposed the imposition of additional regulations on cigarette manufacturers in all the FTC's reports to Congress during his tenure.

WITNESSES

The commissioners heard the testimony of twenty-nine witnesses during three days of hearings. The unpublished record, available to the public at commission headquarters, is 538 pages long.[6] It would have been difficult for any observer to detect differences between what they were watching at the FTC and what they might have watched had they traveled a few hundred yards down Pennsylvania Avenue to the Capitol. The hearing took place in a room similar to a hearing room on Capitol Hill. Members of the commission sat behind a long, elevated bench, and witnesses appeared before them at tables placed at a level down a step or two. The procedures followed were the same as those that would have been followed had this policymaking hearing occurred on Capitol Hill.

Chairman Dixon opened the proceedings by inviting each witness to read or submit his statement for the record, and then the witness was asked to answer questions from the commissioners. Some witnesses were asked no questions at all. The atmosphere of the hearing room was light and friendly toward those who testified in favor of the commission's proposal. But when those who came to question the wisdom of the commission rose to testify, tension crept into the air. At times, opponents were questioned closely, providing some of the same electric drama that television viewers have come to expect in more recent decades after witnessing impeachment hearings of President Richard Nixon in 1974 and President Bill Clinton in 1998, investigatory hearings associated with the Iran-Contra affair in 1987, and the Supreme Court confirmation hearings of Judge Robert Bork in 1987 and Judge Clarence Thomas in 1991. That rule-making hearings are not televised, even today, underscores the idea that the media, pundits, and the American public are generally unaware of or uninterested in a critical source of public policymaking.

The order of appearance of witnesses at a hearing is a clue as to how those conducting the hearings are disposed toward the issue involved. Sympathetic witnesses are scheduled during times when they most likely to be noticed, which is generally early in each day, especially early in the first day. These are the hours when interest is highest and the press is most alert to what is said. The whole tone of the hearings, at least in the public eye, can be governed by what happens first.

It was no accident that the assistant surgeon general of the Public Health Service was scheduled to appear first. He was followed by Senator Neuberger. Thus, the FTC began its hearings with two very strong statements in favor of its proposed rule. The third witness was from the Tobacco Institute, and he was followed by two university research scientists who favored the proposed rule.

The second day of the hearings saw marketing experts, scientists, representatives of advertising, and tobacco growers' associations testify. The third and final day was somewhat more unusual. It was politician's day at the commission. Governors of tobacco states or their representatives and four members of the North Carolina congressional delegation testified. The appearance of congressmen before an administrative agency is a surprising reversal of roles. It is not unusual for a member of Congress to intervene with agencies on behalf of a constituent, but it is unusual for members to testify at an agency hearing, especially when trying to prevent the agency from acting. The appearance of this large a number of elected officials highlights the importance of the rule-making hearing. The commissioners listened patiently and courteously to the elected officials before them. There was little questioning, although some commissioners expressed skepticism that the proposed rule would bring as much economic and social damage as the witnesses claimed it would. Nevertheless, the commissioners understood that elected officials from the tobacco states really had no choice but to testify and vigorously protest a proposal such as this one, which so directly affected their constituents. The congressmen present similarly knew that they were not going to change the commissioners' views simply by testifying against the proposed rule. Instead, they hoped to have the issue transferred from the commission to Congress. In fact, by the time the FTC had announced that it was scheduling hearings, those who opposed the health warning requirement knew that congressional action would be one of the most effective ways, if not the only way, of halting the commission's proposal.

INDUSTRY STRATEGY: CHALLENGE THE AUTHORITY, NOT THE MERITS

One tactic in the strategy to move the controversy to Congress required cigarette manufacturers to publicly ignore and downgrade the importance of the FTC by electing not to personally appear at its hearings. Instead, a lawyer from the prestigious Washington firm of Covington and Burling was retained by the Tobacco Institute to represent manufacturers at the hearings. The lawyer, H. Thomas Austern, chose to ignore the merits of the smoking and health controversy and instead concentrated on the position that the commission did not have general rule-making powers. He insisted that the absence of these powers in the FTC legislation meant that the issue of a health warning requirement would have to be settled by Congress; furthermore, according to Austern, the issue was of too much importance to be decided by an administrative agency. The elected representatives of the people should decide this, he said. Austern warned the commissioners that if they adopted the proposed rule, the Tobacco Institute would take the FTC to court to demonstrate that rule-making powers were not delegated to the FTC by Congress.

With this defense decided on, the attorney for the Tobacco Institute was faced with the task of developing the legal arguments necessary to show that the commission was acting where it lacked the authority to do so. The major thrust of his argument was that if the members of Congress had intended that the commission formulate general rules under the Federal Trade Commission Act of 1914, they would have said so in the act itself. Austern pointed to other laws administered by the commission in which the delegation of rule-making authority was made explicit. Section 8 of the Fur Product Labeling Act of 1945, for example, contains this statement: "The [Federal Trade] Commission is authorized and directed to prescribe rules and regulations governing the manner and form of disclosing information required by this Act." Not able to win on the substantive merits of the situation, the tobacco industry employed a related strategy three decades later in its charge that the Food and Drug Administration lacked the authority to engage in rule making pertaining to nicotine. In the later case, the tobacco industry asserted more narrowly that Congress had explicitly and implicitly proscribed agency regulation of nicotine.

In the earlier labeling controversy, the commission's primary argument, which is discussed more fully later in this chapter, countered that the delegation of rule-making powers was in fact both implicit and explicit in the act. Furthermore, since 1914, judicial interpretation and scholarly opinions of agency authority had pointed to the existence of this authority under the statute that created the FTC. The Tobacco Institute remained adamant in its position throughout the hearings, as was expected. Its opposition, although not well founded in prevailing opinions of the law, served to cast doubt on the commission's authority. Strong tobacco opposition also made it clear that, should the commission promulgate its proposed rule, there would be months of uncertainty as the issue was fought out in Congress, the courts, or both. Most lawyers would not have defended the Tobacco Institute's position if the debate had been strictly academic; the law on administrative rule making is quite clear and favorable to agency powers. Austern, however, was not engaging in an academic debate. His presentation served the useful purpose for which it was designed. The commissioners knew now, if they had not known before, that their rule was due to be reviewed by Congress, an institution where the commissioners were not as likely to receive as sympathetic a hearing as they had become accustomed to receiving in the judiciary over the years.

THE COMMISSIONERS RESPOND

As the commissioners listened to Austern's testimony, it was evident that they were becoming increasingly irritated. Perhaps it was the realization that the powerful tobacco interests might succeed in altering or nullifying their new rule-making procedure by persuading Congress to enact a law specifically removing their rule-making power. Or perhaps they were wearied by the thought of protracted argument in Congress and the courts on the cigarette labeling issue itself. At any rate, the commissioners were lawyers, and they were not receptive to criticism of their action based on their alleged misinterpretation of the FTC's legal mandate.

The patience of the commissioners had worn thin by the second day of the hearings. Anxious to consider the substantive issues involved in the enforcement of their proposed rule, they were tired of defending their authority to act. When Gilbert H. Weil, a representative of the Association of National Advertisers, took up the Tobacco Institute's argument, he elicited this spirited response from Commissioner Elman:

> Lawyers apparently feel that all law is divided into substantive or procedural, or legislative, executive, and judicial, and, therefore they have to talk in those terms. And a lot of lawyers apparently have not read what the Supreme Court and what other students of the administrative process have written on the nature of administrative rule making. I suggest you lawyers read these cases and come to us with a more realistic approach to the real problem that we have here—instead of talking about fantasies and fictions.[7]

The commissioner's displeasure could not mask the fact that during the first fifty years of the FTC's existence, no substantive rules had been written except in a few instances where they had been expressly authorized by laws such as the Fur Products Labeling Act of 1945. Whether the commissioners liked it or not, the opponents of the cigarette rule did have historical justification for expressing their doubt about the validity of the FTC's new procedure. Nonuse gave cigarette manufacturers some support for their argument that general rule-making powers were not delegated by Congress.

Austern, the Tobacco Institute lawyer, began his testimony before the commission by attempting to establish what the intent of Congress had been in creating the FTC in 1914. Discussing selected segments of floor debate that preceded the passage of the act and quoting Representative F. C. Stevens (R-Minn.), one of the five House members who managed the debate, Austern focused on a passage in the debate that seemed to limit the legislative authority of the proposed commission.[8]

The trouble with relying on floor debate to establish congressional intent, however, is that the clear language of the legislation itself and judicial interpretation of that language take precedence over what happened on the floor of Congress. Frequently, remarks that arise in debate are not well thought out. Furthermore, in a lengthy record of debate, one often uncovers statements that support contradictory positions.[9]

Many of the arguments developed in testimony by the Tobacco Institute had been anticipated by the commission. A lengthy document written by the FTC staff contained a detailed history of the smoking controversy, including twenty-four pages of careful argument supporting the FTC's defense of its rule-making authority. The arguments set forth in this document were used to answer the tobacco interests' position at the hearings.

THE FTC'S DEFENSE OF ITS ACTION

The FTC defended its rule-making procedures and authority through three separate but closely related arguments. One was that the rule-making authority had been delegated by Congress both implicitly and explicitly in the act of 1914. The second argument drew on Supreme Court opinions that had encouraged administrative agencies to rely more heavily on rule making rather than adjudicatory procedures. And the third claimed that the commission was not really doing anything very new through its trade regulation rule procedure.

The commission, in support of its first argument, stated that Congress delegated to it the power to prevent unfair methods of competition and deceptive or unfair trade practices. This delegation is contained in section 5(a)(6) of the act: "the Commission is hereby empowered and directed to prevent persons, partnerships, or corporations . . . from using unfair methods of competition in commerce and unfair or deceptive acts or practices in commerce." The delegation of expressed powers to prevent those activities listed indicates that the FTC was to be more than judicial agency acting in a remedial capacity through quasi-judicial procedures alone. In addition, the act gives the commission extensive powers to investigate and inquire. These functions underscored the expectation that the commission was to take affirmative action by exercising rule-making authority.

Another section of the Federal Trade Commission Act empowers the commission to make rules and regulations for the purpose of carrying out the provisions of this act. The FTC claimed that this section embraced the trade regulation rule procedure, even though the section was unnecessary because the basic mandate of the commission could not be fulfilled without rule-making powers. The commissioners wrote, "It is implicit in the basic purpose and design of the Trade Commission Act as a whole, to establish an administrative agency for the prevention of unfair trade practices, that the commission should not be confined to quasi-judicial proceedings."[10]

The logic of the foregoing arguments involving the propriety of rule making as a device for carrying out the purposes of the act was the most persuasive element of the commission's defense of its action on the smoking issue. It was buttressed by the fact that the Supreme Court had accepted this logic numerous times in cases concerning the rule-making authority of agencies. The FTC referred to a 1947 decision involving one of its sister agencies, the Securities and Exchange Commission. In that case, the Court wrote, the choice made between proceeding by a general rule or by individual, *ad hoc* litigation is one that lies primarily in the informed discretion of the administrative agency.[11]

The third of the commission's arguments in support of its new rule-making procedure was not as persuasive as the others. It claimed that although the old trade practices rules, which came out of trade practices conferences, were usually advisory in nature, they did at times form the basis for formal enforcement proceedings. The difference between trade practices and trade regulation rules is one of degree, not of kind. The commission argued further, "The trade regulation rule procedure is not a sudden innovation, but a natural outgrowth of the trade practices rule procedure. It is thus the culmination of more than 40 years of Commission rule making."

One response to this last argument is to ask, Why adopt new procedures if the old ones are nearly the same or almost as good? The answer would have to be that there is a significant difference between what could be accomplished under the trade regulation rules and what could be done with the older, more informal trade practices rules. The commission nearly refuted its own argument when, in a later section of its report, it explained how the new trade regulation rules could be used in adjudication:

> In . . . adjudicatory proceeding(s) the Commission could not use the trade practice rule to resolve any disputed issue of fact, or to dispense with the introduction of evidence required to make out a *prima facie* case. . . . However, in the case of a trade regulation rule, accompanied by and based upon determinations of fact made in accordance with statutory rule-making procedures, the Commission could, in subsequent adjudicatory proceeding, rely not only on the propositions of law contained in the rule, but also on the underlying factual matters determined.[12]

In other words, the new rule-making procedure was much more powerful than the old one. It was enforceable and could be used as the rule of law to be applied in subsequent agency adjudications; the informal trade practices rules were much more limited. The commission, in its explanation of how the new rules could be used in agency adjudicatory proceedings, was making the point that the tobacco interests had already recognized; their understanding of this point accounts, in part, for their opposition to the FTC's proposal.

PROMULGATION OF RULES

The official record remained open for two months after the FTC's cigarette hearings so that those who desired to add additional statements to the official record could do so. After the record was closed, the commission issued its trade regulation rule on June 22, 1964. It was published in the *Federal*

Register less than two weeks later. The commission also published a small announcement of the rule and a summary statement of its background and purpose that was mailed to hundreds of people who had expressed some interest in this proceeding.

Publication of the trade regulation rule in the *Federal Register* marks the formal or official promulgation of the rule by the commission. Some months after it appears in the *Register*, it is published in cumulative volumes called the *Code of Federal Regulations*. All the permanent rules and regulations made by administrative agencies are published in the *Code* and organized according to titles and subject matter. This repository of administrative law is similar in form to the volumes that contain the laws enacted by Congress, the *United States Code*.[13]

The rule that the commission adopted was nearly the same as the initial proposal. It stated that it would consider it an unfair or deceptive trade practice if manufacturers failed to disclose on packages, boxes, and cartons—as well as in advertisements—that cigarette smoking is dangerous to health and may cause death from cancer and other diseases. The only significant departure from the FTC's original position had to do with the wording of the warning itself, which it left to the cigarette companies to compose.

EXPANDING DELEGATION AND DIMINISHING ACCOUNTABILITY

By the time the FTC held its rule-making hearings, procedures to ensure accountability of agencies for its decisions were firmly in place. Procedures had been established for fair and open hearings and transparency of decision making. The appeals to the courts that the cigarette companies were about to make, based on the idea that the commission had exceeded its delegated authority, were to fall on deaf ears. The system had adjusted; the need for agencies to make policy decisions was widely though grudgingly accepted.

Looking back at the cigarette labeling decisions, one has the feeling that the arguments made against agency rule-making authority were almost quaint, given the growth in delegation to government and to quasi- and nongovernmental agencies today. The expansion of agency policy powers has grown enormously in the forty years since the labeling requirement. Policymaking power has been widely dispersed to bureaucratic agencies and at a dizzying pace. The number of government corporations and quasi-government agencies, like AMTRAK and the U.S. Postal Service, has grown rapidly.[14] Scholars of public policy recognize this dispersion of policymaking power and are raising the same questions of accountability for these entities as they had raised earlier for standard government agencies. The popularity of concepts like governance and new public management is an indicator of this trend.[15]

Perhaps the largest expansion of power to nontraditional policymaking entities has occurred over the past few years with the enormous expansion of government contracting out a vast array of powers to private vendors. In theory, the lines of accountability are still intact given that agencies supervise and ultimately control the contracts. But the sheer enormity of the volume of contracting raises serious questions about the possibility of holding contractors accountable for their activities. In 2001, about $107 billion was contracted out by the federal government for services alone, not for goods, such as aircraft, missiles, and ships. This total, for the first time in history, exceeds what the government pays for salaries and fringe benefits for all the civilians on the payroll. This shift has been occurring gradually over the years, and it passed the halfway mark in 2001.[16]

In the mid-1960s, however, such a dramatic expansion could not have been foreseen. And the idea that formed the basis of the tobacco interests' objections to the FTC's actions now seems hopelessly outdated. The delegation argument has been decided by explicit court decisions and by the passing of time. Congress can delegate policymaking powers to agencies. And, as long as those agencies operate under the rules of fairness spelled out in the Constitution and followed by Congress and the courts, their decisions become law.

TOBACCO INTERESTS OBJECT TO THE RULE

The cigarette ruling was to take effect on January 1, 1965, about six months after the FTC published it in the *Federal Register*.[17] In the period between the commission's hearings and January 1, the cigarette interests mobilized in earnest. Within a month after the conclusion of the hearings, the industry announced the creation of a voluntary code.[18] This voluntary code was intended to signify to Congress and the public that the industry was interested in regulating itself and that the action of the FTC was an unnecessary obstacle to self-regulation.[19]

Friends and foes of tobacco industry and its allies in Congress reacted nearly as swiftly to the FTC's newly promulgated rule as the cigarette manufacturers themselves did. After the announcement, members of Congress introduced thirty-one bills in the House and four in the Senate. All the Senate bills were intended to support the FTC and strengthen government regulatory powers over cigarette producers. The House, which often responds more quickly to the pressures of special interests, found itself with six bills designed to strip the FTC of some of its powers to regulate cigarette advertising. The remaining twenty-five House bills were designed either to set up government research programs on smoking and health or to strengthen the FTC.

The fact that the vast majority of the bills were favorable to the FTC's rule was not an indication of congressional support of the commission. Instead, congressional reaction, overall, was overwhelmingly negative, and it quickly became apparent from speeches on the floor and newspaper accounts that the FTC's action would not stand unchallenged. It is not unusual for bills to be introduced to reverse decisions of administrative agencies; however, most die without the formality of committee action. The cigarette interests had too much political muscle to allow the quiet death of the bills challenging the FTC. The first public indication of tobacco power in Congress came from Congressman Oren Harris (D-Ark.). Harris, then chairman of the House Interstate and Foreign Commerce Committee, requested that FTC Chairman Dixon delay implementation of the rule until the 89th Congress, which would convene in January 1965, had an opportunity to study it. Congress, according to Harris, feared prolonged litigation over the rule and thought that legislation was needed to clarify the situation. Harris's arguments were the same as those made by Austern, the tobacco lawyer, at the commission hearings.

Commissioners at the FTC need not have worried about losing a court battle to the tobacco companies because the tobacco threat—voiced numerous times in the FTC hearings and in press releases—was hollow. The tobacco companies' case was weak and most certainly would be decided by the courts in favor of the commission. At the same time, the commissioners knew that an appeal to the courts could take two to three years to resolve: this could have meant postponing implementation of the rule for at least that long. The postponement itself would have been no small victory for the cigarette manufacturers. Consequently, Chairman Dixon chose to yield to congressional pressure and agreed to postpone the effective date (January 1, 1965) of the FTC rule while Congress considered the matter. Subsequently, congressional hearings were scheduled to begin in March in the Senate and April in the House.

As lines were being drawn for the cigarette battle in the ensuing months, it became clear that, although support for the tobacco interests remained strong, the tobacco policy subsystem was showing signs of weakness. The cigarette manufacturers had in the past been able to rely on Congress to kill any serious attempt by government agencies to interfere with their business. Now circumstances were different. The antismoking forces had the surgeon general's report and a ruling by the FTC to bolster their position. Furthermore, a rather impressive number of senators and representatives had begun to associate themselves with the commission's action. A prelude to the difficulties that the tobacco interests were to face had arisen unexpectedly shortly before the FTC hearings in the spring of 1964. An amendment was attached to a crop support bill in the Senate that would have abolished the tobacco support and acreage control programs. It was defeated, handily, by a vote of sixty-three to twenty-six, but this frontal assault shook the representatives of tobacco, and the amendment took them by surprise. This was the first floor test of cigarette sentiment since the surgeon general's report. It showed the tobacco lobbyists that they would have to work diligently to keep the sympathy they were accustomed to finding in Congress. To that end, the industry mobilized a very impressive lobbying team, a team that was at work well before the 89th Congress convened in January 1965.

NOTES

1. For a detailed discussion of the differences between rule making and adjudication, see David L. Shapiro, "The Choice of Rulemaking or Adjudication in the Development of Administrative Policy," *Harvard Law Review* 78. (1965) 921–972.
2. *Penn Tobacco Company*, 34 Federal Trade Commission 1636 (1942).
3. *Hearings before the F.T.C. on Cigarette Labeling and Advertising*, vol. 7, March 16, 1964, 61 (typewritten).
4. In 1966, in light of growing public and congressional interest in the possible health implications of tar and nicotine, the FTC reversed itself and notified cigarette manufacturers that they were at liberty to advertise tar and nicotine levels provided that they made no health claims with respect to them. A year later, after standardized measurement techniques had been agreed on, the commission announced the opening of a smoking laboratory to measure these levels.
5. Quoted in Maurine B. Neuberger, *Smoke Screen: Tobacco and the Public Welfare* (Englewood Cliffs, N.J.: Prentice Hall, 1963), 58.
6. A great number of such documents are now available on the web, see, for example: *Official Transcript of the Proceedings before the Federal Trade Commission in the Matter of Proposed Rulemaking Proceeding for Requiring Health Warning in Cigarette Advertising on 2nd July, 1969*, available at http://tobaccodocuments.org/rjr/503807687-7875.htmlzoom=750&images.
7. Federal Trade Commission, *Hearings on Trade Regulation Rule on Cigarette Labeling and Advertising*, D. 215-8-7, March 17, 1964 (typewritten), 190. Much of the narrative in this section relies on the record of these hearings.
8. In the debate, a colleague asked if the new agency would, in any sense, exercise legislative functions such as those exercised by the Interstate Commerce Commission. Representative Stevens answered, "We desired clearly to exclude that authority from the power of the Commission." The Tobacco Institute pointed to this statement as evidence that the FTC was not meant to have rule-making powers. See *Congressional Record*, 63rd Cong., 2nd sess., June 13, 1914, 11084.
9. Senator Newlands, a sponsor of the Federal Trade Commission Act in the Senate, made it clear in the debate, for example, that he expected the commission to use discretionary rulemaking power. He argued that it would be up to the proposed FTC to affix meaning to the term *unfair competition*. And he went on to indicate his reliance on the Interstate Commerce Commission (ICC) as a model for the FTC. If the ICC could successfully determine rate structures and other regulatory matters through its rule-making procedures, it could be assumed that the FTC could perform a similar function for the matters within its jurisdiction.
10. *Trade Regulation Rule for the Prevention of Unfair or Deceptive Advertising and Labeling of Cigarettes in Relation to the Health Hazards of Smoking and Accompanying Statement of Basis and Purpose of Rule*, FTC document (n.d.), 141.
11. *Securities and Exchange Commission v. Chenery Corporation*, 332 U.S. 194, 203 (1947).
12. The three quotations are from the FTC document *Trade Regulation Rule for the Prevention of Unfair or Deceptive Advertising*, 143, 144, 246.
13. Before 1948, there was no codification of the rules of administrative agencies that appeared in the *Federal Register*. The *Code of Federal Regulations*, which is the responsibility of the National Archives, has brought some order to the chaos that previously existed. Now it is possible for legal researchers to work systematically with administrative rules and regulations in much the same way they work with congressional enactments.
14. An excellent study of this increase can be found in Ronald C. Moe, "The Emerging Federal Quasi Government: Issues of Management and Accountability," *Public Administration Review* 61, no. 3 (May/June 2001): 290. See also Catherine E. Rudder, "The Ethics of Public Policy Making by Private Bodies: The Case of Independence of the Accounting Industry in the U.S." (paper prepared for the Triennial World Congress of the International Political Science Association, June 28–July 4, 2003, Durban, South Africa).
15. See Lester M. Salamon, ed., *The Tools of Governance: A Guide to the New Governance* (Oxford: Oxford University Press, 2002), and the work of Paul C. Light, especially *The True Size of Government* (Washington, D.C.: The Brookings Institution, 1999).
16. These figures are from the Federal Procurement Data System, U.S. General Services Administration, August 2001. Similar shifts have occurred at the state and local levels of government.

See Sheila Suess Kennedy, ed., *To Market, to Market: Reinventing Indianapolis* (Lanham, Md.: University Press of America, 2001).

17. The package warning label was required to appear on January 1, 1965, and the advertising warning six months later, July 1, 1965.

18. Nine major producers were signatories to the code: American Tobacco, R. J. Reynolds, Brown & Williamson, Larus and Brother, Liggett & Myers, P. Lorillard, Philip Morris, Stephano Brothers, and U.S. Tobacco. By 1968, code membership had dropped to six. For various reasons, P. Lorillard, American Tobacco, and Stephano Brothers quit the organization, which removed about one-third of total cigarette advertising revenues from code supervision.

19. This attempt at self-regulation was somewhat duplicative of the code administered by the National Association of Broadcasters, especially after the revision of that code during the summer of 1967.

6

CONGRESSIONAL POWER AND AGENCY POLICYMAKING

The point I'm asking is . . . that some day, some day our kids and grandchildren are going to say . . . how did you let them get away with it? How did you let them get away with it?

—STANLEY ROSENBLATT, PLAINTIFF'S LAWYER ADDRESSING A FLORIDA JURY
IN *LIGGETT GROUP V. ENGLE*[1]

When he was Senate minority leader, Everett McKinley Dirksen spoke lyrically of the place of Congress in the government system at a meeting of the American Political Science Association. In his engaging manner, he directed the thoughts of his audience to article 1, section 8, of the Constitution, which says, "Congress shall have the power . . ." Looking heavenward, the senator said wistfully, "I love those words."

Among the implications of the senator's comment is the suggestion that Congress has the strength to control the powers it delegates to administrative agencies. Although this view might accord with the formal constitutional distribution of powers, it inaccurately describes the realities of contemporary politics. Members of Congress might dream of a parliamentary Camelot where they control, direct, or perhaps substantially influence all the actions of the 1.9 million civilians who work in the bureaucracy, but the hard facts of the modern policy process often shatter that dream.[2]

CONGRESSIONAL OVERSIGHT

Article 1, section 8, enumerating the powers of Congress, has not been repealed, nor has the constitutionally prescribed executive power vested in the president. The line between congressional interference, sometimes derisively called micromanagement and Congress's power to oversee the activities of administrative agencies, is not a clear one. These agencies exist because Congress created them; they make policy because Congress delegates the authority for them to do so and appropriates funds for their continuing operation.

As issues have become more complex and Congress's agenda has expanded to address more of society's problems, it has turned to delegation as a solution to an impossible workload. Congress as an institution has more in its purview than the activities of any single agency. Even if it could become more specialized to compete with bureaucratic expertise, it would be hard pressed to find time to keep up with the voluminous productivity of the agencies. So Congress (or its component parts) has to choose the issues it wants to concentrate on and carefully prepare itself to question the agencies on these issues. A great deal of congressional time and thought goes into making decisions regarding which policies are to be scrutinized. Nevertheless, agencies are sensitive to the *potential* that Congress may review anything that they do. They are acutely aware that Congress has the ability to punish them through legislative action and the power of the purse and to embarrass agency officials by bringing them before Congress to explain their actions.

Although Congress's delegation of legislative power has been explicitly recognized by the courts, it has considerable difficulty controlling, in meaningful, constructive ways, the agencies it creates. Nor is Congress systematic in its approach in monitoring agency work. Congress can harass and can block temporarily, but it has difficulty sustaining its influence over the long term. Agencies are more nimble and persistent than their cumbersome congressional parent. And they have the advantage of expertise derived from the ability to concentrate on a limited group of related issues until they understand the issues and their ramifications better than anyone else.

Congressional oversight is multilayered. It has evolved in tandem with the increasing delegation of the past fifty years. Today, two bodies, the House Government Reform Committee and the Senate Governmental Affairs Committee, have the authority to oversee virtually the entire federal government. These two committees rely heavily on reports of the Government Accountability Office, a congressional agency, and the office of the inspector general in each agency that reports both to Congress and to the agency head. Regular congressional oversight of agency operations in nearly all cases is the responsibility of the committees or subcommittees within an agency's policy subsystem.

Authorizing committees fulfill their authority to engage in oversight in a variety of ways. For example, some committees have formed explicit oversight subcommittees, though, as a practical matter, committee oversight cannot be contained in a single subcommittee. Formal oversight can occur in annual appropriation hearings, hearings on proposed legislation, or occasional investigations.[3] The quality of oversight varies across issue areas; some agencies are subjected to detailed scrutiny of expenditures down to specific, minor grants and contracts that catch the attention of a particular legislator; others receive more general and enlightened policy guidance.[4]

The fact that subcommittees are generally responsible for oversight means that, from the agency's point of view, a few representatives and senators (and their professional staff) are more important than Congress as a whole. Exceptions to this observation arise when congressional leadership takes an interest in an agency's activities or when an agency action touches a widely felt political nerve. The emergence of historically strong party leadership in the House in the twenty-first century has come at the cost of a weakened committee system and chairmen who now are expected respond to the demands of the leadership. As a result, committee chairmen often do the bidding of their party's leadership on any issue that interests the Speaker or majority leader, including matters of oversight.[5]

On the whole, then, agencies operate with the knowledge that their oversight committees and, particularly, the leaders of these committees can wreak havoc on their programs. This knowledge frequently leads to over-cautious agency administration that is concerned more about responding to the wishes of a few members of Congress than about what might be the general, though perhaps unarticulated, desire of Congress or the needs of the nation as a whole.

Overdependence on small numbers of important elected officials can lead to unethical and even illegal interference in agency matters by powerful members of Congress on behalf of a constituent. Individual member intervention in agency affairs or informal oversight could be quite innocent in appearance. Yet even an innocent congressional query can have unsavory overtones. What if a member queries the chair of a regulatory commission about progress in awarding a certain license? This might be a perfectly innocuous question, but it could lead to an unfair advantage for that congressman's constituent in a situation where there was competition for that license.[6]

In short, it is difficult to generalize about the nature, quality, and ethics of congressional oversight. It can be weak in terms of both general policy guidance and influence on the millions of policy decisions that bureaucrats make. On the other hand, it can be devastating to an agency that out of ignorance or hubris defies the wishes of its small but powerful and important congressional constituency.

THE FEDERAL TRADE COMMISSION'S OVERSIGHT STRUGGLE

The actions of Congress against the Federal Trade Commission's attempts to require health warnings for cigarette smokers were unusual both in their form and in their severity. When Congress passed the federal Cigarette Labeling and Advertising Act (CLAA) of 1965 (see Figure 6.1), it reduced in very specific terms a small portion of the FTC's powers. Oversight legislation of a punitive nature is frequently introduced by an irate member, but it

FIGURE 6.1 THE CIGARETTE LABELING AND ADVERTISING ACT (CLAA) OF 1965

Warning Labels

The act required the surgeon general's health warnings on cigarette packages. It mandated cigarette warnings for all packages that read, "Caution: Cigarette Smoking May Be Hazardous to Your Health." Although the act is titled the Labeling and Advertising Act, it did not extend to advertising.

The Preemption of State and Local Regulations

This act was seen as a minor defeat in a large victory for the tobacco industry, as the act made for federal preemption of state and local regulation of advertising. This meant that no state or local government could pass a more restrictive advertising ban than the federal government's advertising restrictions. The act prohibited additional labeling requirements at the federal, state, or local level. The CLAA states, "No requirement or prohibition based on smoking and health shall be imposed under State law with respect to the advertising or promotion of any cigarettes the packages of which are labeled in conformity with the provision of this chapter."

Establishment of a New Secretariat

The secretary of the Department of Health and Human Services was established to carry out research on the effects of smoking and launch programs to inform the public of any dangers to human health presented by cigarette smoking.

Annual List of Cigarette Ingredients

The manufacturers and packagers of cigarettes were required to submit to the secretary of the Department of Health and Human Services an annual list of ingredients that they add to tobacco. The secretary would then transmit a report to Congress if he or she feels that such ingredients pose an additional health risk to consumers. The secretary shall treat such information as trade secrets and would not reveal it without the expressed consent of the producers.

(Excerpted in part from the original legislation.)

seldom is passed or even given serious committee consideration. Normally, reprimands of agencies are informal, handled by committees through threatened action or by an actual reduction of an agency's budget. These occurrences may take place without introduction of legislation or without public hearings.

Open controversy between Congress and an agency is almost always avoided, an indication that those within a subsystem know each other's attitudes and positions fairly well before an agency tries something new. But in the mid-1960s, the pressure exerted on the FTC by the health interests and the surgeon general's report encouraged the commission to take an action that was to invoke the full wrath of Congress. The threat of a warning being required on cigarette packages and in all advertising was more than Congress was prepared to accept. It appeared that no one in the FTC had bothered to check its proposed cigarette rule in advance with the appropriate members of Congress. Perhaps the rule had not been cleared on Capitol Hill because of the newness of the rule-making procedure and the commission's inexperience with it.

The resulting congressional reprimand of the FTC was unexpectedly severe in its intensity. It involved lengthy hearings in both houses of Congress on the substance and wisdom of the FTC action. The legislation that emerged from those hearings specifically negated the commission's rule and temporarily took away its rule-making powers relating to cigarette advertising.[7] In addition, the commission was prohibited from requiring or even considering the requirement of a health warning in cigarette advertising for four years. The jurisdiction of the commission under the 1914 act was not changed; its new, controversial trade regulation rule procedure was left intact except as it applied to cigarette regulation. The pinpoint accuracy of the congressional oversight was so unusual that old-timers on Capitol Hill could not remember when or if it had ever happened that way before.

At the same time, the FTC's health warning requirement did pass muster with Congress and became part of the statutory law with passage of the CLAA. The FTC may have been stung by the volume of criticism directed its way, but it did walk away from the battle with half of what it was originally after. The FTC lost on the advertisement warning issue but won on the package warning requirement, even if the warning itself was a watered-down version of what the commissioners had had in mind.

No Victory for Health

Congress was not acting alone when it moved against the FTC on the cigarette and health issue. It was assisted by the skills, both rhetorical and organizational, of the Tobacco Institute and the allies it had recruited. The lobbying effort mounted by this group was brilliantly conceived; it indicated that the cigarette manufacturers had the good sense to adapt their approach to the changing tides of public demand in the health field. The manufacturers saw the beginning of a breakdown of the tobacco subsystem, and they had the political acumen and sensibility to shift their tactics to cope with it. They turned what could have been a substantial threat to the steady expansion of cigarette sales into a limited victory. As a result, ironically, the CLAA passed by Congress in 1965 was more of a victory for cigarettes than it was for health.

The cigarette manufacturers realized that public demands for action in response to the research on smoking and health were much stronger than they had been in the past. The health forces had been strengthened by the surgeon general's 1964 report on smoking and health. And it was becoming increasingly clear that the cigarette manufacturers would no longer be able to bury or ignore the criticisms of the health people as they had in the past. The industry's attempts to find a safer cigarette and to mitigate the adverse findings of health research by counter, pro-cigarette research had resulted in very little data favorable to smoking. Consequently, promises for even more research, voluntary advertising codes, and a less dangerous cigarette could no longer be used to stay the momentum that the antismoking people had been able to build. Armed with the FTC rule, the surgeon general's report, and some public support, the health groups had many things going for them in 1965. The carefully constructed walls of tobacco defense were beginning to crack as health advocates took advantage of American federalism by working at the subnational level as an alternative to national action.

The political assets of the health people in Washington were enhanced by the successes some of their colleagues were having with state and local governments. Cigarette package warnings had been proposed for New York City by the city health commissioner. Similar suggestions were being considered by New York, Massachusetts, and other states. The governor of California had created a cigarette smoking advisory committee, and in several jurisdictions pressure was growing to enforce laws already on the books that banned cigarette sales to minors. Indeed, one month before President Johnson signed the CLAA (on July 27, 1965), Governor Nelson A. Rockefeller of New York signed into law a requirement that all cigarette packages sold in his state carry a health warning. If there was anything the cigarette companies wanted less than federal regulation, it was state requirements that health warnings appear. This could have meant as many different labels as there were states, creating an obvious marketing problem.

In the face of mounting concern over cigarette smoking as a health hazard, there was genius in the CLAA bill from the industry point of view. The bill contained just enough regulation to pass as a health measure; and while the bill required a health warning, it also contained provisions to supercede state and local regulations and to dismantle an important part of the work of the FTC. Its most significant provision in these terms was the section that temporarily eliminated the FTC's rule-making power in the cigarette advertising field.

The bill as originally introduced permanently banned such FTC action. When the bill was passed, Congress had reduced the length of the ban to four years, or until July 1, 1969. Another important provision of the bill prohibited other federal agencies, such as the Federal Communications Commission, from taking any action regarding health warnings in advertising in that same time period. State and local action was also blocked or preempted by congressional action. Foreclosing the possibility of state and local regulation was a major attraction of the bill for the cigarette manufacturers.

Despite the inclusion of these provisions, the bill was written in terms of protecting public health. The text of the act begins by declaring that it was the intention of Congress to establish a federal program to inform the public of the possible health hazards of smoking. To this end, Congress appropriated $2 million shortly after the labeling act was passed to establish the National Clearinghouse for Smoking and Health. This agency, which was part of the Public Health Service (PHS), was directed to carry out educational campaigns and collect data on smoking and health research in the United States. (The successor agency, now located in the Centers for Disease Control and Prevention, is called the Office on Smoking and Health.) In a sense, this was the only significant provision of the bill for the health interests. The package labeling requirement was thought by most to be rather insignificant as long as no warning had to appear in advertising. As the controversy over the bill developed in Congress, it became clear that the tobacco interests thought they had little to fear from the labeling requirement. On the contrary, a suitably discrete package warning was very much in the interests of the tobacco manufacturers. With all the emerging data on the health consequences of smoking, manufacturers began to view a mild warning as shielding them from liability claims down the road (which, indeed, it did) while having only a marginal long-term impact on sales.

As the final votes neared, there was virtually no opposition to the bill from the cigarette manufacturers. Rather, they seemed to be supporting it. The bill passed the Senate by a vote of seventy-two to five, with most of the tobacco-state senators voting for it. Senators who argued that what was being sold as a public health measure was little more than a boon to the cigarette interests voted against it.[8] Even those who often raised objections to bills that granted the national government regulatory powers instead of allowing the states to have them were quiet on the labeling bill. There were no recorded southern or conservative objections to that part of the bill that prohibited the states from adopting similar or related regulatory legislation.

The House adopted the bill by voice vote under circumstances that were designed to limit debate and dissension. The bill was brought to the floor and passed on a Tuesday afternoon when there were only a few members present. The chief opponent of the bill, Representative John Moss (D-Calif.), had been informed earlier that the vote would come on the following Thursday. When the vote was taken, he was in a commercial aircraft over the Atlantic flying back from Europe. This switch in scheduling violated the gentleman's agreement that governs such matters in Congress. Congressman Richard Bolling (D-Mo.) spoke of the questionable tactics of bringing the labeling bill to the floor early:

> [T]he Committee [Interstate and Foreign Commerce] was able to get through this House of Representatives a piece of legislation which it agreed upon, when the only person who opposed the legislation strongly enough to sign a minority report was known to be away and unable to return.[9]

The committee chairman, Oren Harris (D-Ark.), denied having any knowledge that his dissenting committee member was out of the country. This episode and other earlier signs discouraged Moss and his liberal colleagues from protesting loudly or fighting with any enthusiasm against the labeling bill in the House. The liberal Democratic Study Group, sensing the overwhelming support for the cigarette manufacturers, decided against organizing any opposition to the bill.[10]

The House was considerably more pro-cigarette than the Senate. Realization of this factor by all parties shifted the scene of the most intense activity to the Senate, especially the Senate Commerce Committee. The Senate could be expected to go along with that committee's very powerful and popular chairman, Warren Magnuson (D-Wash.). The strength of the tobacco interests in the House, as opposed to the Senate, could be seen in the conference that followed the passage of the bill in each chamber. The House had passed a permanent ban on the FTC's involvement in cigarette advertising; the Senate conferees forced their House counterparts to accept a maximum four-year limit. In the bargaining, the House refused to accept the Senate provision that the printed warning appear on the front of cigarette packages; instead, the conferees agreed to leave the decision concerning where the warning would appear up to the manufacturers.

On balance, the passage of the CLAA can be seen as a victory for cigarette manufacturers and their allies. The unwary might find that reading of events difficult to accept, yet this interpretation can be supported. First, the CLAA negated the more sweeping FTC trade regulation rule and specifically restricted the FTC from making decisions on the advertising issue for four years. Second, the warning label requirement was watered down, and the states were preempted from enacting more onerous warning laws. Third, the warning label took the wind out of the health lobby's sails while shielding the manufacturers from product liability suits and from further regulation by the states for a period of time. Given the mood of the country and the shifting nature of tobacco politics at the time, the manufacturers could have hardly asked for more. As one observer commented, "In fact . . . the bill is not, as its sponsors suggested, an example of congressional initiative to protect public health; it is an unashamed act to protect private industry from government regulation."[11]

STRATEGY FOR SUCCESS

How did the cigarette manufacturers manage to win such an impressive victory? What led to their success in persuading Congress to do what the FTC could not be persuaded to do? These enviable accomplishments were designed and executed under the able leadership of former Senator Earle C. Clements of Kentucky.

Former Senator Clements's experience on Capitol Hill provided him with both the knowledge of congressional operations and the personal support from members he needed to be effective. His one-time executive directorship of the Senate Democratic Campaign Fund enabled him to draw on the assets of old political favors. Aside from his power in Congress, the former senator was one of the few men who could keep President Johnson out of the controversy. Johnson had as good, if not better, a record on consumer legislation than any president in memory. Yet he made no public attempt to support the FTC in its struggle on Capitol Hill. He was uncharacteristically silent during the whole affair, from the announcement of the congressional hearings through the bill signing formality.

Clements was hired by the six largest cigarette manufacturers in 1964. Reinforcing the strategy to downgrade the FTC's rule-making authority, Clements was at work in Congress well before the commission adopted its rule. The first thing he had to do was coordinate the thinking and strategies of the cigarette manufacturers and their allies within the tobacco policy subsystem. He knew that success could very well depend on how quickly and firmly he could forge a united front among the manufacturers, tobacco-state congressmen, growers, advertisers, and other friends of the cigarette business.

Clements rightly sensed that this time the cigarette companies were going to be forced to give up something; the protestations of the health groups were too strong to be ignored. He decided to persuade his employers to accept the label on packages in return for a ban against a similar requirement in advertising and a ban against state action requiring health warnings. This strategy, which seems so sensible in light of its success, did not seem as sensible when the former senator began his work.

Shortly after Clements arrived in Washington, he scheduled regular weekly meetings with the Tobacco Institute's attorneys, public relations firms, and friends. The public relations firm of Hill and Knowlton had been on retainer to the institute since its inception. While not registered as lobbyists, Hill and Knowlton represented the Washington interests of firms estimated at that time to account for more than 10 percent of the gross national product.[12] At these meetings, detailed plans were worked out for the FTC hearings, for congressional lobbying, and for a possible appeal to the courts should all else fail. Once it was decided that Congress should be the prime target, it was obvious that the Senate Commerce Committee held the key to victory.

Clements knew that both houses could be expected to follow the dictates of their committees. Generally, the whole body affirms the work of its committees; moreover, floor revolts were even less likely than usual against the commerce committees because of their important jurisdictions. Members were not anxious to jeopardize a favorable relationship with these committees by failing to heed their recommendations.[13]

The Interstate and Foreign Commerce Committee was, at the time, a rather conservative force in the House, and southerners held key positions in 1965. The chairman, Oren Harris, represented a rural area in Arkansas, and the second-ranking member, Harley Staggers, was from a similar area of West Virginia. Seven other members of the thirty-three-member committee were from tobacco regions, including North Carolina Congressman Horace R. Kornegay, who was a vociferous advocate for the tobacco companies. After Kornegay decided not to run for Congress in 1968, he assumed the post of vice president and counsel of the Tobacco Institute in January 1969 and later became chairman of the organization.[14]

The Senate Commerce Committee was more consumer oriented than its House counterpart. It was beginning to develop and report out bills on a series of consumer matters unrelated to cigarettes except for their common purposes of strengthening protection of the public from business abuses. The membership of the committee was closely divided over the cigarette issue, making the chairman, Senator Magnuson, of crucial importance to both the smoking and the health forces. He was careful to avoid committing himself to either group at an early date.

Senator Maurine Neuberger (D-Ore.) worked strenuously to rally support for the health forces among her colleagues on the committee. Her work was destined to be unproductive because she faced a united Republican opposition under the leadership of Thurston Morton, the popular senator from Kentucky. Meanwhile, Senators Vance Hartke of Indiana and Ross Bass of Tennessee, both Democrats, were unsympathetic to the pleas of their colleague. Senator Bass had a sizable tobacco constituency, and Senator Hartke was indebted to Earle Clements for his aid as director of the Senate Democratic Campaign Fund. Hartke was subject to no strong pressures from his constituency on either side of the smoking issue, so he displayed some loyalty to those who had been loyal to him. The six Republicans and two Democrats united in opposition to Senator Neuberger, plus some wavering Democrats unenthusiastic about the health position, made the Oregon lawmaker's attempt to give congressional approval to the FTC ruling impossible. It became clear as the hearings began that the FTC action would be either reversed or substantially modified in the Senate Commerce Committee. The health advocates could not rally the necessary political support to prevent Congress from changing the FTC's rule.

The antismoking forces were not nearly as well organized or as well financed as the cigarette interests. Lobbyist David Cohen of the Americans for Democratic Action characterized the contest between the tobacco people and the health people as similar to a match between the Green Bay Packers and a high school football team. The tobacco state congressmen had powerful reasons to reverse the FTC action, namely, their constituents' support. On the other hand, there were few if any "health" congressmen. Those members who did champion the health cause had no substantial constituent interest to back them up.

In the absence of support from special interest constituencies, congressmen find it difficult to vote for regulatory measures that are unpopular across the whole business and industrial spectrum, even when a change in policy could benefit the public at large. Consequently, they find it relatively easy to vote funds for health research but difficult to vote for programs that would end or reduce those hazards that are identified in the research they sponsored, as indicated in this statement:

> The lawmakers enthusiastically vote hundreds of millions of dollars—more, usually, than is requested—for health research, for when it is simply a matter of research, what congressman is against health? However, when the officials go to Capitol Hill with proposals to put research findings into effect—to curb air pollution or discourage smoking—they are skunks at the lawn party. For on these issues there are large economic issues at stake.[15]

THE HEALTH LOBBY

The efforts of health organizations outside of Congress were no more successful than they were inside. Those who might have benefited from the cigarette legislation were confirmed or prospective smokers, and neither group was particularly interested in creating any government program geared to pointing out the group's foolishness. In reviewing the relative weakness of the large health nonprofits, tobacco specialist and health activist Dr. Stanton Glantz, the anti-cigarette health crusader, avers that the groups have been timid and are run by people fearful of losing donations to their organizations lest they push anti-tobacco positions too aggressively.[16] At the same time, the public health interest groups in the mid-1960s had very small constituencies, usually coalitions of the various professionals in fields related to medicine and health. These people found it difficult to devote the time and resources necessary to put their complex, technical reasoning before the public and convince them of its validity. Instead, their activities were confined primarily to research and fund-raising. Consequently, these groups—the American Cancer Society, the American Heart Association, the National Tuberculosis Association, and others—restricted most of their activities to the hearing rooms.[17] Effective grassroots groups like Action on Smoking and Health and Campaign for Tobacco-Free Kids were still in the distant horizon. Nor had the most of the resources and federally funded research dedicated to exposing the hazards of tobacco use yet materialized, as would be the case two decades later.

The health- and consumer-oriented agencies in government were similarly weak in the face of organized congressional opposition. The FTC, for example, had little clout with committees on Capitol Hill because it had virtually no constituent base from the industries it regulated. Without good congressional connections or an active clientele group, the commission was in a poor position to do battle with Congress.[18] Paul Rand Dixon, chairman of the FTC, had little desire to stir up more controversy in Congress than the commission had done already with the adoption of the rule. He testified on behalf of the commission, but there is little evidence of any meaningful activity on his part outside the hearing room. There are good reasons for commissioners to confine most of their activities to the commission hearing room.

Members of regulatory commissions wear two hats. They sit as judges as they listen to cases brought before them under the formal procedures of the Administrative Procedure Act. And they perform as policymakers as they decide which issues to pursue and how to pursue them. These two roles are incorporated in one individual nowhere in government except in the persons of appointed commissioners of the independent agencies.[19] It is difficult to keep the two roles separate, as one might easily imagine. Should the roles become closely intertwined, a commissioner runs the risk of being disqualified from voting on a case on the grounds that the judicial dictum against prejudgment has been violated.

Meanwhile, the PHS was ill equipped to lead a legislative struggle to protect the sanctity of its smoking and health report. The PHS had a large annual budget it wanted to preserve; furthermore, it had never demonstrated much competence in lobbying for substantive legislation, and its parent organization, the Department of Health, Education and Welfare (HEW), had declared at an earlier date that it would not wholeheartedly support the action of the FTC.

The health groups acted as if they knew there was little hope for legislation supporting the ruling of the FTC. They too sensed the opposition in the House and devoted very little time to attempting to overcome what was insurmountable opposition. Instead, they devoted most of their time to the Senate, but given the House opposition, they knew that their efforts in the upper chamber held little promise of bringing a strong piece of legislation out of Congress. The remainder of their efforts was dedicated to taking their case directly to the public by way of a new coalitional organization, the National Interagency Council on Smoking and Health, created in July 1964.[20]

The chairman of the council during the labeling hearings was Emerson Foote, described by the Tobacco Institute as a "one-time advertising man, and 'reformed' smoker, who made a small fortune peddling cigarettes."[21] The characterization did not do justice to the career of this unusual man. Foote came to Madison Avenue in 1936 and began one of the advertising industry's most successful promotional schemes. He handled the Lucky Strike account and wrote most of the slogans that not only made his client prosperous but also popularized smoking throughout the nation. When he decided to join the health forces, he was chairman of the board of McCann-Erickson, one of the country's largest advertising firms. Foote explained that his decision to switch rather than fight for the cigarette manufacturers did not grow out of a dislike for cigarettes: "I am not against tobacco. I am against cancer, heart disease and emphysema."[22] Foote testified at the hearings and worked hard, but with no visible signs of success, to support the FTC's action.[23]

The council, on paper, looked like a powerful lobbying organization. *Barron's*, a national financial weekly, accused it of being a front for the bureaucracy, particularly the PHS.[24] There is some substance to this charge. Two of the three officers of the organization during the labeling hearings were staff members of the PHS, and for five years the headquarters of the council was maintained at PHS offices in suburban Washington. Yet this coalition of health organizations was no match for the cigarette manufacturers. As the date for the congressional hearings approached, it seemed that the antismoking people were politically outclassed by the cigarette group. Cigarettes had high-priced talent, exceptional political experience, a tight organization, and powerful, entrenched support in Congress. Antismoking forces lacked large measures of these vital ingredients.

THE CONGRESSIONAL HEARINGS

The Senate Commerce Committee hearings attracted more attention than those of its counterpart committee in the House. The publicity that accompanied these hearings, coupled with the fact that some of the membership of the Senate committee were uncommitted on the smoking and health issue, underscored their importance. Those who supported the FTC rule were given favorable positions in the scheduling of their testimony, a sign that committee leadership was sympathetic to the commission's ruling. For example, the first slot of the second morning was given to a representative of the American Cancer Society. This early position helped ensure him of newspaper and television coverage. A spot later in the day would have drawn less public attention.

One of the difficulties that plagued the health groups throughout the congressional hearings was the absence of agreement on just what they wanted Congress to do. They agreed that cigarette smoking was harmful to health and that the government should do something about it. All the health witnesses stressed these points. Members of Congress, bureaucrats, physicians, and the representatives of the public interest groups knew the medical arguments well and presented them with feeling. But this is where their agreement ended. Their failure to agree on a plan of action reflected their lack of political know-how and inability to organize a cohesive campaign. Former Senator Clements, on the other hand, had made certain the cigarette manufacturers avoided any disunity.

That the health groups did not have a unified plan for action became obvious early in the hearings. The surgeon general suggested that the FTC was not the most appropriate agency to enforce the labeling and advertising requirement. He noted that HEW could provide the type of regulatory approach required for enforcement of the cigarette labeling regulations. Chairman Dixon of the FTC did not take immediate exception to the surgeon general's point of view. Nevertheless, he did stress in his testimony the necessity of FTC involvement because the absence of a health warning was an unfair or deceptive trade practice. Prevention of such practices was within the jurisdiction of the FTC, Dixon reminded the committee.

The health forces were further split on the wording of the warnings that they wanted to appear on packages and in advertising. Senator Neuberger favored "Caution—Habitual Smoking Is Injurious to Health"; Senator Bennett and Congressman Moss would have preferred this statement: "Warning: Continual Cigarette Smoking May Be Hazardous to Your Health." A third suggestion was proposed by the American Heart Association: "Caution: Habitual Cigarette Smoking Frequently Constitutes a Serious Hazard to Health."

These disputes were in sharp contrast to the smooth coordination and scenario employed by the cigarette interests. The case that the cigarette people made in support of their position was a good one. Their arguments were detailed, coherent, and generally persuasive.

THE CIGARETTE INDUSTRY TESTIFIES

The cigarette lobbyists' testimonies before Congress were contrasted with the presentations they had made at the FTC hearing. Before the congressional committees, they covered all aspects of the argument: the surgeon general's report, other studies on the health consequences of smoking, the importance of unfettered competition to the economy and the American creed, tobacco's contribution to the nation, and the proper policy role of Congress vis-à-vis the states and administrative agencies. This full complement of arguments contrasted sharply with the limited legal argument presented at the FTC hearings.

Another significant difference in approach by the tobacco forces between the FTC and congressional hearings was the number of witnesses who appeared for cigarettes. At the FTC, one lawyer represented the manufacturers. In Congress, dozens of witnesses from a variety of professional fields appeared. The testimony of these witnesses was skillfully orchestrated by Earle Clements.

The heart of the industry case was given to each of the congressional committees by Bowman Gray, chairman of the board of the R.J. Reynolds Company, a competent and effective witness. His voice never rose above conversational tones. For two hours at the witness table of each committee, he chain-smoked his way through what proved to be a thoughtful synopsis of the industry arguments that were to follow. And although Gray disclaimed any medical expertise, he carefully laid the groundwork for the prosmoking medical arguments. He touched base with the economists by noting that "unwise legislation in this field could produce repercussions which would be felt throughout the country's economy." He went on to warn that the balance-of-payments problem might even be exacerbated if exports of tobacco products fell.

Ideological and philosophical objections also appeared in Gray's testimony. Policy in a democracy should be made by Congress, not an administrative agency, and the will of the people embodied in their elected representatives should be supreme, he continued. On other philosophical questions, Gray argued that there was a right to advertise—a right that he labeled "an essential commercial" one. He acknowledged that he believed the FTC rule was "step one in the [government's] trying to get control of one industry." And, he added, it was "a first step to get control of other industries."

After Gray came the parade of witnesses, the largest number of whom were medical doctors and professionals from allied fields. All of them cast doubt on the surgeon general's report. The report, they claimed, was based on statistical rather than clinical evidence and was not sufficient proof that smoking caused diseases. A Virginia pathologist argued that the evidence "submitted . . . by proponents of the theory that lung cancer is caused by smoking . . . does not constitute scientific proof of this theory." Darrell Huff, author of *How to Lie with Statistics*, talked darkly about the surgeon general committee's work. He pointed to a number of statistical and methodological "warning signals" that perhaps indicated that some conclusions in the report were not warranted by the facts.

The majority of witnesses at the congressional hearings testified against the surgeon general's report and the FTC's rule. Most of the professionals who testified identified their employers as independent research associations. However, nearly two years after the hearings, it was disclosed that a few of the witnesses had not properly or fully identified themselves. Senator Daniel Brewster (D-Md.) mailed questionnaires to those who testified on behalf of the cigarette industry. Sixteen of the thirty-seven questionnaires he sent were returned. Some of those answering admitted that they had received large fees from the tobacco interests for their testimony. This came as a surprise to some members of the committee who thought they were hearing professional opinions untarnished by any possible financial connection with the industry. Senator Brewster suggested that there be a committee investigation of any possible conflicts of interest that might have arisen at the labeling hearings, but the request died quietly and quickly.[25]

Cigarette manufacturers had a number of well-organized allies in Washington. While the Senate Commerce Committee was holding its hearings, the National Association of Broadcasters held its annual convention in town. Over 500 radio and television executives attended. At a reception, more than 400 of the 535 members of Congress were entertained by these executives and treated to their views on the right to advertise. It has been estimated that more than one-third of the members of Congress owned major stock holdings in radio and television stations. This could account for some of the sympathy in Congress for those who were threatened by government regulation of cigarette advertising.[26]

After the hearings, the Senate Commerce Committee quickly voted down Senator Neuberger's bill to accept the FTC's approach to the regulation of cigarette labeling and advertising. The members of the committee, instead, reported out a bill very similar in form and content to the one eventually passed into law. Senator Neuberger attempted to amend the bill on the floor, but she was unsuccessful.

The act went to President Johnson on July 13, and he maintained his silence on the legislation as he had done throughout the controversy. On July 27, within hours of the time the bill would have become law automatically without the president's signature, he signed the act. Eight disenchanted members of Congress, in league with lobbyists for the Americans for Democratic Action, attempted to persuade the president to veto the bill. Their efforts were to no avail. The president signed the legislation in the privacy of his office. There were no guests, no glitter, and no souvenir pens, which ordinarily accompany the signing of a major piece of legislation. The bill was signed without ceremony, and the president's press secretary released the news without benefit of comment.

The passage of the CLAA marked the end of a well-organized campaign to move Congress to adopt an unusual oversight measure. The skills of the Tobacco Institute, enhanced by the sympathies of many members, helped to remove any doubts that might have existed in the FTC or elsewhere as to where ultimate policymaking authority resided. Congress is effective in disciplining errant agency policymakers, particularly when those agencies challenge the interests of powerful economic groups. Although the lengths to which Congress went to discipline the FTC were unusual, it is not unusual for members to prevent similar agency actions through less stringent, more informal methods.

THE FTC RESCINDS ITS RULE

The day after the president signed the bill, the FTC issued an order vacating its trade regulation rule. In this order, the commissioners took note of the fact that the legislation did not change the findings or conclusions that were the basis of the labeling and advertising rule. Manufacturers were warned that any advertising that attempted to undermine the warning that was required on packages would be unfair and deceptive and could be stopped by the commission. Although the legislation prohibited the FTC from requiring a health warning in advertising, the July 28 commission order stated, "[The commission] will continue to monitor current practices and methods of cigarette advertising and promotion, and take all appropriate action consistent with the Act to prohibit cigarette advertising that violates the Federal Trade Commission Act."[27]

The legislation marked the end of a turbulent excursion into congressional politics for the FTC. In the summer of 1965, the commission settled down to its more normal routine and put to one side, at least temporarily, any plans for mounting a new rule-making proceeding in the cigarette and health field until the ban against its doing so expired in the summer of 1969. The commission set up its legislatively mandated tar and nicotine laboratory and began gathering information for its yearly reports to Congress on cigarette smoking and advertising.

Although things around the FTC grew quieter, the cigarette controversy continued. The nonsmoking genie was out of the bottle, and it began to appear and reappear in other, often unexpected, places. Congress had succeeded in silencing the FTC for a while, but it was about to hear from some of its sister agencies on the same subject in slightly different garb. The congressional action had won cigarette manufacturers some time, but the question of smoking, its relationship to health, and what the government might do about it was far from settled.

NOTES

1. This quotation was brought to our attention by Professor Roger Magnusson of the University of Sydney, who includes it on his syllabus on critical issues in public health law.
2. This estimate excludes the March 2003 figures from the Postal Service (U.S. Department of Labor, Bureau of Labor Statistics), available at http://stats.bls.gov/oco/cg/cgs041.htm.
3. See Walter Olezek, *Congressional Procedures and the Policy Process*, 5th ed. (Washington, D.C.: Congressional Quarterly Press, 2000), esp. chap. 10.
4. For an example of extreme micromanagement by Congress, see Jeff Brainard, Stephen Burd, and Kelly Field, "U.S. House Approves Spending Bill That Would Close Loophole and Cut 2 NIH-Approved Studies," *Chronicle of Higher Education*, June 27 2005 http://chronicle.com/daily/2005/06/2005062701n.htm
5. For an excellent assessment of Congress in the early years of the twenty-first century, see Kirk Victor, Richard E. Cohen, and David Baumann, "The State of Congress," *National Journal*, January 10, 2004, 82–104.
6. For one recent example of the haziness of the line between propriety and impropriety, the reader is referred to charges of undue influence leveled against members of Congress involved in the savings and loan debacle of the 1980s. Former Speaker of the House Jim Wright (D-Tex.) and Senators Alan Cranston (D-Calif.), Dennis DeConcini (D-Ariz.), John Glenn (D-Ohio), John McCain (R.-Ariz.), and Donald Riegle (D-Mich.) all were implicated for intervening, unfairly, with the Federal Home Loan Bank Board (the agency responsible for regulating the savings and loan industry) on behalf of specific thrift institutions. The lawmakers claimed that their actions fell in the category of legitimate casework and were motivated by a desire to alleviate unnecessarily burdensome restrictions on constituents who operated struggling thrifts. As such, the members argued that their machinations fell well within the realm of ethical behavior. Many others, in both public and private spheres, disagreed. See Martin Mayer, *The Greatest-Ever Bank Robbery: The Collapse of the Savings and Loan Industry* (Toronto: Scribners and Sons, 1990).
7. Public Law 89-92 (1965), U.S.C., sec. 1331. The ban on FTC action in the area of advertising was extended for another two years in 1970. At that time, Congress also required that the FTC give six months' notice of, and supporting evidence for, any future plans to adopt trade regulation rules regarding cigarettes. See Public Law 91-222 (1970), 15 U.S.C., sec. 1331.
8. Four of the opposition votes were cast by liberal Democrats: Paul Douglas of Illinois, Robert Kennedy of New York, Gaylord Nelson of Wisconsin, and Joseph Clark of Pennsylvania. The fifth was from a Republican, Senator Wallace Bennett of Utah, a Mormon and longtime foe of cigarette smoking.
9. *Congressional Record*, H 15962, July 13, 1965.

10. Organized in 1956, the Democratic Study Group (DSG) consists of House Democratic liberals who organize oppose the dominant conservative leadership in the House. The group first indicated its strength and principles when called on to oppose the Southern Manifesto of 1956, a document sponsored by nearly all southern Democrats that opposed civil rights measures. The DSG proved effective in winning some liberal reforms in the early 1960s and early 1970s. For more on the DSG, see Richard Bolling, *House Out of Order* (New York: Dutton, 1965), 54–58, and Mark F. Ferber, "The Formation of the Democratic Study Group," in *Congressional Behavior*, ed. Nelson W. Polsby (New York: Random House, 1971).

11. Elizabeth Brenner Drew, "The Quiet Victory of the Cigarette Lobby: How It Found the Best Filter Yet—Congress," *The Atlantic Monthly*, September 1965, 76.

12. It is difficult to be certain about how much is spent on the institute's lobbying campaigns in any one year. By 1994, data pegged advertising and promotional spending by the tobacco industry at about $4 billion a year (*USA Today*, June 9, 1994, 1), and a significant percentage of that amount was devoted to lobbying efforts.

13. In the most recent Congresses, the majority's party leadership, rather than the fact of powerful committees, provides the impetus for voting for or against a particular piece of legislation.

14. This practice of former members of Congress staying in Washington and working for business lobbies has become increasingly common perhaps because of extended active life spans. Such lobbying and advisory positions are often extremely lucrative. Whether the possibility of assuming such jobs after leaving Congress influences members' actions while on Capitol Hill is a matter for empirical research.

15. Drew, "The Quiet Victory of the Cigarette Lobby," 79.

16. For a fascinating description of some of Glantz's work, see Stanton A. Glantz et al., eds., *The Cigarette Papers* (Berkeley: University of California Press, 1996).

17. The American Medical Association (AMA) did not testify in Congress, although it took the position publicly that Congress, not the FTC, should regulate the cigarette industry, if there had to be any regulation at all. This position drew criticism from the more liberal members of the organization who wanted the AMA to speak out on this health problem.

18. See Norton E. Long, "Power and Administration," *Public Administration Review* 9 (autumn 1949): 257–64.

19. For good discussions of the law and politics governing the work of the federal independent regulatory agencies, see Robert A. Katzmann, *Regulatory Bureaucracy: The Federal Trade Commission and Antitrust Policy* (Cambridge, Mass.: MIT Press, 1980), and David M. Welborn, *Governance of Federal Regulatory Agencies* (Knoxville: University of Tennessee Press, 1977).

20. The following groups were members of the council: American Academy of Pediatrics; American Alliance for Health, Physical Education and Recreation; American Association for Respiratory Therapy; American Cancer Society; American College of Chest Physicians; American College Health Association; American College of Radiology; American College of Surgeons; American Dental Association; American Heart Association; American Hospital Association; American Lung Association; American Medical Student Association; American Pharmaceutical Association; American Public Health Association; American School Health Association; Association of State and Temporal Health Officers; Boys' Club of America, March of Dimes Birth Defects Foundation; National Association of School Nurses; National Board of Young Men's Christian Association; National Congress of Parents and Teachers; National Jogging Association; National League for Nursing; National Medical Association; National Student Nurses Association; Society of Surgical Oncology; U.S. Department of Defense; U.S. Department of Education; U.S. Department of Health and Human Services; Office on Smoking and Health; Public Health Service; and Veterans Administration.

21. From a speech by Franklin B. Dryden, assistant to the president, Tobacco Institute, Inc., before the 21st Tobacco Workers Conference, January 17–20, 1967, Williamsburg, Va., 12 (mimeograph).

22. Roy Parker Jr., "Ad Whiz Has New Target," *Raleigh News and Observer*, January 12, 1965.

23. Foote was succeeded as president of the National Interagency Council by former Surgeon General Luther L. Terry, who in turn was succeeded by his former assistant surgeon general, James L. Hundley. Hundley served as assistant chairman of Terry's Advisory Committee on Smoking and Health. The council devoted most of its efforts to holding conferences and promoting educational campaigns designed to discourage smokers from continuing their habit.

24. "Best Foote Forward?" *Barron's*, January 18, 1965, 1-2.
25. Congress itself pays only the expenses of those witnesses it asks to testify; others pay their own expenses. The problem of witnesses paid by special interests is not serious so long as they disclose their connections. The problem of undisclosed connections is an ethical one; its implications remain unexplored by Congress.
26. Roy Parker Jr., "Cigarettes Have Friends in Labeling Battle," *Raleigh News and Observer*, March 25, 1965.
27. "Vacation of Warning Requirements in Trade Regulation Rule concerning Advertising and Labeling of Cigarettes," *Federal Register* 30 (1965): 9484.

7

THE BUREAUCRACY, CONGRESS, AND THE PRESIDENT

BALANCING ACTS

Politics is like a tennis game. You can move to the right or to the left, but you always have to come back to the middle.

—NANCY PELOSI (D-CALIF.), HOUSE MINORITY LEADER

The Federal Trade Commission's (FTC's) activism on cigarettes was quieted by Congress only temporarily by the moratorium imposed in the Cigarette Labeling and Advertising Act. The FTC, joined by its growing health constituency and other bureaucratic agencies, continued to work for acceptance of the idea of requiring a health warning in advertising even though the congressional ban against making such a requirement remained in effect until July 1, 1969.

In the years since Congress chose to exercise its oversight prerogative over the FTC, the antismoking agencies gathered public support, found an ally in the Federal Communications Commission (FCC) and other parts of the federal government, and achieved more unity in pressing for their goal of strengthening the health warning and extending it to advertising. By the 1990s, leadership in the efforts to regulate tobacco had moved from the FTC and the FCC to a newly invigorated Food and Drug Administration (FDA). Virtually every major agency in government was enveloped in the question of what to do about tobacco.

Meanwhile, the reputation of the tobacco companies gradually eroded as new health studies traced ever more serious medical consequences to cigarette smoking. The position of the manufacturers deteriorated in the eyes of many because the industry did not voluntarily alter the direction of their advertising campaigns, which still portrayed smoking as good clean fun. Despite their massive marketing and strategic philanthropy, by the 1990s their focus on children and teenagers was to become their Achilles' heel.

The introduction of the 100-millimeter cigarettes in 1967 and 1968— giving the smoker more smoke for the same price as regular or king-size cigarettes—was taken by some members of the FTC as proof of the callous disregard by the manufacturers for government attempts to curtail smoking.

THE FCC ENTERS THE FRAY

As the evening variety show ends and the late news is about to begin, a panorama of traffic signals, danger signs, and cautionary flashing lights dance across the television screen. A chest X-ray appears, a man coughs, and a voice announces, "We receive many warnings in our lives." The camera then closes in on a cigarette package so that the viewer can read, "Caution: Cigarette Smoking May Be Hazardous to Your Health." Today there are no cigarette ads on television, but by the late 1960s such presentations as this one were common fare for U.S. television. They were brought to the American public or, more accurately, were mandated by the FCC—not by Congress but by a federal regulatory agency. The action was subsequently upheld by the federal courts and constituted only the first step of the FCC in its effort to set national, binding policy on cigarette advertising by public broadcasters.

Probably the most important event to occur during the four-year moratorium on the FTC was this dramatic entrance of the FCC into the smoking and health debate. This commission, like the other independent regulatory bodies, had generally shown very little interest in moving against the wishes of those it regulates. Yet with relatively little prodding, the FCC was persuaded to require that broadcasters air antismoking publicity more frequently. The FCC's action favoring the antismoking people, against the wishes of the broadcasting industry, is intriguing politically because of the very limited support it had in any quarter, including the health groups themselves. Perhaps the FCC commissioners saw the matter as one of principle that should override parochial political interests and as one on which they had the authority to act. Agencies are not unaffected by the larger informational environment. Moreover, regulatory agencies tend to listen to arguments presented to them. In this case, an independent policy entrepreneur, John F. Banzhaf III, who abhorred cigarettes, was the originator of the idea to apply the fairness doctrine to cigarette advertising.[1]

A New York lawyer at the time, Banzhaf wrote the FCC requesting the commission to require that WCBS-TV in New York City give, without charge, the same amount of time to responsible health groups as that sold to tobacco companies for the purpose of promoting the virtues and values of smoking. In effect, Banzhaf had the unusual idea of persuading the FCC to apply its fairness doctrine to cigarette commercials. Application of the fairness doctrine in this case meant that any station that carried cigarette ads was obliged to inform its listeners of the health hazards of smoking. The FCC agreed with Banzhaf. The agency's decision did not require that precise amounts of exactly equal time be given, but it did require stations to provide "a significant amount of time for the other viewpoint."[2]

The commission's pronouncement came as a surprise to nearly everyone. The president of the National Association of Broadcasters called the action an "unwarranted and dangerous intrusion into American business."[3] Members of Congress were caught off guard by the FCC's announcement. One tobacco-state congressman, Walter Jones (D-N.C.), attempted to rally support for the cigarette manufacturers among other industries, the advertising of whose products he claimed might in the future meet a fate at the hands of the FCC similar to that of cigarette advertising. Using the "slippery slope" argument to build support from parties outside the tobacco debates, he warned that other groups, such as those opposing the consumption of alcoholic beverages, might soon request that the fairness doctrine be applied to them.[4] Senator Warren Magnuson (D-Wash.), on the other hand, announced his support for the FCC action, terming it a major victory for health forces.

There was some surprising opposition to (or at least nonsupport for) the FCC action from some of the health groups. While the initial reaction of these groups was favorable, they later started having misgivings that surfaced when appeals were filed in the U.S. Court of Appeals for the District of Columbia by two venerable Washington law firms—Covington and Burling and Arnold and Porter—on behalf of the cigarette manufacturers. The reluctance of groups like the American Cancer Society was based on the fear that the courts might agree with the complaint and dismiss the FCC opinion. They would then be in the position of having been antagonistic to radio and television stations and the networks on whose goodwill they depended for the free announcements that promoted their own fund-raising drives. The fears of the health groups were unjustified, however. On November 21, 1968, the court of appeals decided that the FCC could use its fairness doctrine to require free time for antismoking commercials.[5]

However, this pattern of caution was to characterize the old-line, generalist groups until public opinion had clearly shifted many years later. In the meantime, the older groups' timidity provided an opportunity for antismoking policy entrepreneurs to create their own organizations dedicated specifically to their cause. Dr. Stanton Glantz, the University of California Medical School professor who was the driving force in 1997 of the university library's publishing on the Internet the damning Brown and Williamson papers that Merrill Williams had purloined, commented on a PBS *Frontline* show that the health groups were a disappointment in the battles with the tobacco industry.[6]

Thanks to the FCC's decision to apply the fairness doctrine to cigarette advertising, an amusing variety of antismoking ads began to appear on radio and television. Informative and dramatic, it seems certain that they contributed to the reduction in cigarette consumption noted first in 1968. The American Cancer Society reported that, after the ruling, it distributed four times as many prerecorded antismoking commercials for radio and television than it had prior to the FCC's action.[7] Banzhaf's strategic maneuver to persuade the FCC to apply the fairness doctrine to cigarette commercials led to the ban enacted by Congress on airwave advertising that became effective in 1971, discussed later in this chapter.[8]

Activists like John Banzhaf and Ralph Nader (and the numerous organizations that they, most notably Nader, created and inspired) have taken advantage of the policymaking powers of administrative agencies to bring about changes in policy favorable to consumers. Crusades to eliminate dangerous products from the marketplace and deceptive practices in advertising rely on agency action for their support. The consumer movement that began in the 1960s gave greater force to administrative law as a tool of social change. The procedures and the laws that agencies used for policymaking were not new for the most part. What was new was their use by organized, professionally staffed consumer groups. Agency power marshaled for the consumer is often less than enthusiastically received by Congress. As one study notes, "the administrative process proved to be the key element in consumer protection policy, and the implementation of that policy invariably has taken a different path than that envisioned by its original proponents."[9] The agencies and Congress often define their agendas differently in the field of consumer protection. Of course, business groups have come to realize the power of administrative law. As a result, consumer interests do not necessarily hold the upper hand today.

THE FCC INTENSIFIES THE BATTLE

As the July 1, 1969, expiration date of the Cigarette Labeling and Advertising Act of 1965 (CLAA) approached, the FCC unexpectedly announced in February a proposed rule that would go a step further than applying the fairness doctrine to cigarette advertising. Instead, the proposed directive prohibited cigarette advertising on radio and television altogether.

The FCC announcement at a news conference and in the *Federal Register* put Congress on notice that it would have to act before the July 1 expiration date if it wanted to extend the moratorium on agency regulation of cigarette advertising. The antismoking interests found themselves in an unusually good position because for once they could advance their cause by seeing that Congress failed to act.

The tobacco lobby, however, was fully prepared for the expiration date and committed to seeing that Congress act to protect manufacturers from agency action but overplayed their hands in the House. The resulting Public Health Cigarette Smoking Act was not entirely to the liking of the industry (see Figure 7.1). The compromise legislation banned cigarette ads from radio and television beginning January 2, 1971, and strengthened the warning on packages. The act gave the FTC the authority to consider the warning requirement for all printed advertising after July 1, 1971. Balancing those provisions

FIGURE 7.1 PUBLIC HEALTH CIGARETTE SMOKING ACT OF 1969
(Became law in 1970.)

Required New Package Warning Labels

Substituted "Caution: Cigarette Smoking May Be Hazardous to Your Health" label with "Warning: The Surgeon General Has Determined That Cigarette Smoking Is Dangerous to Your Health."

Temporarily Preempted the FTC Requirement of Health Labels on Advertisements

Struck out provisions relating to the authority of the FTC with respect to unfair or deceptive advertising acts or practices and reports to Congress by the Secretary of Health, Education and Welfare and the Federal Trade Commission.

Prevents States or Localities from Regulating or Prohibiting Cigarette Advertising or Promotion for Health-Related Reasons

Substituted the provision that no statement relating to smoking and health should be required in the advertising of any cigarettes whose packages are labeled in conformity with the provisions of this chapter with the provision that no requirement or prohibition based on smoking and health should be imposed under state law with respect to the advertising or promotion of any cigarettes whose packages are labeled in conformity with the provisions of this chapter.

Prohibited Cigarette Advertising on Television and Radio (Authority to the Department of Justice)

It shall be unlawful to advertise cigarettes on any medium of electronic communication subject to the jurisdiction of the FCC.

(Excerpted in part from the original legislation.)

---

desired by health advocates, important concessions were made to the tobacco interests, including the requirement that the FTC give Congress six months' notice of any rule-making activity pertaining to cigarettes. Hence, if the proposed rule were not to the liking of Congress, it could block FTC action. Another important victory for tobacco interests, preemption of state action, was incorporated in the legislation, like the CLAA before it. As a result, states could not enact laws, stronger or weaker, that regulated cigarette advertising.

Six radio station owners appealed the broadcast prohibition to the courts. In March 1972, the Supreme Court upheld the congressional action. The cigarette manufacturers did not join in the appeal, largely because, once again, just as in 1965, congressional action in the cigarette controversy provided manufacturers with some distinctive advantages. Most important, the complete ban on cigarette commercials reduced the impetus for the networks to air antismoking ads, a consequence apparently unappreciated by the successful antismoking groups. The tobacco companies, on the other hand, supported the broadcast ban specifically because they anticipated that the broadcasters would be less likely to air the detrimental antismoking ads that had been effective in discouraging smoking.

FITFUL PROGRESS: THE EFFORTS OF A PERSISTENT FTC

Soon after the moratorium on FTC action on cigarette advertising was lifted, the agency shifted back into forward motion. The congressional ban on broadcast advertisements went into effect in January 1971. Three months later, the FTC had the cigarette companies back at the bargaining table and consenting, in a voluntary agreement, to include a health warning in all their printed advertising, similar to that already appearing on cigarette packages. And by midyear, the FTC was hammering away at the manufacturers again, threatening to initiate adjudicatory procedures for false and deceptive advertising if the cigarette companies did not agree to make their ad warnings more prominent.[10] Within six months, the FTC had succeeded in forcing six major cigarette companies to agree to a consent order that required ad warnings to be "clear and conspicuous" in all printed advertisements. Finally, eight years after the surgeon general issued his seminal 1964 report and eight years after the FTC announced its rule-making intentions, the regulatory policies that the FTC had proposed were adopted in their entirety.

Up to the 1990s, the FTC, either advancing the cause of regulation or retreating in the face of opposition, was in the center of the debate, causing consternation for the tobacco industry. The FTC's forward progress was hardly smooth or uninterrupted, not only because of the opposition of the tobacco industry to the agency's activism. For example, in April 1972, a U.S. district court cast a shadow of doubt on the FTC's entire policymaking capabilities. The federal court ruled that the commission could not require the posting of octane ratings on gasoline pumps. The decision was later reversed by the U.S. Court of Appeals for the District of Columbia, however, and the Supreme Court denied *certiorari*, allowing the appeals court ruling in support of the FTC to stand. The FTC, bolstered by this decision legitimating its rule-making power, was successful in urging Congress to ban ads for "little cigars" shortly thereafter in the fall of 1973.[11] Attempting to change the rules of the game to create strategic advantage is a standard in the repertoire of political strategies.[12] Despite the FTC's ultimate vindication, at the time the outcome was far from set, and some of the agency's energies had to be diverted from regulating businesses to defending itself in court.

In 1975, the FTC's policymaking powers were made more explicit by Congress. President Ford signed the FTC Improvements Act, a law providing the commission with a statutory basis for rule making and providing easier access to FTC proceedings for consumers. The goodwill and congressional trust apparent in this legislation did not last for long, however, for by the late 1970s, the FTC was back on the defensive for taking too much of an activist, consumer-oriented approach to its responsibilities. Several attempts were made by Congress to restrict the FTC's jurisdiction and cut back its appropriations. On two occasions in 1980, Congress actually allowed funding for the commission to expire.

Congressional (and industrial) opposition grew to such intensity in this period that the FTC was frequently singled out as the prime reason to push for the reform of government regulatory processes in general. Congressional discontent with the FTC peaked when the commission began to take on some of the most politically well-connected groups in the country, including segments of the insurance, drug, funeral, and advertising industries. Finally, on May 28, 1980, Congress passed a second FTC Improvements Act to reign in the agency.

This legislative slap in the face proved to be only a temporary setback for the FTC, for the commission was back in front of Congress in May 1981 with calls for a new, more effective health warning system for cigarette packaging that would include sterner language and larger type. The commission's 1981 staff report on cigarette advertising highlighted the fact that large portions of the population were not fully aware of the dangers of smoking. Support grew for stricter regulation.[13] The FTC's advocacy on these issues did not produce immediate results, but the commission's energy did ultimately bear fruit when, on October 13, 1984, President Reagan signed the Comprehensive Smoking Education Act into law (Public Law 98-47). Among other things, the new law replaced the 1970 version of the package warning with a series of four stronger, more specific warnings. The FTC may have been restricted or dissuaded from acting on its own by the FTC Improvements Act of 1980, but the commission proved to be an effective advocate for change nonetheless.[14]

KEEPING THE PRESSURE ON: THE POLITICS OF INFORMATION

When building support for a position against a more powerful opponent, the development and effective dissemination of credible research can be a useful strategy, one followed by the health advocates both in and out of government. Such information can be drawn on to build public support and a case for a change in public policy.[15] Pressure is, as a result, put on elected officials either to change the law or to limit their interference with bureaucratically induced policy change.

Until recently, the bureaucracy has had no serious contenders in the battle for information. One of its primary responsibilities is to keep data current and stay on top of issues. A second significant source of reliable information is the academic world, whose findings can prove inconvenient to the business world, although the rising practice of using corporate funds to support university research can create serious credibility questions for research findings. Another source of information is the think tank, a rapidly growing sector. The stratagem, however, of creating and funding think tanks, most of which support free enterprise and limited government, has produced a barrage of studies of varying quality largely supporting business interests. Despite the general intrusion of corporate interests into research, in the case of tobacco, the deleterious impact of smoking was becoming impossible to dispute.

Over the years, reliable scientific evidence amassed in a crescendo that continues to build: smoking is harmful both to the smoker and to those who must breathe their smoke (including fetuses), is associated with numerous illnesses, and shortens one's life span by an estimated thirteen years. In 1998, the *Journal of the American Medical Association*, which had as recently as the 1950s featured tobacco advertising claiming positive health effects of smoking in its pages, published a major study that linked both active and passive smoking to irreversible artery damage.[16]

By 2004, the surgeon general's report informed readers that smoking negatively affects every major organ of the body. Information countering industry claims and pointing the way toward tobacco control has poured in over the past decade: nicotine is as powerful a drug as heroin and cocaine; people who smoke typically begin during adolescence before they are sufficiently mature to envision their own mortality; in the 1990s, friendly Joe Camel was more recognizable to young children than Mickey Mouse; the higher the price of a pack of cigarettes, the less likely a youth will buy one and hence acquire an addiction that for some proves virtually impossible to cast off; and after one year of a smoking ban imposed in New York City—contrary to the alarmist claims of the cigarette manufacturers—no negative financial impact on restaurants and bars could be detected, and the ban was found to enjoy greater support than did the popular New York Yankees baseball team, suggesting that elected leaders need not fear a serious backlash from such restrictions.[17]

As early as 1968, the only "controversy" about the health effects of cigarettes was that created and claimed by the industry through its Tobacco Institute. The medical evidence, however, like information in general, did not speak for itself. Nor did it stand alone. Employing their own version of information politics, the tobacco companies flooded society with countervailing, if largely counterfeit, declarations of their own.

During the time between the publication of Surgeon General Luther Terry's report in 1964 and thirty years later when tobacco seemed on the ropes, the health subsystem was strengthened, thousands of studies were accumulated and reported in the press, antismoking interest groups were formed and gathered strength, bureaucratic agencies chipped away at the industry, policy entrepreneurs in and out of government executed strategies to curtail tobacco use, whistle-blowers leaked damaging information showing the industry to be disingenuous in their assertions and activities, and the cigarette companies and smokers were, as a result, vilified. Even then, fighting this industry seemed next to impossible. The most successful corporation, Phillip Morris, with 50 percent market share, made $63 billion in 1993 alone. In that same year, the tobacco companies spent over $6 billion to promote their cigarettes. The industry consistently contributed huge amounts of money to the political parties and members of Congress.[18] It engaged in major philanthropy that built loyalty to the industry among groups that might otherwise have responded more negatively and vigorously to the deleterious effects of tobacco use. It provided research dollars and other forms of support that institutions were loathe to turn down. If information were speaking for itself, it would not be heard until an enormous, patient effort was made on many fronts over many years by many people, not least federal bureaucrats, to lay the necessary groundwork.

THE SURGEON GENERAL: INFORMATION, NOT REGULATION

The 1965 CLAA provided an important opening for laying this foundation through information politics. Specifically, the bureaucracy was authorized to keep attention focused on the smoking and health issue through the seemingly harmless requirement that both the FTC and the Public Health Service submit annual reports to Congress on smoking. According to the act, these reports were to contain current information concerning smoking and health together with recommendations for further legislative action. The reports opened the door for both agencies to make very strong appeals for further action to curb smoking. Both the 1967 and the 1968 reports of the Department of Health, Education and Welfare, led by its energetic Secretary Wilbur Cohen, called for warnings to appear in advertising along with the disclosure of tar and nicotine content.

Concurrently, the reports of the surgeons general grew increasingly emphatic about the adverse effects of smoking. It is hard to imagine the debate over tobacco regulation getting started at all if it had not been for Surgeon General Terry and his well-orchestrated release of the Advisory Committee report on smoking and health in 1964. Since that time, the surgeon general has been at the front of the pack in leading the regulatory charge against the tobacco subsystem. The surgeon general's office may not have had the regulatory tools of the FTC to work with, but the country's chief public health officer does have credibility and legitimacy in the eyes of the public, and his or her pronouncements are inevitably perceived as newsworthy by the media. This combination of legitimacy and exposure make it possible for the country's preeminent health authority to make claims about smoking that help shape public opinion and construct a social reality that enabled regulators in all three branches of government to contemplate formulating restrictive policies they would never consider otherwise.[19]

Among the more prophetic of these reality-shaping pronouncements came with prescient emphasis on the dangers of environmental smoke in 1972. Important grassroots movements to ban or limit smoking in designated public spaces can trace their beginnings to the early 1970s when the surgeon general began making these sorts of pronouncements about the health hazards of secondhand smoke.[20]

This authoritative statement on the detrimental effects of secondhand smoke also gave federal bureaucrats cause for action. In May 1973, the Federal Aviation Administration began requiring that smokers and nonsmokers be segregated by section on commercial airlines. The Interstate Commerce Commission (ICC) restricted smoking to the rear 20 percent of all commercial interstate buses in May of the following year. In 1976, the ICC extended its ruling to trains, and executives in the General Services Administration (GSA) began issuing smoking guidelines for buildings in which nearly one million government employees worked. Step by step, smoking was being restricted as people were no longer free to smoke anywhere they chose.

Another round of regulation along these lines was inspired by release of the surgeon general's annual report in 1986. Many of these reports over the years have focused on a specific theme, and this one renewed and updated charges relating to the problem of secondhand smoke first raised a decade and a half earlier.[21] Later that same year, the GSA, the Department of Defense, and the Veterans Administration all took steps to establish smoke-free rules for common areas under their jurisdiction, while the Environmental Protection Agency (EPA) issued its own draft report citing secondhand smoke as carcinogenic and proposed that it be classified as a class A carcinogen.[22] Each of these actions was made possible, at least in part, by the pathbreaking claims issued by the nation's leading government authority on health, the surgeon general, who, in turn, relied on numerous government- and privately funded studies on the health effects of tobacco and the behavioral elements underlying smoking.

By 1994, smoking was prohibited on all regularly scheduled interstate buses because of rules promulgated by the ICC. Congress banned smoking on all domestic flights, regardless of length (excepting flights to Alaska and Hawaii). The Department of Defense prohibited smoking in all indoor spaces on military bases worldwide (except in restaurants, recreational areas, and domiciles).[23] Even more inclusive rules were announced by the Department of Labor's Occupational Safety and Health Administration to prohibit smoking in the roughly six million enclosed business sites under its jurisdiction nationwide (including restaurants and bars where food is served).

Each of these bureaucratic initiatives gained significant impetus, it can be argued, from the surgeon general's pronouncements on the dangers of secondhand smoke—and smoking in general—over the years. And each action, with the exception of the congressional ban on airline smoking, was promulgated by a government agency acting outside what is traditionally thought (and taught) to be the normal legislative process.

Each subsequent year brought worse medical news about smoking from the surgeons general, the National Institutes of Health (NIH), the Centers for Disease Control (CDC), and universities in the United States and abroad. By the turn of the twenty-first century, former smokers outnumbered smokers in the United States, the rate of smoking had been cut in half, and most people who did smoke reported that they wanted to quit. By 2005, most Americans must have known about the ill effects of smoking. No one has a monopoly on information, however. Information use is not a one-way street, as the health interests were about to see.

THE INDUSTRY FIGHTS BACK: POLITICS TURNS INFORMATION ON ITS HEAD

The tobacco industry was far from defenseless and fought back vigorously, often through its propaganda arm, the Tobacco Institute, until its doors were closed by the tobacco settlement. In 1998, for example, the British American Tobacco Company (BAT) leaked its misleading interpretation of a study by the International Agency for Research on Cancer (IARC), an affiliate of the UN World Health Organization, on the effects of passive smoking. BAT erroneously claimed that IARC found the impact of environmental smoke to be illusory. On the contrary, the study reported that breathing secondhand smoke increased the risk of lung cancer by 16 percent, a figure in line with previous research. Because the study had too few participants, however, the findings were statistically insignificant. Relying on the public's innumeracy, BAT said that "statistically insignificant" meant that no link with cancer was found.[24]

Current science itself, however, is not always correct—a fact that makes the public susceptible to claims that science is wrong even when it is not, as in the cases of global warming and the theory of evolution. For example, scientific evidence suggested that lower tar and nicotine content in cigarette smoke reduced the harmful effects of smoking. This canard, though reflecting current science forty years ago, continues to be perpetrated by a hard-fought public policy that required the FTC laboratory to measure the quantities of these ingredients in every brand.[25] The results of these tests (now performed by the tobacco companies) are published regularly and distributed by the commission but today are largely considered of little use and misleading. Manufacturers were encouraged to include the test results in their advertising, and since early 1971, all of them have done so. This official, government focus on tar and nicotine has, no doubt, contributed to the fact that the four-fifths of all smokers in the United States today buy so-called light cigarettes, apparently deluding themselves that they are limiting the damage smoking is causing to their bodies.[26]

The tobacco companies used the technique of attacking the adequacy of the science underlying information unfriendly to the industry after the EPA issued a report in 1992 on secondhand smoke. The EPA was excoriated by the tobacco industry. In the following year, industry leader Phillip Morris reprinted in full, in six full-page ads in major newspapers throughout the country, an article titled "Passive Reporting on Passive Smoke," by Jacob Sellum, versions of which had originally appeared in *Forbes'* MediaCritic and the *Wall Street Journal*. The headline of the ads read, "Secondhand Smoke Facts Finally Emerge: How Science Lost Out to Politics on Secondhand Smoke." The essence of the article was an attack on the scientific validity of the EPA report.[27]

Such efforts of the manufacturers have a long history and continue worldwide. As recently as 2002, Phillip Morris commissioned a study it released in the Czech Republic that purported to demonstrate that smokers, rather than being drains on public funds because of their health care needs, actually save the state money—by the fact that smokers die prematurely. The brouhaha surrounding this seemingly cynical effort to appeal to public officials' fiscal concerns at the cost of more humanitarian considerations reverberated throughout the world, though Phillip Morris chief executive officer Geoffrey Bible soon apologized, in the United States at least, for the report.

THE ROLE OF THE PRESIDENT

Although the tobacco companies retained much of their clout in the courts and in Congress through the mid-1990s, a counterbalance to tobacco interests was provided by those health and regulatory professionals in the bureaucracy who were committed to actively and aggressively promoting public health and truthful advertising. To what degree, however, does the bureaucracy actually carry out the wishes of the president, and to what degree is it acting independently?

The answer to this question varies, but, analogous to Congress in its oversight role, no administration can fully control agency professionals whose loyalties diverge from presidential (or congressional) preferences. Some administrations, like that of George W. Bush, have reputations for paying more attention to the actions of agencies than some other administrations have.[28] He has also actively used rule making and executive orders, especially after 9-11, to effect his will in public policy. That President Bush in effect issued a go-slow signal to the bureaucracy on tobacco control is apparent in, for example, the drastic reduction in the Justice Department's request for damages under the Racketeer Influenced and Corrupt Organizations Act (see chapter 8). President Jimmy Carter, unenthusiastic about Secretary of Health, Education and Welfare Joseph Califano's antismoking crusade in

1978, wrote in the margin of a staff memo that urged him to support the elimination of tobacco subsidies, "I refuse to be drawn into this fruitless issue."[29]

President George H. W. Bush's FDA Commissioner Kessler said that he did not feel free to proceed on tobacco control rule making with a pro-tobacco president at the helm. On the other hand, following the lead of President Ronald Reagan in his dealings with Surgeon General Everett Koop's call to arms on tobacco,[30] President Bush did not interfere with Secretary of Health and Human Services Louis Sullivan's outspoken advocacy of the anti-tobacco cause, a fact suggesting the difference between publicizing a problem and moving to regulate an industry. For example, the secretary asked sports fans and promoters to boycott sports events sponsored by tobacco companies, and he was a severe critic of smokeless tobacco. Through health care pronouncements such as those made by Sullivan, together with education programs initiated by the Department of Health and Human Services, political appointees have proven able to set priorities different from those of their presidents and to create a climate conducive to policy change.[31]

Nevertheless, modern presidents, in general, have important means of control, first, through the appointment process, which allows them to place loyal compatriots in the lead positions of the bureaucracy, and, second, through the Office of Management and Budget (OMB), through which all budget requests, agency rules, and legislative proposals must be vetted. (Of course, the OMB is itself composed largely of career bureaucrats who perform the technical work, most of which has policy implications.) Presidents can appoint loyal allies and people with histories consistent with the views of the chief executive. However, control through the appointment process is neither exact nor complete. In choosing their cabinets, for example, presidents must balance a number of political considerations, such as pleasing interest groups helpful in their election victory and getting their nominees approved by the Senate. Presidents do not have the luxury of considering policy views to the exclusion of everything else. Moreover, it is difficult to anticipate an appointee's views on issues that have not yet emerged in the policy process, as President Carter discovered when Secretary Califano began his anti-tobacco crusade. This is a problem confronted by presidents most visibly when considering whom to nominate to the Supreme Court.

Sometimes presidents or their assistants issue direct orders to agencies on certain policy matters, as apparently was the case when the chief auditor for Medicare was told that he could not tell Congress his deal-killing estimate of the price tag of the Medicare prescription bill in 2004.[32] Whenever the professionals in the bureaucracy are working on a presidential priority, one can be sure that the president and his aides will be paying attention. However, most matters cannot be a presidential priority. Here, the president must rely on the good judgment of his appointees to ensure that his wishes are carried out. The appointees, most of whom are not subject-matter experts in the matters under their agencies' jurisdictions, must themselves rely on none other than the civil servants in the bureaucracy.

Some agencies are more subject to direct presidential control than others. Regulatory bodies like the FTC and the FDA; medical agencies like the CDC, NIH, and the Office of the Surgeon General; and scientific advisory commissions are staffed by medical and science professionals and are less likely to be politicized, though they may be. They can be and are influenced through the appointment process to varying degrees, depending on the president. Moreover, the regulatory agencies must submit proposed rule making to the Executive Office of the President for review and approval prior to taking action. Health and scientific agencies, in particular, are typically staffed by apolitical professionals committed to their crafts and dedicated to their profession, not a particular administration. President Reagan's surgeon general, C. Everett Koop, provides a preeminent example of this phenomenon. No better exhibit, however, for this kind of professional orientation can be found than at the FDA, both a health and a regulatory agency, under the leadership of David Kessler in the 1990s.

BIG TOBACCO UNDER SIEGE: MULTIPLE VENUES

Over time, the tobacco companies were under siege in a variety of other policy arenas beyond the federal bureaucracy. Even Congress did not entirely sit on its hands. Supplied with information on the harms of smoking and pressed by growing antismoking forces, between 1986 and 1994 it passed five pieces of legislation aimed toward tobacco and passive smoke control, including one on smokeless tobacco (a scourge that had led to a spate of highly publicized cases of oral cancer in male teens), two acts banning smoking on domestic airline flights of specific durations, another law mandating the states to impose and enforce restrictions on cigarette sales to minors, and a final piece of legislation requiring all federally funded children's services to be provided in smoke-free environments.

Multiple venues are afforded not only by the constitutional structure of checks and balances but also by federalist principles. At the state level, Mississippi Attorney General Michael Moore linked up with experienced private plaintiffs' litigators to devise a new legal strategy. State and local governments too had climbed on to the no-smoking bandwagon and outlawed smoking in government buildings. At the local level, ordinances proscribed indoor smoking in public places in an increasing number of localities, and a mounting number of private businesses came to the conclusion that smoking at the workplace was too costly to their bottom lines. These trends were to continue over the following decade until only a few laggards remained.

Public opinion, too, shifted, even in the dwindling number of tobacco states where pro-tobacco loyalties were deeply rooted and cultivated by the extraordinary philanthropy of big tobacco. Increasing awareness that the companies were focusing their advertising efforts on children and teens was extremely damaging to the industry.

If, however, tobacco executives felt that they had reached a nadir by 1994, they were wrong. Still, the companies did have at least one reason for optimism. Congress changed hands after the congressional elections of 1994. Representative Henry Waxman's (D-Calif.) series of highly publicized hearings on behalf of the health subsystem were brought to an end by the elections of 1994. When the Republicans took over the House, Waxman lost his subcommittee chairmanship and, hence, his platform from which to attack tobacco interests. Fortunately for tobacco interests, the full Commerce Committee would now be chaired by Thomas Bliley (R-Va.), whom antagonists sometimes derisively called "the congressman from Phillip Morris."

The midterm elections brought in a Republican majority to the House of Representatives for the first time in forty-two years. Both the Senate and the House would be organized and led by the Republicans. Committee chairs would be Republican, and big tobacco had reason to cheer. They had contributed in excess of $3 million to the Republican Party to help bring about this result.[33]

Although tobacco was back in the driver's seat on Capitol Hill, policy entrepreneurs FDA Director David Kessler and Attorney General Janet Reno provided a significant counterforce, just as the attorneys general were doing in the states. Given the policymaking powers of government agencies, tobacco's worries were far from over. Nor would the industry find its interests safe from injury in that formerly friendly arena: the courts.

NOTES

1. Introduced in 1949, the FCC established a rule known as the "fairness doctrine" to require broadcast media to cover "controversial issues" of local interest. The stations also had to provide "a reasonable opportunity for the presentation of contrasting viewpoints. In 1986, a federal court ruled that the doctrine did not have the force of law. Consequently, the FCC terminated the rule in 1987. For an interpretation of the impact of the removal of the fairness doctrine, see Michael Massing, "The End of the News?" New York Review of Books 52, no. 19 (2005) http://www.nybooks.com/articles/18516.
2. Federal Communications Commission, Public Notice, 1188-3, June 5, 1967 (mimeograph).
3. "Wasilewski Opposes Fairness Doctrine Being Applied to Cigarette Spots," TV Code News, 6, no. 6 (June 1967): 3.
4. For more on this common form of argument and its hazards, see Simon Blackburn, Being Good: A Short Introduction to Ethics (Oxford: Oxford University Press, 2002).
5. John F. Banzhaf III v. Federal Communications Commission, 405 F. 2d 1082 (1968).
6. PBS Frontline, "Inside the Tobacco Deal" (1997),available at http://www.pbs.org/wgbh/pages/frontline/shows/settlement/interviews/glantz.html.
7. In the eight months after the FCC's decision, the American Cancer Society distributed 4,723 such commercials. See Robert E. Dallos, "Perry Mason's TV Foe, Dead of Cancer, Left Anti-Smoking Film," The New York Times, September 13, 1968, 55.
8. After bringing his complaint to the FCC, Banzhaf went on to become the founder and executive director of an organization called ASH (Action on Smoking and Health), which endeavored to raise a legal defense fund of $100,000 to help protect and defend the FCC's

decision. Among the sponsors of ASH were many of those individuals associated with the antismoking forces, including Sen. Maurine Neuberger.

9. Mark V. Nadel, *The Politics of Consumer Protection* (Indianapolis: Bobbs-Merrill, 1971), 29.

10. The threat of case-by-case action allowed the FTC to bring pressure to bear on cigarette manufacturers while at the same time avoiding congressional sensitivity regarding the more general rule-making procedures invoked by the FTC in the past.

11. "Little cigars" were cigars made the same size and shape of cigarettes by the tobacco companies to avoid regulation. They were not covered under laws passed by Congress, which applied, according to the letter of the law, only to traditional cigarettes.

12. Deborah A. Stone, *Policy Paradox: The Art of Political Decision Making*, rev. ed. (New York: Norton, 2002).

13. In a survey done for the report, 50 percent of women did not know that smoking could cause miscarriage or stillbirth, and 40 percent of the high school seniors believed that smoking was "no great health risk."

14. Despite passage of the law requiring more stringent warnings, the influence of the tobacco lobby remained strong. Earlier formulations of one of the four warnings specified that smoking could cause death as well as miscarriage in pregnant women. Mention of this possibility was deleted in committee mark-up sessions.

15. Margaret E. Keck and Kathryn Sikkink, *Activists beyond Borders: Advocacy Networks in International Politics* (Ithaca, N.Y.: Cornell University Press, 1998). See also Stone, *Policy Paradox*.

16. George Howard et al., "Cigarette Smoking and Progression of Atherosclerosis: The Atherosclerosis Risk in Communities (ARIC) Study," *Journal of the American Medical Association* 279, no. 2 (1998):119–124.

17. "The Health Consequences of Smoking: A Report of the Surgeon General" (May 27, 2004), available at http://www.surgeongeneral.gov/library/smokingconsequences.

18. Gene Borio, *Tobacco Timeline: The Twentieth Century, 1950–1999—The Battle Is Joined* (2003), available at http://www.tobacco.org/resources/history/Tobacco_History21.html. The Tobacco Timeline was created by Gene Borio's tobacco.org. This Web site is described on the site as follows: "Tobacco.org is a free resource center focusing on tobacco and smoking issues. It features tobacco news, information, assistance for smokers trying to quit, alerts on tobacco control issues, and open consideration of all aspects of the spectrum of issues concerning tobacco, nicotine, cigarettes and cigars. It began in 1988 with Gene Borio's news-posting service on Compuserve (where Borio was a forum leader), Prodigy, and later AOL. A BBS (Electronic Bulletin Board Service) began in 1993, and the website began in 1996. Since 2000 it has been run by Gene Borio and Michael Tacelosky." This site provides a wealth of information on the history of smoking and politics. Another good source is *Frontline's* "Inside the Tobacco Deal" at http://www.pbs.org/wgbh/pages/frontline/shows/settlement/timelines/fullindex.html. For a third excellent chronological source of actions pertaining to smoking and politics, consult the Office of Smoking and Health of the Centers for Disease Control.

19. For a discussion of how authoritative claims made by scientists and government leaders can help construct a mass social reality that is conducive to change, see Ronald J. Troyer and Gerald E. Markle, *Cigarettes: The Battle over Smoking* (New Brunswick, N.J.: Rutgers University Press. 1983), 26, 77, 144. According to Troyer and Markie, claims made by federal officials have a stigmatizing sociological effect that eggs along changes in public attitudes that, in turn, make further regulation by government possible.

20. Today, over 2000 communities in the U.S. ban smoking in restaurants, bars, offices and other public places. In fact, nearly 400 localities have moved to outlaw smoking outdoors as well. (Dennis Cauchon, "Smoke-Free Zones Extended Outdoors", *USA TODAY*, November, 1, 2005, http://www.usatoday.com/news/nation/2005-11-01-smoke-free-zones_x.htm

21. Surgeon General, *The Health Consequences of Involuntary Smoking* (Washington, D.C.: U.S. Department of Health and Human Services 1986) brought to light the importance of "side stream" smoke (also referred to as environmental tobacco smoke [ETS]), noting that ETS was at least as rich in carcinogens as inhaled tobacco smoke. The report also noted that "passive smokers" have significantly higher rates of lung cancer and various other respiratory conditions Robert L. Rabin and Stephen D. Sugarman, *Smoking Policy: Law, Politics and Culture* (New York: Oxford University Press, 1993), 3–4

22. The EPA's final report ("Environmental Tobacco Smoke") was issued in 1992 after being endorsed by an independent panel of experts—some, including the panel's chairman, with close ties to research supported by the tobacco industry. The report confirmed the links

between ETS and elevated rates of lung cancer and other respiratory conditions and estimated that ETS was responsible for approximately 3,000 lung cancer deaths and about
37,000 cardiovascular disease–related deaths per year (about the same number of deaths
attributable to automobile accidents). ETS was also identified as responsible for between
150,000 and 300,000 lower-respiratory ailments in children.

23. Only since 2005 have the rules, strengthened by executive order in 1999, been fully in effect.

24. See ASH Open Letter to PCC (March 1998), available at http://www.ash.org.uk.

25. William G. Meserve, staff counsel to the Senate Commerce Committee, discussed some of
these developments in a speech titled "Cigarettes and Congress" before the California Conference on Cigarette Smoking and Health, October 29, 1967.

26. Borio, *Tobacco Timeline*. Evidence reported by Borio's *Tobacco Timeline* follows: October 17,
1996: "Researchers disclose molecular link between a substance in tobacco tar and lung cancer: a benzo (a) pyrene derivative damages lung cancer-suppressor gene, p. 53, in the exact
'hotspot' associated with lung cancer. *Science* magazine ("No Such Thing as a Safe Cigarette). In 1981, the Surgeon General's annual report concluded that no progress had been
made in the search for a safe cigarette. Even the lower tar and nicotine cigarettes seemed to
constitute a health risk because smokers, believing they were safer than with other cigarettes, smoked more often, covered over the air vents in the filters, and inhaled more
deeply—thereby increasing their health risks." March 22, 2003: "Judge orders Phillip Morris to pay $10.1 billion in damages for misleading smokers into believing that low-tar ciga-
rettes are safer than regular brands. *Susan Miles et al v Phillip Morris Inc.* See:
http://www.tobacco.org/resources/documents/030321milesvmo.html. "The Court finds
that the term 'Lights' not only conveyed a message of reduced harm and safety, but also
conveyed to Class members that the 'Lights' cigarette product was lower in tar and nicotine. . . . Phillip Morris' strategy was to create doubt about the negative health implications
of smoking without actually denying these allegations. . . . The evidence at trial establishes
that Phillip Morris continued this disinformation campaign through the mid-1990s. . . .
Phillip Morris' motive was evil and the acts showed a reckless disregard for the consumers'
rights.—Illinois Circuit Court Judge Nicholas Byron."

27. For a detailed case study of Phillip Morris's attempt to derail EPA regulations through
misinformation politics, see M. E. Muggli, R. D. Hurt, and L. B. Becker, "Turning Free
Speech into Corporate Speech: Philip Morris' Efforts to Influence U.S. and European Journalists regarding the U.S. EPA Report on Secondhand Smoke," *Preventive Medicine* 39, no.
3 (2004): 568–80.

28. In contradistinction to the point about the power wielded by President Bush over the
bureaucracy is his lack of interest on a related front, namely, wielding his power over decisions by Congress, perhaps because, with a Republican Congress, the president has less
need to engage formal mechanisms to accomplish his will. Here, the president has done
very little. Bush has accepted every act of Congress without veto and has not rescinded any
congressional appropriation in five years. Most presidents have used those powers hundreds of times in similar time periods. See Jim Cooper, "Cowed and Profligate Bush Has
Failed in His Fiscal Duty, *Financial Times*, July 15, 2005, 13.

29. Califano was dismissed from his position as secretary of the Department of Health, Education and Welfare after he took up his antismoking crusade, about which tobacco-state
elected officials were apparently furious.

30. In the 1982 report, Surgeon General Everett C. Koop attributed 30 percent of all cancer
deaths to tobacco and called cancer from smoking "the chief preventable cause of death in
our society." The 1984 report said that 80 to 90 percent of all chronic obstructive lung disease and 50,000 of 62,000 deaths were caused by smoking. In the 1985 report, Koop said that
cigarettes were the main peril in the workplace, prompting the AFL-CIO to accuse him of
undermining efforts to improve environmental and occupational health programs. See
Washington Post, December 20, 1985, A9.

31. The Reagan administration waged a continuing battle with Congress about the size of the
budgets of the Public Health Service (PHS), including the Office of Smoking and Health.
While the administration was successful in at least slowing the growth rate of the PHS budget, the bureaucracy found ways to circumvent some of the administration's efforts. For
example, in 1984, when the administration tried to deemphasize activities of the Office of
Smoking and Health, bureaucrats repackaged its antismoking program into an anticancer
program and nested it in the National Cancer Institute (also a part of the PHS), where it was
easier to hide from the knife of the administration's budget cutters.

32. Charles Babington and Ceci Connolly, "Democrats Call for Medicare Drug Inquiry," *Washington Post*, February 10, 2005.
33. In 1995, "tobacco companies give the GOP $2.4 million in 'soft' dollars. The top two soft money contributors to the GOP that year were Phillip Morris ($975,149) and RJR Nabisco ($696,450). Tobacco industry PACs gave $841,120 to Republican members of Congress" (Borio, *Tobacco Timeline*).

8

THE COURTS MOVE INTO
THE SPOTLIGHT

*To cease smoking is the easiest thing I ever did. I ought to know
because I've done it a thousand times.*

—Mark Twain

By the mid-1990s, the tobacco companies found themselves under siege in multiple arenas and at every level of government. Their antagonists were sharing information and strategies with each other and were making uneasy alliance when doing so furthered their ambitions and goals. During this period, the actions in one arena became densely intertwined with those in another, muddling the neat conceptual categories that the words "public," "private," "separation of powers," and "federalism" connote.

For example, documents stolen from the Brown & Williamson Tobacco Company fell into the hands of Mississippi Attorney General Michael Moore. He could not legally use these materials to make his case against the tobacco companies because they were deemed "proprietary" or private. This explosive information found its way to tobacco antagonists in private litigation, in Congress, at the Food and Drug Administration (FDA), and then on the front page of the *The New York Times* and the Internet. As a result, what was once private became public. This transformation was assisted by Moore's having contracted with private plaintiffs' lawyers to fund and prosecute Mississippi's anti-tobacco case. These litigators were fiercely competitive, and they understood that these documents had to be made public in order to be admissible in court. They had no compunction about doing what was necessary to accomplish that goal. They knew that the same documents could also be used by the state attorneys general, by private plaintiffs' lawyers, by members of Congress, by the U.S. attorney general, and by the FDA commissioner to make their cases in court and to persuade the public that the tobacco companies should be held liable for past acts, should pay their fair share of the damage smoking has caused, and should be tightly regulated by the federal government. The documents would help convince the president to support his subordinates in the bureaucracy as they interrupted the practices of a politically powerful industry.

The convergence of these battles over tobacco in the courts is no surprise to anyone familiar with the structure and culture of government in United States. When there is a fight, the courts are often the final arbiters—at least until a new strategy that politically and legally circumvents the court rulings can be devised. Understanding the intertwining of the multitude of activities that culminated in legal contests requires pulling together a number of separate, almost implausible stories.

A NEW ERA IN TOBACCO LITIGATION

Prior to the mid-1990s, lawsuits against the cigarette companies by victims of lung cancer and other tobacco-related diseases had failed to win even a single favorable ruling in the courtroom. In the 1940s and early 1950s, scientific data on the health dangers of smoking were not sufficiently definitive in the judicial eye (especially in the eyes of jurors) to link smoking and cancer. Furthermore, in the early 1960s, manufacturers of cigarettes had some protection against suits because the courts accepted the argument that they had no clear or reasonable way to foresee the harm that cigarettes might do to consumers. After 1965, when warning labels started appearing on packs of cigarettes, the courts found that these words of caution relieved the manufacturers from liability, just as they had predicted.

By 1988, there were about 135 liability cases pending against tobacco companies by smokers or their families. In one case—*Galbraith v. R.J. Reynolds Industries*—nationally known trial attorney Melvin Belli claimed that his client was addicted to tobacco, so that the health warnings on labels were useless. In another highly publicized case, *Marsee v. U.S. Tobacco*, a woman had argued that her son died of oral cancer because he used snuff. Juries in both these cases ruled in favor of the tobacco companies. In a third important case, *Cipallone v. Liggett Group*, a U.S. circuit court of appeals ruled that tobacco companies have limited immunity from liability in such cases because of the warning labels. On January 12, 1987, the Supreme Court upheld this finding by declining to review the case. As recently as the mid-1990s, tobacco companies had never paid any punitive damages for the harmful effects of their products.

The perfect record of the tobacco companies in U.S. courts came to an end in the latter part of the 1990s thanks to the untiring efforts of a state-level elected official working with his own bureaucracy and some good friends from his law school days. Taking advantage of the opportunities for policy entrepreneurship and the multiple policy venues in the U.S. system, Mississippi Attorney General Michael Moore pursued a novel approach to tobacco litigation that ultimately would bring litigants, if not under the control of statutory authority, at least to the negotiating table. Instead of trying to demonstrate that the tobacco companies were liable for the damage their product caused to the health of smokers, Moore would sue the tobacco companies for reimbursement of the costs that the state of Mississippi had borne in treating smokers in its Medicaid program.[1]

Moore's new legal strategy had originally come to him from Mississippi attorney Mike Lewis, a former classmate of his from the University of Mississippi, known fondly as Ole Miss. Lewis had experienced a former client and friend's suffering through a slow and painful death from cancer caused by smoking cigarettes. It occurred to Lewis that the state was bearing an enormous cost in treating people who, like his friend, suffered from smoking-related illnesses and that the states might succeed in holding the tobacco companies responsible for the states' share of the cost of health care for smokers. After all, the state was an innocent party bearing costs generated by a transaction between the smoker who bought and smoked the cigarettes and the manufacturers who sold them. (In economic jargon, such third-party effects are called "externalities.") Lewis soon shared his idea with his friend Attorney General Moore, who was receptive to suggestion.

In the spring of 1993, Moore began assembling a legal team to pursue a case on behalf of the state of Mississippi against the tobacco companies. Lacking the requisite resources and in-house expertise to succeed, the attorney general attracted experienced, top-notch private litigators to assist him. Moore convinced them to use their own money to finance the case but without their usual contingency contract that ensured plaintiffs' lawyers a percentage of the financial judgment if they won the case. Instead, if the case succeeded, the losing side, the tobacco companies, would be required to pay the attorneys' fees, which stood to be enormous. This agreement allowed the state to go head-to-head with a formerly invincible force despite the enormous costs of sustaining a case against these companies. In a sense, the taxpayers of Mississippi were getting for free the best legal counsel that money could buy. The huge legal costs of bringing suit against these companies would not be paid out of proceeds due the state, should it win. Nor would Mississippi have to finance the enterprise. The plaintiffs' lawyers would. Like venture capitalists, the plaintiffs' lawyers were taking on a huge financial risk in exchange for a potentially commensurate payoff. Lead counsel Richard Scruggs, for example, would possibly earn $1 billion for his efforts alone.

Focusing on lawyers' fees rather than tobacco and its effects on public health was to become a major diversionary tactic by tobacco's friends in Congress and elsewhere. Scruggs deflected this issue somewhat by agreeing to let a panel of judges determine his fee. Without the huge gains that the legion of lawyers stood to reap, it is improbable that this caliber of legal talent could have been amassed against the tobacco industry. As Scruggs said in an interview with PBS's *Frontline*, "The money mattered." So did the challenge. For Scruggs and his colleagues, going against a seemingly indomitable force was the legal equivalent of walking on the moon for the first time. "It is not often in life that you have a chance to make a mark on humanity," he said. "And we all got caught up in the opportunity that this presented to us." Scruggs explained their thinking in this regard. "This was an industry that had never been beaten. [It] had fortified itself for decades against litigation. [We] had prepared and covered every conceivable litigation angle. It was sort of like the challenge of climbing Mount Everest the first time. It had never been done. . . . [In] theory you could do it. But nobody had."[2]

Scruggs was the leading lawyer for the state Medicaid reimbursement cases and subsequently the lead negotiator in the global tobacco settlement that was to bring together a massive array of interested parties—across branches and levels of government on one side and across the tobacco industry on the other. Other key members of the team included Don Barrett, Mike Lewis, and the well-known litigator Ron Motley. Dick Scruggs and Motley had successfully tried a massive class-action suit against the asbestos industry. It was during that trial in 1993 that Scruggs mentioned to his colleague the idea that the tobacco companies might be sued to recover costs to health imposed by smoking. "Motley is a quick study and the idea of doing something on that scale inspired him. I mean, he was, he needed sedation after I told him about it," Scruggs later recounted.[3] Don Barrett was a Mississippi attorney experienced in tobacco litigation as a plaintiffs' attorney. He too knew the formidable forces the state would be facing. According to Scruggs,

> the Ole Miss connection among many of the protagonists was a coincidence . . . that we took advantage of. . . . We had money in our pockets as a result of the asbestos litigation, so . . . all of these elements, by chance, came together. And I think that almost simultaneously we realized the potential we had there. With a war chest, with legal talent, [and] with an Attorney General [Mike Moore], a state official who was willing to do it, is enthusiastic about doing it. And some bright legal ideas about how to get it done.[4]

In yet another coincidence, the judge in the Mississippi case was known (but not well) by the members of the legal team, as he was a graduate of—where else?—Ole Miss.

Over the summer of 1993, the legal team began developing the theory and strategy on which they would base the state's case. They also polled public opinion and found that "it would be very problematic to win the case. . . . The poll results were fairly discouraging," according to Scruggs. Undeterred, after spending more than a year researching the case, the group decided to argue in court that the tobacco companies had been unjustly enriched by their sale of cigarettes to Mississippians because the state and not the companies had been forced to pay for the costs of health care for the sick smokers. As a second prong in the strategy, Moore sought an injunction to force the tobacco industry to stop targeting their marketing and advertisements toward children.[5] On

May 23, 1994, Moore filed his lawsuit in a Mississippi court against thirteen tobacco companies as well as wholesalers, trade associations, and industry public relations consultants.

Part of Moore and Scruggs's strategy was vigorously to encourage other states to file their own lawsuits in order to increase the pressure on the tobacco companies. As medical costs were becoming an increasing burden on state budgets, a successful suit not only would bring needed revenues to state coffers but also could further the political ambitions of the attorney general who brought it. Moore energetically lobbied the other attorneys general to bring their own suits. He knew that as more Medicaid actions were filed, the likelihood would increase that at least one case could be won. Moreover, with multiple states suing the companies, even an industry like tobacco, with seemingly inexhaustible resources, would be hard pressed to fight on so many fronts at once. As hoped, once Moore filed his lawsuit in Mississippi, other states followed his lead and filed parallel lawsuits against the tobacco companies. Minnesota was the second state to file in August 1994, followed by Florida in February 1995. Eventually, all fifty states would file claims against the tobacco companies.[6]

NEW PRIVATE LITIGATION: THE CASTANO CASE

On top of the claims brought by the state attorneys general against the tobacco industry, the tobacco companies were also feeling the pressure of new private litigation. Chief among these was a class-action lawsuit, *Castano v. American Tobacco Company*, filed by attorney Wendell Gauthier in the spring of 1994 in New Orleans.[7] Gauthier would subsequently persuade sixty other members of the plaintiffs' bar to pledge $100,000 a year to launch the suit and would turn the case into the largest class-action suit ever against the tobacco companies. This case would also prove to be instrumental in bringing the tobacco industry to the negotiating table in 1997.[8]

Consistent with the reason many other combatants were induced to become active in the anti-tobacco cause, Gauthier was propelled by a personal connection with a victim of tobacco use. Smoker Peter Castano was a friend of Gauthier's who had died of cancer in 1993. Castano's widow asked Gauthier to sue the tobacco companies on her husband's behalf, but Gauthier knew that taking on the tobacco companies with the usual legal arguments would be a losing battle. The announcement in 1994 by FDA Commissioner David Kessler that evidence was mounting that the tobacco industry had manipulated the level of nicotine in cigarettes in an effort to addict smokers provided Gauthier with an alternative to past legal approaches. Gauthier's discovery was strengthened just a few days later by a segment on ABC's *Day One* program that similarly alleged that tobacco companies had spiked their cigarettes with nicotine.

Gauthier realized that this allegation presented the possibility of filing a suit against tobacco based on nicotine addiction. If what Kessler and the ABC program said were true, tobacco companies could no longer argue that smokers had freely chosen to smoke if they were addicted to the nicotine—deliberately manipulated by the companies—in cigarettes. To bring a lawsuit, however, Gauthier would have to prove that nicotine was an addictive substance and that the tobacco companies had taken advantage of this fact. Gauthier needed evidence.

On March 29, 1994, about two months before Moore filed his lawsuit in Mississippi, Gauthier jointly filed *Castano v. American Tobacco Company* with twenty-five plaintiffs' law firms. The defendants included, in addition to the American Tobacco Company, seven of the largest tobacco companies. The complaint included the names of four other plaintiffs, in addition to Castano, who had tried to quit smoking and had failed. Among the complaint's allegations was that the tobacco companies had engaged in fraud and deceit in stating that nicotine was not addictive and had acted negligently in deliberately misrepresenting the contents of their product. The plaintiffs were asking for punitive and compensatory damages as well as funds for the treatment of tobacco-related diseases. Eventually, the *Castano* case, involving a plaintiffs' consortium of approximately sixty law firms, sued on behalf of every addicted smoker in the United States.[9]

If orchestrating this number of lawyers and plaintiffs required sophisticated management skills, then bringing together and negotiating on behalf of state, federal regulatory agency, congressional, presidential, and private interests simultaneously, as Moore and Scruggs were to do, entailed a level of performance unprecedented in American legal practice. First, however, tobacco's opponents needed evidence that they did not have.

THE WHISTLE-BLOWERS

The lawyers in the *Castano* case, the FDA, and the state attorneys general received crucial help from two whistle-blowers: Merrell Williams and Jeffrey Wigand. Without these two, the pressure on the tobacco industry might never have been enough to bring them to the negotiating table in 1997 and again in 1998.

Merrell Williams, a paralegal for a law firm in Kentucky representing Brown & Williamson, had stolen confidential documents belonging to the tobacco company. Over the approximately four years that he worked at the law firm, beginning in late 1987, Williams had taken thousands of confidential papers that showed that for many years the tobacco companies had conducted extensive research on the harmful effects of smoking, including the effects of nicotine and other carcinogenic ingredients in tobacco. Never, however, had the corporations released their findings to the public. If admissible, these materials could be used to support the charge that the tobacco industry had engaged in a widespread and long-term cover-up of its true activities and intentions.

As is frequently the case with whistle-blowers, Williams himself was far from a white knight with pure motives. As Scruggs described him at their first meeting, "He looked like warmed over death. He looked unkempt. Not quite like he'd been sleeping under a bridge but close to it. He was obviously very ill, very nervous, had been drinking." Personally troubled and financially strapped, Williams met with Don Barrett and Dick Scruggs on April 15, 1994, and handed over the Brown & Williamson documents to them. Scruggs swiftly saw the gold mine that the material would be in demonstrating evidence of fraud by the tobacco industry. "I looked at Merrell, and I said, 'These guys are toast.' We've got them," Scruggs recounted. When his colleague Barrett read excerpts from the document at a meeting of the *Castano* lawyers, Gauthier immediately realized their importance in the campaign against tobacco. Never before had such damning evidence been extracted from the industry.

One major obstacle stood in the way of using the documents in court: admissibility. Because these documents had been stolen and were confidential, a judge would be sure to keep them out of court, rendering them useless in the tobacco litigation suits. The challenge for Scruggs and his erstwhile allies was how to get these documents in the public domain and, hence, admissible as evidence.

Of course, in the meantime, Brown & Williamson's legal team was doing everything in its power to put the genie back in the bottle by getting the stolen papers returned and by vigorously pursuing Merrell Williams. In fact, a court had already ordered Williams to return the material to its rightful owner, Brown & Williamson. Uncharacteristically, however, the tobacco company was in the dark, as it did not know how many of their documents or which ones Williams had photocopied.

Scruggs felt the stolen documents contained evidence of fraud and should be sent to Congressman Henry Waxman (D-Calif.), who was at the time investigating and holding a yearlong series of hearings on the tobacco industry. At about the same time, the FDA obtained a set of the 4,000 pages of the same purloined material. The documents were also sent to Congressman Ron Wyden (D-Ore.), who was a member of the Waxman committee. The first story on the papers appeared in a front-page story in *The New York Times* on May 7, 1994, with the headline "Tobacco Company Was Silent on Hazards."

Even more ominous for Brown & Williamson's interests, as well as those of the industry as a whole, a full set of the documents was placed in the library of the University of California, San Francisco, and, from there, on the Internet. Brown & Williamson quickly filed a claim in San Francisco superior court to have the documents from the library returned to them, arguing that they had been stolen. But on June 29, the California Supreme Court rejected the tobacco company's request to prohibit the university from making the documents public. The documents, with the help of Dr. Stanton Glantz, a medical researcher at the university, had been uploaded to the Web for the entire world to see. The papers were now public documents, clearing the way for their use in the cases against the tobacco companies and by FDA Commissioner David Kessler in his novel efforts to regulate the industry.

The other key whistle-blower was Jeffrey Wigand, who had been the head of research at Brown & Williamson from 1989 to 1994. If Merrell Williams were a person of questionable character and prospects, Jeff Wigand was his opposite. As a former vice president of Brown & Williamson and experienced researcher, Wigand could provide insider's knowledge of the activities and intent of the tobacco companies.[10]

Wigand's decision to become a whistle-blower stemmed from his disillusionment with Brown & Williamson, which had hired him to develop a safer cigarette and then changed its direction soon after his arrival. Once competitor R.J. Reynolds had abandoned its efforts in this area, decision makers at Brown & Williamson saw no business need to pursue this line of research either. Eventually, the disappointed Wigand, apparently not a team player in the company, was dismissed. Subsequently, in return for a series of benefits covering retirement and health needs, Wigand signed a confidentiality agreement that prohibited his talking about what he had learned while at Brown & Williamson.

Soon after his dismissal, on March 24, 1993, Wigand was contacted by a producer at CBS who was seeking an adviser for a story on fire-safe cigarettes. Wigand, an expert and in need of a job, accepted the offer. Over time, Wigand and the CBS producer, Lowell Bergman, began talking about Wigand's experience at Brown & Williamson, and Bergman began to realize that he had another, potentially explosive story here. Wigand's willingness to cooperate with Bergman also soon attracted the interest of the anti-tobacco forces, and by the spring of 1994, he and Kessler at the FDA were in contact. The Justice Department and Representative Waxman's office also sought out Wigand as a source of inside information.

In 1995, Wigand agreed to be interviewed for CBS's *60 Minutes* about his experiences at Brown & Williamson. The interview was taped, but as the broadcast date approached in the fall of 1995, CBS's general counsel, worried about CBS's being sued by Brown & Williamson, brought broadcast plans to a halt. Aware that ABC had been successfully sued for its *Day One* program about the tobacco industry, CBS canceled the segment. The broadcaster experienced a great deal of criticism for what seemed to be a caving in to industry demands. Brown & Williamson wasted no time in suing Wigand for breaking his confidentiality agreement. In seeking to defend himself against Brown & Williamson, he found none other than Dick Scruggs, who agreed, perhaps not entirely altruistically, to be Wigand's pro bono lawyer. Scruggs found and paid for lawyers in Kentucky to defend him against the company. As Scruggs had anticipated, representing Wigand was to prove highly beneficial to himself and his colleagues.[11]

In November 1995, Wigand was deposed by Scruggs and Mike Moore for the Mississippi Medicaid reimbursement case. For over two hours, the whistle-blower gave a full account of his experiences at Brown & Williamson. In January 1996, journalist Alix Freedman at the *Wall Street Journal* obtained a copy of the entire transcript. She wrote an article that laid out all of Wigand's allegations, including his statement that his former boss, Brown & Williamson chief executive officer (CEO) Tommy Sandefur, had knowingly lied while under oath to Congress when he swore before Representative Waxman's subcommittee in 1994 that he did not believe that nicotine is addictive. The information in the *Journal* article proved extremely useful for the plaintiffs in the *Castano* case, as the awareness of the impact of nicotine was the basis of their case. Wigand himself became a key witness in that litigation, just as Scruggs had anticipated.

Predictably, the cost to Wigand personally for his disloyalty to his former employer was huge. Brown & Williamson, in no mood for forgiveness for Wigand's violation of the confidentiality agreement, withdrew all payments to him and ruthlessly pursued him in court. The former vice president of a leading American corporation found himself teaching high school science for perhaps $30,000 a year. According to Scruggs, "They unleashed an unprecedented smear campaign against [Wigand]. They hired investigative firms . . . to go into every aspect of his past. Drag out every, every piece of paper or transaction that Jeff Wigand had ever conducted to try to put a false light on it and on him. They tried to show that he was a mental case, that he was a wife beater, that he was a shoplifter. I mean they came in with all sorts of allegations to actually smear him."[12]

In discussing why Wigand stood alone among his many peers in coming forward to expose the industry, FDA Commissioner Kessler observed,

> Certainly if you look at what Jeff Wigand went through, you understand why a lot of people haven't come out and talked. But the one thing that united them all [the industry people we talked to] . . . [was that] they were very scared. They were very frightened. They knew what the industry's modus operandi was. They knew the kind of force that unlimited resources could have on you. They understood the kind of legal proceedings that you could face. Not only today and tomorrow. But for years.[13]

Even Merrell Williams, whose prospects were never promising, was hounded by the industry. He was sued, his strapped financial situation notwithstanding. Dick Scruggs bailed him out financially in what the tobacco companies charged constituted an illegal *quid pro quo* for providing the stolen Brown & Williamson papers to Scruggs.

No one, it seems, was given a reprieve by the tobacco industry. Scruggs was also sued for his involvement with the stolen papers. "They put me under surveillance, did the same to my family," Scruggs said in a PBS interview. "Sued us in federal court. Sued me. Sued Merrell. Sued any other

lawyer, had a long list of John Doe defendants who had seen or had partici-
pated in turning these documents over. . . . And unleashed more or less
a smear campaign of their own [alleging] that we were paying for stolen
documents."[14]

THE FIRST SETTLEMENT: LIGGETT & MYERS
BREAKS RANKS

Yet another unprecedented breakthrough for the tobacco litigators came
when Bennett LeBow, who maintained a controlling interest in the Liggett &
Myers tobacco company, surprisingly broke ranks with the rest of the
tobacco industry and entered into a settlement agreement with the *Castano*
group and five of the states. Never before had the big tobacco companies had
a defector at this level in their midst, as previously they had all toed the same
line that tobacco was not addictive and did not cause cancer, and the companies were working hard to uncover the truth about the effects of smoking.
While Liggett was the smallest tobacco company—with a U.S. market share
of about 2 percent—LeBow's willingness to settle gave needed legitimacy to
the plaintiffs' cases, provided crucial information (previously undisclosed)
on industry practices, and helped shift tobacco politics in favor of the anti-
tobacco forces.

Over December and January 1995–1996, personal injury lawyer Don
Barrett conducted negotiations with Liggett in complete secrecy and independently of members of the *Castano* group and the state attorneys general. In
February, he brought in Scruggs and Moore, while the *Castano* group would
not be brought in until negotiations were almost complete. On March 13,
a proposed settlement was announced between Liggett and the *Castano*
group as well as four of the five states that had filed lawsuits against the
company by that time. Louisiana, the fifth state, would later also sign on to
the agreement.

The groups fighting the tobacco companies constituted an uneasy alliance,
as no one wanted to get the short end of the stick. The plaintiffs' lawyers who
had financed the *Castano* litigation were especially concerned that their monetary interests be protected. A package deal was negotiated that covered the
Castano case, the suits brought by the states' attorneys general, and some of the
FDA's concerns. Under the agreement, Liggett agreed to pay five states—
Florida, Louisiana, Massachusetts, Mississippi, and West Virginia—$1 million
a piece plus between 2 and 7 percent of the firm's pretax income over the following twenty-four years. In exchange, Liggett would be safe from future lawsuits by these states from trying to recoup money spent on smokers in their
Medicaid program.[15] The *Castano* group, in return for being barred from
future lawsuits against Liggett, would receive 5 percent of the company's pretax income for the next twenty-five years. This money would go to programs
to help people stop smoking and not to individual plaintiffs, an important

development that shaped subsequent agreements with the other tobacco companies. The private lawyers would get their huge contingency payments, but their clients, the plaintiffs who had been harmed, would get nothing. Liggett had the right to end the deal, however, if the *Castano* case were not upheld as a class action by the Fifth Circuit Court of Appeals. At the insistence of the attorneys general, Liggett also agreed to adopt a number of the FDA's proposed rules limiting advertising and marketing to minors.

As a crucial part of the settlement—and the final blow that brought the rest of the industry to the negotiating table—Liggett would make available confidential files that the industry desperately wanted to keep private. These files further implicated the other tobacco companies in concealing knowledge of the health effects of tobacco and, once obtainable, would strengthen the hand of the attorneys general and plaintiffs' lawyers in their negotiations with the companies and that of federal authorities—the FDA and the Justice Department—fighting the industry in court.

It appeared that the success of the *Castano* group was to be short lived, however, when just two months later their national class action was decertified by the Fifth Circuit Court of Appeals, nullifying their part of the Liggett settlement. But Gauthier (the lead counsel) and other members of the *Castano* group had expected the unfavorable ruling and immediately began filing parallel individual cases in each state. Within months, they had already filed seven such cases. When negotiations for a "global" settlement between the tobacco industry and all the plaintiffs began in the spring of 1997, Gauthier and other members of the *Castano* group would participate, arguing for compensation for the countless addicted smokers in America, compensation that the addicts or their survivors would never see.[16]

Another problematic case facing the tobacco companies in 1996 was brought by attorney Norwood Wilner in Florida on behalf of cancer victim Grady Carter. Wilner had decided to follow Attorney General Moore's strategy of seeking compensation for the cost of the complainant's medical costs instead of seeking punitive damages. With the Brown & Williamson documents now publicly available, Wilner had evidence that the tobacco companies knew of the dangers of smoking that it had not publicized. This was, in fact, the first case to use the Williams documents in court, and it resulted in a historic reversal for the industry. On August 9, 1996, after a very short trial, the jury in *Carter v. Brown & Williamson Tobacco Corp.* found in favor of Grady Carter, who was awarded $750,000 in damages to cover his medical costs.[17]

The next year, the environmental tobacco smoke (ETS), or secondhand smoke, arguments bore fruit for the first time as the tobacco companies settled with the flight attendants for sickness caused by ETS in *Broin v. The Phillip Morris Companies, et al.* The judicial tide seemed to be turning against the tobacco industry, yet another inducement for the companies to come to negotiating table rather than risk unsustainable losses in the courts. Nevertheless, tides that shift once can be expected to shift again, especially in a world with multiple policy venues and creative minds able to recast issues.

PRESSURE MOUNTS FOR GLOBAL SETTLEMENT

By the late summer of 1996, tobacco executives had become increasingly concerned about the ever-growing expenses of their legal defense. The determined efforts of Attorney General Mike Moore to encourage new states to file Medicaid cases and the loss of the important *Carter* case in Florida meant that these costs were only likely to increase. In addition, the new revelations about the tobacco industry uncovered by the whistle-blowers and the Liggett files, coupled with the campaign by Commissioner David Kessler at the FDA, meant that a settlement might be the best way out. By this time, Janet Reno's Justice Department had also begun five separate grand jury investigations of the tobacco companies.

Scruggs and Moore had begun discussing the possibility of a settlement with the tobacco companies in the spring of 1996. Faced themselves with the mounting costs of pursuing their cases and reading a news report that Steve Goldstone, R.J. Reynolds's CEO, had said that would consider a comprehensive settlement, Scruggs and Moore initiated talks with representatives of the tobacco industry.

The process of negotiating a settlement would eventually involve virtually all the major players in tobacco politics, including the state attorneys general, representatives of the *Castano* group, the Clinton White House, public health groups, and Congress. The FDA's proposed remedies were an important component of the agreement, though Kessler did not directly participate in the negotiations and subsequently objected to the outcome. Despite the enormous number of players involved and the often conflicting objectives among negotiators on both sides, a proposed global settlement between the tobacco companies, the attorneys general from forty-six states, and a number of private plaintiffs was announced on June 20, 1997.

The terms of the agreement required the tobacco companies to pay what eventually amounted to $368 billion to the forty-six states over the twenty-five years. This sum would compensate states for the costs of providing medical care to people suffering from smoking-related illnesses and would also be used to finance smoking cessation programs. The settlement also established new restrictions on tobacco marketing and advertising and required tobacco companies to print warning labels about the addictiveness of nicotine and the danger of smoking on cigarette packages. In addition, it authorized the FDA to regulate nicotine as a drug and cigarettes as drug delivery devices. In return, the tobacco companies were relieved from the dozens of lawsuits currently filed against them by the states and individual smokers. The companies were also granted limited immunity from future lawsuits filed by the states or by individuals. The terms of the settlement would, however, have to be approved by Congress.[18]

Despite the historic agreement, the settlement quickly ran into problems. After reviewing the agreement, David Kessler, by that time the former head of the FDA, and former Surgeon General C. Everett Koop publicly criticized

the settlement, pointing out that it would restrict the FDA's authority to regulate tobacco in that the FDA would be prohibited from regulating the nicotine levels in cigarettes for at least twelve years. Also, before reducing the
allowable nicotine levels in cigarettes, the FDA would have to demonstrate,
with good evidence, that doing so would bring about a significant lowering
of the health risks of smoking and would not create a black market for high-
nicotine cigarettes. This concession seemed unwarranted since U.S. District
Court Judge William L. Osteen Sr. had ruled in April that the FDA *did* have
the authority to regulate tobacco and without the restrictions detailed in the
proposed agreement. Many trial lawyers and public health groups were also
opposed to the agreement's protection of tobacco companies from future
lawsuits seeking punitive damages and from class-action cases.

President Clinton was not taking the lead in pushing the agreement for
passage in Congress, and the necessary congressional support of the deal
was weak despite the early involvement of Senate Majority Leader Trent Lott
(R-Miss.), who had provided many of the national connections Moore would
need in the plan for an agreement.[19]

Nor was it certain that Congress would stick to the bargain struck by the
attorneys general and the tobacco companies. On April 1, 1998, Sen. John
McCain (R-Ariz.) sponsored an anti-tobacco bill that was much tougher than
the global settlement and that did not hold the tobacco companies harmless
from future lawsuits stemming from prior acts. Seven days later, R.J.
Reynolds abruptly pulled out of the June 20 agreement, and within hours the
other companies followed. The tobacco legislation to implement the global
settlement died in the Senate in June 1998.[20] That same month, the U.S. court
of appeals ruled that the FDA did *not* have the right to regulate tobacco,
though the judgment would be appealed to the Supreme Court for a final
determination of the FDA's authority in this specific area.

Despite the failure of the initial settlement bill in Congress, the tobacco
companies still wanted to settle the states' cases. By this time, in fact, Mississippi and Florida, which were not parties to the agreement, had settled independently with the tobacco companies. Texas and Minnesota would similarly obtain settlements in early 1998. The attorneys general from the
remaining forty-six states would themselves reach a new agreement with the
tobacco companies, called the Master Settlement Agreement (MSA), as soon
as November 1998.

This agreement was narrower in scope and generally weaker than the
1997 agreement. In return for the states dropping their suits, the four tobacco
companies agreed to pay the states $206 billion over twenty-five years to
compensate for their smoking-related Medicaid expenses. This was a lower
amount than either the 1997 agreement or the Senate legislation. The states
were granted full discretion in how they would use these funds, though
many stated they would devote much of it to Medicaid. In addition, $1.7 bil-
lion was earmarked for the establishment of the American Legacy Foundation, which was formed to develop programs to decrease teen smoking and

smoking in general.[21] The MSA also required that the Tobacco Institute be disbanded and barred cigarette ads that targeted minors, including ads that featured Joe Camel and other cartoon characters. Tobacco ads on billboards were also banned. In addition, the tobacco companies would have to maintain a Web site for at least ten years that would include all documents that had been produced in smoking and health–related lawsuits. The four tobacco companies that settled via the MSA would not receive limited immunity from future lawsuits as in the 1997 agreement. The MSA did not mention FDA regulation, an intentional omission that meant that the agreement could be implemented without new legislation from Congress.[22] At the same time, the legality of the FDA's attempt to regulate tobacco would be held in legal limbo until the Supreme Court made a final determination in 2000.

DEVELOPMENTS IN WAKE OF THE MSA

The MSA altered the terrain of an industry already in transition from the declining importance of tobacco in Congress, the entrance of new CEOs representing a larger worldview than their predecessors, and the growth of international markets and competition. The four companies in the settlement lost some of their market share because small makers of cigarettes—not having been a part of the MSA—could enjoy a competitive advantage and sell their products for less, though they did not have the big companies' advantage of brand loyalty. While the MSA granted the four tobacco companies immunity from additional lawsuits from the states involved in the settlement, it did not shelter them from future lawsuits filed by other parties. In 2005, three major cases were still in progress. Two of these were class actions brought in Florida and Illinois, and the third was a federal conspiracy suit.[23]

The federal suit, *U.S. v. Phillip Morris*, was a conspiracy case originally brought by the Clinton Justice Department. After the Waxman hearings in 1994, the Justice Department began investigating whether the seven tobacco company CEOs, who had testified under oath before the committee that nicotine was not addictive, had committed perjury. Reversing course, on January 29, 1998, the tobacco executives returned to Congress and conceded that nicotine is, in fact, addictive and that smoking may cause cancer.

While criminal indictments were never brought against the executives for lying to federal authorities, in 1998 the Justice Department did begin studying the possibility of recovering costs the federal government had spent in its Medicare program in treating smoking-related sickness. Arguing that the basis for such a suit would be ill founded, the tobacco companies assiduously lobbied the Justice Department to discourage the Civil Division lawyers from going forward with the effort. Beholden only to their professional interpretation of the law and answerable primarily to Attorney General Janet Reno and President Clinton, the career civil servants were unmoved by the companies' imprecations. Reno and Clinton approved bringing suit, and at his January 19, 1999, State of the Union Address, the president announced the decision to go forward. The demand for Medicare reimbursement, combined with the efforts of the FDA to regulate tobacco as a drug, "represented the federal government's most aggressive actions ever against the tobacco industry," according to *Congressional Quarterly*.[24]

As promised, on September 22, the Justice Department filed a civil suit— *U.S. v. Philip Morris*. The federal government charged the tobacco companies with conspiring since the 1950s to defraud and mislead the public about the dangers of smoking under the Racketeer Influenced and Corrupt Organizations (RICO) Act, a highly creative use of RICO not anticipated by its congressional authors. The claim relied heavily on the documents uncovered during the states' cases. Like the states, the federal government was further seeking reimbursement for medical expenses to treat people with smoking-related diseases.[25]

In September 2000, U.S. district judge Gladys Kessler (no relation to David Kessler, the former commissioner of the FDA) dismissed the Justice Department's petition to recover the costs of medical care but allowed the novel claim under the RICO Act to go forward. The government had adequately demonstrated that in concealing the health risks of cigarettes from smokers, the tobacco industry had engaged in racketeering, Judge Kessler ruled. When President George W. Bush took office in 2001, his attorney general, John Ashcroft, pushed to reduce the resources devoted to the case. He tried to reach a settlement, but, over the next four years, his department's career lawyers continued to prepare for trial. Opening statements began in September 2004.

On June 7, 2005, during closing arguments of the now six-year-old lawsuit, the Justice Department made a surprise announcement that the government would not seek the $130 billion to fund smoking cessation programs.[26] Instead, overriding objections of career lawyers in the Justice Department involved in the case, they would seek less than 10 percent of that amount, just $10 billion. This decision not only shocked anti-tobacco activists but also created a "growing political liability for the Bush administration."[27] Then, in another about-face, the government announced that it would request the original $280 billion in damages, the largest ever sought in a civil racketeering trial, after all.[28] By then, however, it was too late to reverse course, as the Supreme Court declined to review a separate appeals court decision that the Justice Department was now permitted under the federal racketeering statute only to seek $10 billion in penalties for misleading the public about the dangers of smoking.[29] While $10 billion is a large sum, it is one-twenty-eighth the original maximum penalty sought; this amount was only the theoretical figure should the four companies involved lose the suit and have to pay the maximum.[30]

No matter which way the legal winds blew in the United States, the tobacco companies, ever nimble, had long ago begun to eye international markets for both production and sales. The world loomed.

NOTES

1. Michael Janofsky, "Mississippi Seeks Damages from Tobacco Companies," *The New York Times*, May 24, 1994; Carrick Mollenkamp et al., *The People vs. Big Tobacco* (Princeton, N.J.: Bloomberg Press, 1998), 25, 28–29, Peter Pringle, *Cornered: Big Tobacco at the Bar of Justice* (New York: Henry Holt, 1998), 7. Pringle's book and Mollenkamp's work are thorough and well-documented analyses of tobacco and the courts. The account in this chapter relies heavily on their interpretations of the events leading up to the tobacco cases being heard in the courts.
2. PBS *Frontline*, Scruggs, "Inside the Tobacco Deal" (1998), available at http://www.pbs.org/wgbh/pages/frontline/shows/settlement/interviews/moore.html.
3. PBS *Frontline*, "Inside the Tobacco Deal."
4. PBS *Frontline*, "Inside the Tobacco Deal."
5. PBS *Frontline*, "Inside the Tobacco Deal"; Pringle, *Cornered*, 7, 31.
6. PBS *Frontline*, "Inside the Tobacco Deal"; Janofsky, "Mississippi Seeks Damages from Tobacco Companies"; Kenneth Jost, "Closing In on Tobacco," *CQ Researcher* 9, no. 43 (1999): 12; Mollenkamp et al., *The People vs. Big Tobacco*, 30, 52–53; Pringle, *Cornered*, 55.
7. Civil Action No. 94–1044.
8. Pringle, *Cornered*, 6–7, 42–43.
9. Pringle, *Cornered*, 6–7, 42–43.
10. When they used the tactic of the document dump—that is, responding to requests for documents in the discovery phase of a lawsuit by delivering a truckload of papers (why do the work for one's opponents?)—Wigand could tell investigators just where to look among the mass of material for what they needed.
11. The award-winning movie *The Insider* (Touchstone, 1999) documents this series of events. The movie, directed by Michael Mann, starred Al Pacino, Russell Crowe, and Christopher Plummer.
12. Scruggs on *Frontline*, "Inside the Tobacco Deal."
13. Kessler on *Frontline*, "Inside the Tobacco Deal."
14. Scruggs on *Frontline*, "Inside the Tobacco Deal."
15. Alix Freedman et al., "Breaking Away: Liggett Group Offers First-Ever Settlement of Cigarette Lawsuits," *Wall Street Journal*, March 13, 1996; Jost, "Closing In on Tobacco," 12; Pringle, *Cornered*, chap. 12.
16. Mollenkamp et al., *The People vs. Big Tobacco*, 57–58, Pringle, *Cornered*, 263.
17. Mollenkamp et al., *The People vs. Big Tobacco*, 48–55.
18. John Broder, "Cigarette Makers in a $368 Billion Accord to Curb Lawsuits and Curtail Marketing," *The New York Times*, June 21, 1997; Mary H. Cooper, "Tobacco Industry: Do Ads and New Products Still Target Teen Smokers?," *CQ Researcher* 14, no. 13 (2004): 1025–1048. Jost, "Closing In on Tobacco"; Pringle, *Cornered*, 305.
19. In the continuing series of Mississippi connections in this saga, Lott was brought into the picture by his brother-in-law Dick Scruggs, Attorney General Moore's law school classmate and his lead counsel. It was Senator Lott who originally introduced Scruggs to Dick Morris, President Clinton's pollster, whom the Mississippi legal team was to hire to assess the attitudes of the state's public about asbestos in 1989 and then, in 1993, tobacco. Lott's participation helped convince the parties that Congress would be willing to act should an agreement be reached.
20. Martha A. Derthick, *Up in Smoke: From Legislation to Litigation in Tobacco Politics*, 2nd ed. (Washington, D.C.: Congressional Quarterly Press, 2005), 121; Jost, "Closing In on Tobacco"; Pringle, *Cornered*, 305–7; Jeffrey Taylor and Suein Hwang, "From the Ashes: The Big Tobacco Deal Gains New Momentum despite Early Setbacks," *Wall Street Journal*, October 23, 1997.
21. According to the *American Journal of Public Health* (March 2005), the American Legacy Foundation can be credited with accelerating the overall decline in youth smoking by 22 percent in the first two years—2000 through 2002—of their TRUTH campaign aimed at teenage smokers. As of this writing, tobacco companies and their allies continue to attack the American Legacy Foundation for misuse of funds and the states for not expressly using the payments for the settlement for the "intended" use and instead balancing state budgets with the tobacco money windfall.
22. Cooper, "Tobacco Industry," 13.

23. The Florida class action is a personal injury case, and in Illinois, Phillip Morris is defending itself against a charge of fraudulent marketing of Marlboro Lights and Cambridge Lights in the claim that these two brands are safer to smoke than regular cigarettes. As of the summer 2005, *Howard A. Engle v. Liggett Group* was under review by the Florida Supreme Court. In Illinois, *Sharon Price v. Phillip Morris* was also in appeal by the state supreme court.

24. Cooper, "Tobacco Industry,"13.

25. Marc Lacey, "Tobacco Industry Accused of Fraud in Lawsuit by U.S.," *The New York Times*, September 23, 1999.

26. The original suit asked for $280 billion to cover both smoking-related Medicare costs plus penalties under RICO for misleading and defrauding the public for fifty years (Kenneth Jost, "Can the Industry Survive the Latest Battles?",*CQ Researcher* 9 no. 43[1999]: http://library.cqpress.com/cqresearcher/document.php?id=cqresrre1999111200&type=hit list).

27. Eric Lichtblau, "U.S. Seeks Higher Damages in Tobacco Industry Suit," *The New York Times*, July 19, 2005. Nevertheless, according to reporter Ira Tanowitz in *Advertising Age* (July 4, 2005), the sanctions, which the Justice Department was seeking in its filing with the federal district court in the District of Columbia, "would represent the most draconian marketing curbs ever imposed by government on private industry." The requested sanctions included ending the marketing light cigarettes, price promotion for major brands, and motor sports sponsorships anywhere in the world (for the first time covering marketing outside the United States). The companies would also be required to "to resume and boost by one-third annual funding for the American Legacy Foundation's anti-tobacco ads." Despite the huge reduction in request for monetary penalties, the reaction of tobacco executives to the proposed sanctions was decidedly negative.

28. Gina Holland, *Court Won't Let Bush Push Tobacco Penalty*, Associated Press Online, (October 17, 2005). http://www.sfgate.com/cgi-bin/article.cgi?file=/n/a/2005/10/17/national/w073505D08.DTL&type=printable.

29. Linda Greenhouse, "Justices Reject Appeal in Tobacco Case," *The New York Times*, October 18, 2005; Mark Sherman, "U.S. Again Seeks $280b in Tobacco Profits" *The Washington Post* July 18, 2005. http://www.washingtonpost.com/wp-dyn/content/article/2005/07/18/http://AR2005071800859.html.

30. The defendants in the lawsuit are Philip Morris USA Inc. and its parent, Altria Group Inc.; R.J. Reynolds Tobacco Co.; Brown & Williamson Tobacco Co.; British American Tobacco Ltd; Lorillard Tobacco Co.; Liggett Group Inc.; Counsel for Tobacco Research—U.S.A.; and the Tobacco Institute. In a subsequent development, Sharon Eubanks, the lead trial lawyer in the government's law suit resigned abruptly. She said her superiors' unwillingness to support her work on the case led to her decision. "The political appintees to whom I report made this an easy decision," the twenty-two year Justice Department veteran explained. (Pete Yost, "Justice Department Lead Lawyer Quits" Associated Press Financial Wire, December 1, 2005, http://www.cbsnews.com/stories/2005/12/01/national/main1090650.shtml).

9

POLICY ENTREPRENEURSHIP
IN THE BUREAUCRACY AND BEYOND

If you want something done, ask Kessler.

—From Former FDA Commissioner David Kessler's High School Yearbook[1]

David Kessler was appointed commissioner of the Food and Drug Administration (FDA) by President George H. W. Bush in 1990. Armed with an M.D. from Harvard University and a law degree from the University of Chicago, Kessler had impeccable academic credentials even though his management experience was limited. Camouflaged by his thick, horn-rimmed glasses and his boyish looks, Kessler's keen interest in public health and his political acumen were easy to underestimate. He was a policy entrepreneur.[2]

The entrepreneur is one who takes advantage of the power of position to aggressively tackle an issue and strategically advance it. Public entrepreneurs do not "go by the book," or, in less colloquial terms, they do not necessarily follow the bureaucratic rules if those rules are obstacles to achieving the desired goal. Willing to take risks in advancing an issue, entrepreneurs may elevate their own judgment over that of their superiors or may bypass nominal superiors to reach the ultimate decision makers. The risks they take are those that may result not only in failure for the issue at hand but also in loss of their jobs. Thick skins that bounce off severe criticism, persistence in the face of long odds, and confidence in one's abilities and in the rightness of one's cause are all qualities that assist the successful entrepreneur. Predictably, entrepreneurs are notoriously difficult to manage, and their superiors must ultimately determine whether tolerating a maverick is worth the consequences. Whether entrepreneurial behavior is appropriate in a public bureaucracy is a matter of debate.

The term is borrowed from the private sector, where one sees most entrepreneurship occurring, usually in start-up companies and at the head of a business enterprise. In the public sector, however, there are many heads of agencies, bureaus, and offices, and the role of the entrepreneur is less well defined and understood. Although increasingly appreciated as a vehicle for change, the public entrepreneur does not fit well within a bureaucratic culture. Typically, public servants should not be in business for themselves, even when they deem that business to belong to the public. The primary reason for bureaucratic rules and procedures is to ensure accountability and appropriate behavior, but these same rules can lead to sclerotic, unresponsive government whose denizens follow the rules without advancing public interests effectively. Kessler was a master in the application of entrepreneurial leadership to his work in government.

Kessler took his job seriously, and soon after his arrival, it became clear that he planned to shape up his sleepy agency. Exhibit number one was the case of Proctor and Gamble, which had at first ignored an FDA order and then suffered unexpected, severe repercussions from an enforcement action initiated by Kessler.[3] From early in his tenure, Kessler's sights were set on tobacco. The proximate catalyst was the death of the father, a heavy smoker, of the FDA spokesman, who had asked Kessler to put cigarette control on his agenda.[4] Kessler assembled his demoralized FDA staff, many of whom became enthused at the prospect of taking on the tobacco industry and proceeded to show Kessler the heartfelt letters and petitions that the FDA had received over the years. Over 100,000 signatories had importuned the FDA to regulate tobacco.

Kessler would hold off doing so, however, both because he needed more information to make the case that FDA could legally regulate tobacco under the Food, Drug and Cosmetic Act of 1938 and because President Bush, his boss, was pro-tobacco. When Bill Clinton became president and reappointed the commissioner, Kessler had a better shot at succeeding in his quest. Ironically, the debacle of Clinton's failed health care reform plan did open a window of opportunity for Kessler. Clinton might prove receptive to a plan to forge a positive legacy in the field of public health for his presidency.

Kessler's first order of business was to establish the FDA's authority to set rules for cigarette production and advertising. The FDA, which today functions simultaneously as a scientific, regulatory, and public health agency, was created by Congress under the Food and Drugs Act in 1906, superseded in 1938 by the Food, Drug and Cosmetic Act. Today, the FDA's powers are derived from 1938 statute and amendments to it. Unfortunately for Kessler's case, the passage of the 1906 act was secured by way of a compromise that excluded nicotine from the list of regulated drugs. While the 1938 act again made no mention of nicotine, it did cover medical devices used to deliver drugs. Kessler, the lawyer, understood the parsing of legal language, the ways of legal argument, and the need to use the opening in the 1938 law by finding convincing evidence that cigarettes were under his agency's jurisdiction. Cigarettes would have to be shown to be delivering nicotine, a drug, to the bloodstream. This demonstration was no small task, especially since he had little evidence at first to prove his case and since Congress had explicitly prohibited regulation of tobacco by agencies no fewer than four times in the 1970s.[5]

When he decided to take on the cigarette industry, however, he was repeatedly warned off. "'It's impossible. It's a fool's errand.' No matter whom you asked you got the same answer. 'You can't do that. They're just too powerful. You can't take on the tobacco industry,'" Kessler said he was told.[6] Representative Newt Gingrich (R-Ga.), who was to become Speaker of the House after the 1994 elections, characterized Kessler as being "out of his mind" for trying to regulate the industry.[7]

At the start of his quest, Kessler did not have the proverbial smoking gun of irrefutable evidence that the tobacco companies were treating nicotine, tobacco's key ingredient, as a drug. "Throughout the years the industry had maintained that tobacco was not a drug, that the companies did not try to get people hooked on cigarettes or other tobacco products, and that in fact cigarettes were not addictive," Kessler commented in an interview in conjunction with the PBS television program *Frontline*. With regard, however, to taking on the industry, Kessler said,

> We weren't ready to do it. We didn't, we had not thought through what it would take. We hadn't done our homework. It took us 2 to 3 years to write a simple three page letter. We issued that letter in February 1994. That letter turned out to be a critical turning point. It was the first time that the Federal government would consider regulating tobacco products. [It was the] first time in 30 years since the Surgeon General's report in 1964 that linked smoking and cancer. The Federal government would consider regulating tobacco products if there was evidence that the nicotine in cigarettes and smokeless tobacco were drugs under the federal law.[8]

On February 25, 1994, Kessler went public. He threatened to regulate cigarettes as a drug if it could be determined that cigarette manufacturers manipulated nicotine levels in their products over the years in an effort to better "hook" consumers. In April 1994, testifying before Henry Waxman's (D-Calif.) health subcommittee in the House, the chief executive officers (CEOs) of every major U.S. tobacco company responded by swearing under oath that they did not believe that cigarettes were addictive. Most denied that smoking causes cancer. While juries may not have been willing to hold cigarette corporations responsible for smokers' addiction and cancer, few people denied that cigarettes were addictive and caused cancer. That the seven leading CEOs of these companies seemed to have lied under oath was galling to many.

"Outrage" is not too strong a word for the effect on some people of the executives' apparent misrepresentation. In fact, Jeffrey Wigand, the former head of research for the Brown & Williamson tobacco company, discussed his reaction on seeing the hearings on C-SPAN: "When that TV image replayed in my mind, I realized that, by my silence, I was not that far removed from the men on my screen."[9] It was Wigand's information (both before and after the CEOs' congressional appearance) that helped bolster

Tobacco company executives testifying under oath before Representative Henry Waxman's health subcommittee that cigarettes are not addictive (April 1994; National Institutes of Health photo).

Kessler's case to regulate the industry, damage the industry's position in the courts, and bring the big companies to the bargaining table with the state attorneys general.

After issuing the letter on the FDA's concern about tobacco use, Kessler had his staff begin to collect medical and behavioral evidence that would assist him in making his case. Fortuitously, Kessler's effort was advanced by two surprising developments in 1994. First, the FDA received an anonymous call in March 1994 suggesting that they look at recently issued foreign patents.[10] Following this lead, FDA investigators discovered that a new strain of tobacco, labeled Y-1, had been developed in Brazil for Brown & Williamson and that fifteen pounds of Y-1 seeds had been exported to the United States to Brown & Williamson and then back to Brazil for cultivation. This discovery provided the missing crucial evidence that Kessler needed, as these special seeds produced tobacco with 6 percent nicotine content—twice that permitted to be grown in the United States under existing bureaucratic rules. Moreover, after an exhaustive search of customs records up and down the East Coast, an FDA investigator found that the Y-1 seeds had in fact been brought into the United States. When questioned about Y-1 by the FDA, Brown & Williamson explained that this tobacco was mixed with low-tar tobacco.[11]

To Kessler, this revelation constituted the smoking gun he had been seeking. Reducing tar in a cigarette also reduces the nicotine. Brown & Williamson was apparently making up for that loss by adding the Y-1 tobacco and hence was manipulating the level of nicotine, something that the industry had consistently denied. Instead, adding nicotine to low-tar cigarettes was said to improve the taste, an assertion patently untrue, as nicotine has a bitter taste, according to the respected *Merck Index*.[12]

The second development in the spring of 1994 supported and amplified what Kessler had uncovered. In May, the internal papers that Merrell Williams had stolen from Brown & Williamson were leaked to key members of Congress, the FDA, and the press. The documents supported the claim that the industry knew as early as the 1940s—and certainly by the 1960s—that cigarettes were addictive and that tobacco company executives had known of health problems related to smoking that they did not reveal publicly.[13] Among the papers, a 1963 memorandum was discovered. In it, general counsel Addison Yeaman inadvertently provided a second smoking gun. "Nicotine," he wrote, "is addictive. We are, then, in the business of selling nicotine, an addictive drug."[14] The documents also pointed to the Y-1 patent, applied for by Brown & Williamson, for the genetically engineered tobacco plant to increase nicotine content. As evidence that the industry was aware of the addictive nature of and intentionally manipulated nicotine, Kessler's case for regulation was building.

GETTING THE PRESIDENT ON BOARD

After four years of investigation and study, Kessler and his troops at the FDA were ready to act. Kessler's energy was nothing short of remarkable, a characteristic common among successful policy entrepreneurs. His courage was a *sine qua non* for someone prepared to take on an industry whose strategic wall of invincibility had barely been dented over years of persistent ramming by personal injury lawyers and by federal health and regulatory bureaucrats and their occasional allies in Congress.

When asked several years later whether he felt threatened by the tobacco industry and its power to destroy his career, Kessler responded, "What would you have done? This wasn't about careers or risks to individuals. We asked a question and we started looking at the evidence and once we started down that path, it was evidence that we saw that just was overwhelming. And that's what persuaded us." But Kessler was no simple true believer who would self-destruct over a principle, even that of public health, in which he deeply believed. His political acuity was impressive.

By 1994, Kessler and his investigators had accumulated sufficient evidence to declare that nicotine is an addictive drug. Since he was not privy to the highly damaging Brown & Williamson papers until later in the year, much of his evidence was developed by simply scouring past scholarly research and connecting the mounting studies—a task no one had apparently tackled prior to Kessler and his troops doing so. The fact that nicotine was shown to be addictive in numerous scientific studies was enough to jump-start an announcement that the agency would consider regulating tobacco, but much more would be needed to move to the next step of proposing and implementing a practicable regulation.

The shot over the bow came in the form of a letter from Kessler to the Coalition on Smoking and Health.[15] "We issued . . . a very simple three page letter. It said that we would consider regulating nicotine if we could establish that the companies intended [to create] nicotine's pharmacological effects," he explained.[16] The lengthy, painstaking preparation of this document was propelled by Kessler's belief that "[t]he letter had to be 100 percent accurate, totally unassailable." Even then, Kessler's action was risky. His head of the legislative affairs office and liaison with Congress, Dianne Thompson, warned him soon before the letter was issued that "you will be all alone if the reaction is unfavorable. I don't think you can count on anybody to back you up if things go wrong." If he were seen as overreaching or acting from personal motives to increase his power, he would not be supported from any quarter. He could not expect assistance from his superiors at the Department of Health and Human Services (HHS) or in the White House. "When we issued that letter in February of 1994, no one asked the White House permission," Kessler later bragged. "But, in fact, I told the Assistant Secretary for Health [at HHS] Phil Lee, my boss, but no one really focused on it."[17]

The release of the letter was carefully orchestrated by a highly experienced head of public affairs for the FDA, Jim O'Hara. The strategy was to place phone calls to two outstanding science reporters at *The New York Times* and *The Washington Post* and contacts at the television networks. He would call each one and then fax the letter. According to Kessler, the reporters recognized immediately the care with which the letter was written and the enormity of its implications. In suggesting that the FDA may have a legal basis for regulating cigarettes, his letter signaled, according to Phil Hilts of *The New York Times*, "a complete break with the past."[18] Similarly, John Schwartz was reported to have said that he "knew immediately that the whole world had changed."[19] As word quickly spread inside the Beltway, the reaction was high pitched, from the tobacco industry's total surprise (and bewilderment that they had had no forewarning from their intelligence sources) to Federal Trade Commission's career lawyers being "stunned and elated. We thought an atom bomb had gone off in Rockville [Maryland, a Washington, D.C., suburb and headquarters of the FDA]," said one.[20]

Kessler knew that if he wanted to be successful in regulating tobacco under the Food, Drug and Cosmetic Act, he would need the ear and then the support of the president. "It's one thing when a regulator goes out and says nicotine is a drug," he observed. "It's another thing when a regulator and a President of the United States make that statement." Moreover, even to issue a regulation, Kessler needed White House clearance. Further, he had a huge problem on his hands: how was he going to regulate tobacco use and not outlaw it as the law would normally require of any drug that causes the degree of harm that tobacco use does? Kessler was keenly cognizant of the impracticality of prohibition. He needed to devise a way to stop people (mostly kids) from starting but in doing so not create a black market.

At least by the end of 1994, Kessler had the most of the evidence he needed. "We were able to see what [the tobacco companies] knew, I mean for years, that, in fact, [they knew that] nicotine was an addictive drug. And it was that evidence . . . which was absolutely critical. Without that evidence we couldn't have gone anywhere. Now . . . just having evidence is not necessarily going to get you where you want to get to." He had two challenges. One was the need for political support from the highest level, and the other was the need for an approach to regulating tobacco that would pass legal muster, allow regulation of advertising, and obviate outright prohibition.

The president was needed for both legal and political reasons: "We made a decision that nicotine was a drug under the Federal Food, Drug and Cosmetic Act. That was our [the FDA's] decision. We didn't ask for permission to make that decision, we didn't ask for clearance on that decision," Kessler observed. "But we did, as is normal policy, have to get a clearance on any regulation. So we brought the regulation through the normal channels."[21] After issuing the February 1994 letter, Kessler had tried to work through his own department, HHS, to move to the next level of actually issuing the regulation, to no avail. Normal channels were not working for Kessler.

Fortunately, the FDA letter had brought the agency's intention to the attention, not expressly positive, of the White House. The next year, according to Kessler, "someone in the White House asked, 'How did this start?'" But Kessler needed more than the president's attention—he needed Clinton's active support. Kessler had not originally been President Clinton's appointee but rather that of his 1992 opponent and had been only grudgingly reappointed by the new president. Was Kessler to be trusted? Was he a Republican Trojan horse in the Democratic administration? Kessler chose to use the vice president, whom Clinton trusted, as his willing conduit to the president, unofficially bypassing HHS altogether. "The Vice President was absolutely critical," Kessler later observed.[22]

In seeking the president's support, Kessler had already established backdoor links with White House staff, including White House Counsel Abner Mikva and presidential consultant and confidante Dick Morris. Judge Mikva had served with Kessler earlier in the decade on a visiting committee of the University of Chicago Law School, a coincidence that facilitated contact. In a second coincidence, Mikva had been one of the judges to uphold the FDA in its decision not to regulate cigarettes in *ASH v. Harris* in the 1980s.[23] As they talked one day in Mikva's office in the West Wing of the White House about the FDA's jurisdiction over tobacco use, Mikva went straight to a volume of the *Federal Reporter* in his bookcase and began to read a footnote from the *ASH* case, a footnote that Mikva himself had penned two decades earlier: "Nothing in this opinion should suggest that the Administration is irrevocably bound by any long-standing interpretation. . . . An administration is clearly free to revise its interpretations." Judge Mikva was signaling that Kessler needed to simply provide a "reasonable basis" for reversing the FDA's course and asserting its authority to regulate tobacco use.[24]

While the judge provided helpful substantive guidance to Kessler, Dick Morris had the weight to move the president. Kessler's connection came indirectly by way of Mike Moore, the Mississippi attorney general. He came to visit Kessler in Washington, and his lead counsel in the state Medicaid case, Dick Scruggs, accompanied him. Kessler felt certain that his letter to the Coalition on Smoking and Health had encouraged the litigators in the Medicaid cases and in the private injury suits. According to Kessler, "We stayed in touch as their litigation advanced, becoming allies in our related battles."[25] During the meeting, Scruggs's direct line to Dick Morris became apparent, and subsequently he connected Morris and Kessler. Morris had been pressing on Clinton the idea that the administration should "take on the tobacco industry" as part of a positive alternative to Republican Newt Gingrich's Contract with America and the Republican takeover of Congress after the 1994 elections. Despite the urging of Morris and the vice president, a number of Clinton's advisers and political allies were dead set against the FDA action.

In August 1995, Vice President Al Gore brought the issue to President Clinton and facilitated a meeting among Clinton, Gore, White House Counsel Mikva, Chief of Staff Leon Panetta, and Kessler, accompanied by HHS Secretary Donna Shalala. In addition to the tobacco companies' knowing that nicotine was addictive "long before the FDA" did, Kessler explained, the evidence showed that they marketed cigarettes to children and youth. That's where, according to Kessler, the president's interest piqued and the "debate . . . changed" both for Clinton and for the public. The argument that smoking was a free choice collapsed under the weight of the evidence that the industry intentionally manipulated nicotine levels and targeted kids, most of whom, once they started smoking, could not manage to quit even though they wanted to. No one believed that addiction is freedom.

Clinton had undoubtedly followed the momentous events of 1994, including the Waxman hearings and the public release of damning confidential documents of Brown & Williamson. He had also read the 1995 issue of the *Journal of the American Medical Association* that detailed the extensive, damaging health effects of smoking. The White House knew, too, that because of the "overwhelming weight of scientific evidence," blocking an FDA regulation would be politically unwise. Kessler's resigning over this issue, a real concern given Kessler's entrepreneurial behavior, might be politically damaging.

The president, however, was about to face a reelection fight and needed to carry at least some of the remaining five tobacco states to win. Earlier, Clinton had decided to poll those states to see what kind of leeway he had.

The findings were revealing. After all the negative reports generated by the bureaucracy and health community through the years, even the public in these states would be willing to see tobacco controlled, especially if government action were focused on preventing tobacco use by children. Armed with this information and nudged along by Dick Morris in private, late night White House briefings for President and Mrs. Clinton (an admirer of Kessler), Clinton got on board the anti-tobacco train. His focus and that of the FDA would be children, a winning political issue.[26]

Before Kessler met with the president in late July 1995, he and his staff had untied the Gordian knot of crafting a rule that would regulate but not outlaw tobacco use. Staff attorney Ann Witt suggested that the FDA focus on cigarettes as drug delivery devices, a term of art in the Food, Drug and Cosmetic Act, rather than on nicotine per se. With this approach, the FDA could regulate advertising, an action not possible otherwise, and the agency could "assert jurisdiction over the product without banning it."[27]

On August 10, 1995, Clinton held a news conference in the East Room of the White House with Kessler sitting at his side and children surrounding the president. Clinton himself had decided to announce his support for the proposed regulations, "an initiative that most people outside the FDA would have thought unimaginable only months before."[28] If upheld, this action would be the first time that a regulator (or any other government authority) would impose substantive rules on the tobacco industry. The president's announcement was the culmination of hard work, persistence, excellent agency staff, an entrepreneurial agency head willing to take risks, and a large dose of luck.

It would be the first time that any president had confronted the formidable tobacco industry. "When Joe Camel tells our children that smoking is cool, when billboards tell teens that smoking will lead to true romance, when Virginia Slims tells adolescents that cigarettes will make them thin and glamorous," Clinton intoned, "then our children need our wisdom, our guidance, and our experience."[29] To say that the response from the tobacco industry was as harsh as the nicotine in their cigarettes is an understatement.

KESSLER PRESSES ON

Launching a yearlong rule-making proceeding, the *Federal Register* immediately published the proposed rule. As promised, the FDA's proposal for regulating tobacco focused on preventing children and teenagers from becoming users of tobacco. The new rules would make selling cigarettes to anyone under eighteen a federal offense. They imposed new restrictions on the advertising and marketing of tobacco products. Tobacco-friendly members of Congress were not amused. In response in the spring of 1996, a quarter of the House and a third of the Senate each signed a strong letter to the FDA that objected to Kessler's proposal. They threatened that 10,000 jobs could be lost and that the FDA's rule would "trample First Amendment rights to advertise legal products to adults."[30] These members were participating in the public comment requirement for every proposed federal regulation. During this period, the proposed rule drew more than 710,000 comments, sixteen times the number of responses any FDA proposal had ever received. Under the Administrative Procedure Act, every comment had to be given "full and serious consideration" by the agency, which had to either explain why it rejected a suggestion or incorporate the idea into the proposed rule. The work was backbreaking, but hard-charging Kessler was determined to complete the task as quickly as possible. He rented a warehouse and hired temporary workers working in two shifts to sort and classify the comments. "It was a scene of noise and confusion, but there was no other way to get the job done," Kessler observed. Because the tobacco industry had decided to bury the agency in comments, "[t]he slightest letup would have sunk us in a sea of paper."[31]

Then, in August 1996, after the arduous rule-making proceeding, the FDA formally adopted the rule that retailers were required to verify by photo ID the age of anyone under the age of twenty-seven who was purchasing cigarettes or smokeless tobacco (see Figure 9.1). The new rule banned vending machines and self-service displays except in facilities that were completely inaccessible to minors. It forbid billboards within 1,000 feet of schools or playgrounds and limited other advertising, such as in stores or no buses, to black-and-white text-only message. Also banned was brand-name sponsorship of sporting or entertainment events.[32]

The tobacco companies quickly filed suit in federal court in North Carolina, a tobacco-growing state and a potentially friendly venue, to halt the FDA in its tracks. Echoing the two letters from the members of Congress during the comment period, they argued that the FDA lacked the legal authority to regulate tobacco and that the restrictions on advertising constituted an infringement of their First Amendment protections for free speech. In April 1997, Judge William L. Osteen Sr. found that the FDA did have the statutory authority to regulate access to tobacco but did not have the authority to regulate marketing and promotion activities. Although both sides would appeal, the ruling constituted a significant defeat for the tobacco industry. The case was next taken up by the Fourth U.S. Circuit Court of Appeals in June 1998. This time the court decided in the tobacco industry's favor, finding that Congress did not intend to delegate jurisdiction over tobacco products. The Justice Department appealed to the Supreme Court. In a decisive blow to the FDA's activism on tobacco, on March 21, 2000, the Court narrowly decided, five to four, that the FDA did not have the authority to regulate tobacco.[33] The majority ruled,

> No matter how important, conspicuous, and controversial the issue, and regardless of how likely the public is to hold the Executive Branch politically accountable, an administrative agency's power to regulate in the

FIGURE 9.1 THE RULE OF THE FDA REGULATING CIGARETTES

The FDA rule reduces children's easy access to tobacco products by:

- Requiring age verification by photo ID for anyone under the age of twenty-seven purchasing tobacco products.
- Banning vending machines and self-service displays except in "adult-only" facilities where children are not allowed, such as certain night-clubs totally inaccessible to anyone under eighteen.
- Banning free samples and the sale of single cigarettes and packages containing fewer than twenty cigarettes.

The FDA rule limits the appeal of tobacco products to children by:

- Prohibiting billboards within 1,000 feet of schools and playgrounds. Other advertising is restricted to black-and-white text only; this includes all billboards, signs inside and outside of buses, and all advertising in stores. Advertising inside "adult-only" facilities, such as nightclubs, can have color and imagery.
- Permitting black-and-white text-only advertising in publications with significant youth readership (under eighteen). Significant youth reader-ship means more than 15 percent or more than two million readers under eighteen; there are no restrictions on print advertising below these thresholds.
- Prohibiting sale or giveaways of products like caps or gym bags that carry cigarette or smokeless tobacco product brand names or logos.
- Prohibiting brand-name sponsorship of sporting or entertainment events (including teams and entries) but permitting it in the corporate name.

These provisions will be phased in between six months and two years from the date of publication in the *Federal Register* to give businesses adequate time to comply.

Source: Federal Register, August 1990.

public interest must always be grounded in a valid grant of authority from Congress. . . . Congress, for better or for worse, has created a distinct regulatory scheme for tobacco products, squarely rejected proposals to five the FDA jurisdiction over tobacco.[34]

It is important to note that the Court did not reject its earlier, more expansive decisions on delegation and deference to agency policymaking authority. The key factor in the previously cited case is that Congress *explicitly* denied the power to regulate tobacco to the FDA (and other agencies). To maintain their opinions in other delegation cases, the majority of the Court wrote,

Such deference [to administrative agencies] is justified because the responsibilities for assessing the wisdom of such policy choices and resolving the struggle between competing views of the public interest are not judicial ones.

After the loss in the Supreme Court, federal regulatory activism against tobacco was stopped in its tracks. Supporters in Congress for tobacco regulation have unsuccessfully sought to pass legislation giving authority to the FDA to regulate tobacco. In October 2004, such a provision was passed in the Senate but not in the House.[35]

As the Constitution clearly states, Congress shall make the laws. The federal bureaucracy, in effect, makes policy with the force of law through delegation of authority to the agencies. However, if Congress, as the ultimate arbiter, makes clear that the bureaucracy does not have the authority to regulate an activity, Congress trumps the agencies. Until enough leverage can be applied within Congress to regulate tobacco by law or until a new strategy can be devised that will pass legal muster, analogous to the FCC's applying the fairness doctrine to cigarette advertising, anti-tobacco forces will have to move to venues outside the bureaucracy and even outside the United States. The tobacco industry has itself changed into a global enterprise, opening a whole new area of bureaucratic opportunity to regulate tobacco in the international arena.

COMBINED IMPACT OF 1998 MASTER SETTLEMENT AGREEMENT AND KESSLER

Trying to attribute causation with certainty is perilous. How can one be sure that an outcome is caused by a particular antecedent? Results may emanate from a process or a series of events occurring over time and interacting with each other rather than from a single, clearly identifiable factor. The matter is further complicated by the murkiness of the antecedents. The Master Settlement Agreement (MSA) of 1998, for example, did not have the force of law but simply was an agreement that did not include the entire tobacco industry, and it was watered down in a number of ways from the original, failed bargain set in 1997. As for the impact of the FDA, it *lost* its case and its ability to regulate tobacco as a drug, although many of the FDA's proposed practices were incorporated in the MSA and instituted by state and local governments. Factors unconnected to either the FDA effort or the MSA, such as the growing social unacceptability of smoking, probably had an independent effect on smoking rates. Nevertheless, it is fair to say that the combination of events, including the MSA and the aggressive effort of the FDA to regulate tobacco as a drug, helped lead to reduced cigarette consumption in the United States. Tobacco sales "plummeted."[36] By 2001, three years after the MSA took effect, smoking among children and teens had declined by 40 percent and in the overall population by almost 20 percent. Overall, per capita consumption had declined by half since its peak in the early 1960s, suggesting a large cumulative effect of information politics, the MSA, and regulatory efforts of the bureaucracy.

Because price increases dampen cigarette smoking, continued declines were anticipated as many of the states increased excise taxes on cigarettes to meet fiscal needs. Since 2002, over thirty states increased excise taxes on cigarettes. New Jersey was the first state to break the $2.00 tax barrier (total tax, including federal excise tax, on a single pack). By 2003, the average cost of a pack of cigarettes in the United States was $3.59, an increase of 77 percent since 1998.[37] The tobacco companies, no longer united, followed different political strategies.

Still protected by Congress, Philip Morris changed tack by actively seeking FDA regulation, apparently with the goal of improving its negative public image, which, according to one study, "has a damaging impact on the company's stock price, political influence, and employee morale."[38] This effort echoed the reversal of the industry's opposition to the FTC proposal to place health warnings on cigarette packs as the corporations realized that such warnings could protect them from liability caused by cigarette smoking. Similarly, FDA regulation could help make the industry unassailable to liability suits from individuals claiming that the industry had misled them.

THE INTERACTION OF MARKETS AND POLITICS

Despite substantial support from Congress, a string of uninterrupted successes in court until the *Carter* case, and the eventual decimation of the FDA's bold strategy to regulate tobacco as a drug, several forces were converging in the 1990s to reposition the tobacco companies' sights toward the international arena. First, with the growing success of the free-trade movement, huge new markets, along with fierce new competition, appeared on the horizon. Second, in response, tobacco companies were continuing to merge and go global, and with this development the farmer–manufacturer alliance, so effective in Congress, was gradually collapsing. As trade barriers loosened, the companies were importing cheaper tobacco rather than exclusively buying domestically, and they were increasingly producing cigarettes outside the United States. By the turn of the twenty-first century, farmers and the tobacco companies were battling each other in court. In a class-action suit in 2003, 500,000 farmers settled with six tobacco companies for manipulating the price they paid for tobacco.[39] By 2005, in an effort to bail out tobacco growers financially and to decrease U.S. tobacco production, the U.S. government was offering tobacco farmers $10 billion to quit growing tobacco. American farmers were going out of the tobacco business.

Third, demonstrating the limits of negotiated deals compared with the comprehensiveness of laws, the 1998 MSA with the state attorneys general was binding only on those companies involved in the deal. The costly agreement bypassed their competitors who could, as a result, undercut them in price in the United States. The agreement, however, did not address the activities of *any* company, including those who had signed on to the MSA, outside the boundaries of the United States, allowing even the corporations that were part of the MSA to engage in all the practices, such as misleading advertising and attracting children to smoke, permissible in much of the rest of the world. Compounding this factor is the fact that U.S. tobacco exports are not subject to most federal laws and regulations pertaining to products harmful to health, to packaging and labeling laws, and to advertising restrictions that apply in the United States.

Fourth, the average price of cigarettes went up in the United States not only because of the 1998 agreement but also because of the increase in state excise taxes. At the highest end, the price of a pack in New York City exceeded $7.00 by 2003. (Overall, however, U.S. excise taxes on cigarettes are low compared to a number of other affluent countries.)

Fifth, while more than 20 percent of the American public still filled the industry's coffers to support their habit, elements of the settlement, along with public pressure against smoking and increasing knowledge of its injurious impact on smokers and nonsmokers alike, led to large decreases in smoking. In the end, the concerted, incremental efforts of the health and regulatory agencies to inform the public of the dangers of smoking were successful.[40]

The United States was and is a shrinking, if still significant, market. In comparison, the world, especially Asia, represents the future. Internationally, the figures are staggering. According to the World Health Organization (WHO), 1.1 *billion* people smoke, 95 percent of them outside the United States.[41] This global number is expected to increase by 45 percent within the next twenty years if current trends are unchanged.[42] By the time of the first, abortive tobacco agreement in 1997, the major U.S. tobacco firms were already selling one-third of their product abroad, with Philip Morris and R.J. Reynolds selling two-thirds of their cigarettes to markets outside the United States. Ironically, while the 1997 and 1998 agreements covered only the major firms in the United States—and only for practices within the United States— the initial settlement was called a *global* agreement. However, large payouts—$246 billion over twenty-five years—meant higher cigarette prices in the United States and hence lower per capita consumption. At the same time, the manufacturers simply passed on the cost of the payouts and of later increased state excise taxes directly to the consumer. As a result, though smoking, as measured by a percentage of people who smoke, in the United States declined, profits remained buoyant. With population increases, the decline in consumption did not directly translate, one for one, into a commensurate decline in sticks of cigarettes smoked. Still, the 1998 binding, out-of-court agreement may have accelerated an existing trend of cigarette makers' marketing their products elsewhere.[43]

The United States became the largest exporter of tobacco products in the world, and U.S. tobacco companies transformed into multinational corporations by exporting, purchasing formerly state-owned tobacco companies, engaging in joint ventures, and creating networks for distribution and sales.

According to one estimate, the three major multinationals, Philip Morris, R.J. Reynolds, and British American Tobacco (BAT), already owned or leased plants in fifty countries around the world by the time of the first, abortive 1997 agreement.[44] Moreover, foreign markets have been opened to U.S. companies by means of threatening retaliatory trade sanctions. According to one reliable report, this technique has been effective in forcing open previously closed markets, an occurrence that led in four documented countries (Japan, South Korea, Taiwan, and Thailand) to an almost 10 percent increase in per capita smoking.[45]

Today, to speak of big tobacco is no longer to refer to U.S. firms. In fact, the largest, only purely national firm is the government-owned China National Tobacco Company (CNTC), which prospers in a country where there are more male smokers than the entire population of the United States.[46] With 31 percent of the world market, CNTC is followed by Philip Morris (17 percent), BAT (13 percent), R.J. Reynolds (6 percent), and Rothmans International (4 percent).[47]

The implications for the health community of these developments are clear. As Nancy J. Kaufman stated in her October 2000 submission on behalf of the Robert Wood Johnson Foundation to the WHO Framework Convention on Tobacco Control (FCTC), "Tobacco is now a global product, sold and marketed throughout the world. It can no longer be contained or controlled by any single nation. Protecting the public's health requires a global approach to a global epidemic."[48]

BUREAUCRATS' NETWORK: THE HEALTH COMMUNITY GOES INTERNATIONAL

The government bureaucrats were not sitting on their hands while U.S. tobacco companies went global. Obviously, if tobacco were to be controlled, purely national strategies were not going to work. Tobacco is emblematic of the problems arising from the globalization of markets and the internationalization of issues. As markets become global in scope, the need for and the difficulty of regulation at the global level become apparent.

Because authoritative government is largely national, a yawning incongruence has emerged between national governance and global markets. Other than the World Trade Organization, international institutions typically lack the authority and the enforcement capability necessary to govern effectively. The German scholar Wolfgang identifies the problem as a governance gap that is filled in adventitiously by informal, consensual global public policy networks.[49]

One form that these networks take is that of multinational activist networks working to change practices of nations (and, through nations, entities like corporations). Such networks may work through international organizations, such as the WHO, which is staffed by 3,200 bureaucrats and has established elaborate governance mechanisms that include nonvoting participation by recognized nongovernmental organizations (NGOs or nonprofits). Typically, the activist movements are composed of subject-matter experts, NGOs, foundations that help fund these networks, international organizations, and national government bureaucrats who share an interest in changing policies and practices in a particular area, such as human rights, the environment, and health.[50] These loose networks of people and organizations use techniques—like applying information politics, working incrementally, and looking for openings that will lead to change—familiar to and practiced adeptly by health advocates and career bureaucrats in the U.S. health and regulatory agencies over the past forty years on behalf of tobacco control.

Despite the inability of these bureaucrats to regulate tobacco in the way they might have liked in the United States, other public servants and elected officials have been shaping policy in their own countries, sometimes in conflict with other domestic agencies and elected officials and sometimes with their cooperation. Following the lead of U.S. health bureaucrats, using much of the research generated in the United States, and working with and through transnational activist and health networks, by the 1990s other nations began to act on the dangers of tobacco use. Everyone seemed to realize the likely unfortunate consequences of banning smoking altogether, as the experience with prohibition of alcohol had demonstrated. The approaches to regulation that other nations have applied corresponded with those proposed in the United States in, for example, the 1997 and 1998 tobacco agreements, but soon after the turn of the twenty-first century, a number of countries had gone further than anything politically possible in the United States. For example, in 2004, in what Prime Minister Bertie Ahern called a "world leading measure," Ireland barred smoking in most public places, including bars, throughout the nation.[51] Soon countries ranging from New Zealand to Sweden and Norway and Bhutan were following suit. The European Union, operating largely through bureaucrats, had the previous year prohibited companies from indicating "light" or "mild" on cigarette packages and required that health warnings must cover 30 percent of the front and 40 percent of the back of cigarette packages, reflecting the provisions of the WHO's treaty provisions for tobacco control. Going a step further in 2003, the Philippines became the first country to comply with the WHO treaty requirements, although it was agreed that Philip Morris Philippines would help write the regulations. Botswana, Mongolia, South Africa, Estonia, Niger, Sweden, Finland, Norway, Thailand, Lithuania, Singapore, and Tonga have all placed total bans on tobacco advertising and marketing.[52]

That the battle over tobacco control is as contentious elsewhere as in the United States can be seen in India, where in 2004 the bureaucrats in the health ministry ordered a ban on showing smoking in films and television. The reaction of the Censor Board and of the information and broadcasting ministry, which would enforce the ban, was none too positive. The Censor Board chief, Sharmila Tagore, charged that the "decision [was] taken in haste and very unaesthetic in taste."[53]

Canada is also following an aggressive course with tobacco companies. The Supreme Court of Canada announced a decision that allows the government of British Columbia to sue tobacco companies for the cost of treating smoking-related diseases. The $245 billion settlement in the United States inspired this move, according to newspaper accounts. The decision is a serious blow to cigarette manufacturers.[54]

Countries representing most of the world's people have not come aboard the anti-tobacco train, however. In the developing world, a number of nations, such as Zimbabwe, Brazil, and Malawi, are dependent on tobacco revenues. Tobacco leaf exports, for example, account for almost 9 percent of the gross domestic product of Zimbabwe. These countries rely on the tobacco business to generate needed foreign exchange, and tobacco taxes help fund their governments. The largest producer and consumer of tobacco in the world, China, relies on tobacco taxes for 8 to 10 percent of its national budget. This dependence may account for health claims made on the state-owned monopoly's Web site that deny the link between smoking and cancer and herald smoking as a way to prevent ulcers, improve brain power, reduce chances of Parkinson's disease, and treat schizophrenia.[55] When the SARS (severe acute respiratory disease) epidemic in Asia broke out in 2003, rumors spread in China, Singapore, and the Philippines that smoking would prevent this life-threatening disease.

Thus, despite progress in many areas of the world, overall smoking is declining in industrialized countries rising in developing ones.[56] Currently, five million people die each year from the effects of smoking, according to the health bureaucrats at the WHO. Unchecked, this figure will rise by 2020 to ten million a year with an estimated 70 percent of the victims from the developing world. Researchers estimate that half the people currently smoking, 650 million, will die of a smoking-related disease.

Like health and regulatory civil servants in the United States, bureaucrats in international organizations like the World Bank and the WHO (working through country representatives and assisted by career health experts, economists, and scientists) and transnational activist networks like the Framework Convention Alliance for Tobacco Control have employed information politics to press their case against tobacco use. The signal achievement of the international community has been the successful completion of a treaty on tobacco control, the world's first in the area of public health, called the Framework Convention for Tobacco Control of the WHO. The pact is aimed at reducing the health and economic effects of tobacco use and includes measures familiar to anyone with a passing knowledge of the proposals and studies produced by U.S. bureaucrats and the larger health community over the past forty years. As described by the WHO,

[K]ey provisions in the treaty encourage countries to:

- Enact comprehensive bans on tobacco advertising, promotion and sponsorship;
- Obligate the placement of rotating health warnings on tobacco packaging that cover at least 30 percent (but ideally 50 percent or more) of the principal display areas and can include pictures or pictograms;
- Ban the use of misleading and deceptive terms such as "light" and "mild";
- Protect citizens from exposure to tobacco smoke in workplaces, public transport and indoor public places;
- Combat smuggling, including the placing of final destination markings on packs; and
- Increase tobacco taxes

The FCTC also contains numerous other measures designed to promote and protect public health, such as "mandating the disclosure of ingredients in tobacco products, providing treatment for tobacco addiction, encouraging legal action against the tobacco industry, and promoting research and the exchange of information among countries."[57]

Despite barriers put up by U.S. officials representing the president of the United States, this treaty was approved in May 2003 by all 192 nations at the WHO's World Health Assembly in Geneva, Switzerland. Signed by 168 nations, the agreement gathered sufficient national ratifications to take effect in February 2005. By midsummer, seventy-eight nations had become parties to the treaty. Representing the president, HHS Secretary Tommy Thompson signed the Framework Convention on behalf of the United States, but as of mid-2005, President Bush had not submitted—and was not expected to submit—the treaty to the U.S. Senate for ratification. "The U.S. repeatedly made proposals that would weaken critical provisions of the FCTC and severely undermine its potential to reduce the death and disease caused by tobacco around the world," one anti-tobacco organization reported in 2002.[58] Once again, the health and regulatory bureaucrats in the United States were bested by elected officials, in this case the president, whose political interests diverged from the concerns of the health community.

Enforcement is the responsibility of the individual parties to the treaty. Decidedly weak as a result, the force of this pact will be in its use by tobacco control advocates in each country and in the transnational networks to encourage public officials to live up to their treaty obligations by enforcing it. Called "accountability politics" by Keck and Sikkink, this approach is a component of the patient, incremental strategy that has led to a 50 percent drop in smoking in the United States.[59] Anti-tobacco firebrands may not be pleased with the pace, but those health advocates who understand politics and social change and the ferocity of an industry that sells six trillion cigarettes a year know the size of the task before them. Worldwide, 47 percent of men and 12 percent of women currently smoke, and that number is rapidly increasing.

NOTES

1. Peter Pringle, *Cornered: Big Tobacco at the Bar of Justice* (New York: Henry Holt, 1998), 96.
2. A review of the developing scholarly literature on public sector entrepreneurship suggests that scholars are just beginning to understand this multidimensional phenomenon. Here, we are emphasizing one element: the policy entrepreneur. A similar approach is followed by the work of Luc Bernier and Taïeb Hafsi of the École nationale d'administration publique in Quebec. See, for example, "The Changing Nature of Public Entrepreneurship" (paper prepared for the Midwest Political Science Association Conference, Chicago, April 2003). For a related perspective, see Gordon E. Shockley, Peter M. Frank, and Roger R. Stough, "Toward a Theory of Public Sector Entrepreneurship" (paper delivered at the NCIIA 7th Annual Meeting: Big Ideas in a Small World, Boston, March 20–22, 2002).
3. David Kessler, *A Question of Intent: A Great American Battle with a Deadly Industry* (New York: Public Affairs, 2001), 108; Carrick Mollenkamp et al., *The People vs. Big Tobacco* (Princeton, N.J.: Bloomberg Press, 1998).
4. Mollenkamp et al., *The People vs. Big Tobacco*, 109.
5. The Controlled Substances Act of 1970 excluded tobacco from the definition of a "controlled substance." The Consumer Product Safety Act of 1972 did not cover tobacco products as a "consumer product." The 1976 amendment to the Federal Hazardous Substances Labeling Act of 1960 included a statement that "hazardous substance" did not apply to tobacco products. The Toxic Substances Control Act of 1976 excluded tobacco products from the term "chemical substance."
6. PBS *Frontline*, "Inside the Tobacco Deal" (1998), available at http://www.pbs.org/wgbh/pages/frontline/shows/settlement/interviews/moore.html.
7. Mollenkamp et al., *The People vs. Big Tobacco*, 115.
8. *Frontline*, "Inside the Tobacco Deal." In July 1997, Kessler became dean of the Yale University School of Medicine. He is currently at the University of California School of Medicine, the home of Stanton Glantz, who made available the stolen Brown & Williamson papers to the University Library and the Internet.
9. Mollenkamp et al., *The People vs. Big Tobacco*, 111. From the *Frontline* introduction of Wigand interview: "But Wigand paid a price for blowing the whistle. He lost his $300,000-a-year job at Brown & Williamson and any chance to be hired as a high-level researcher. By June 1997, Wigand's marriage had fallen apart; he was teaching high school science and living on $30,000 a year. Industry-paid detectives were following him and he was facing a lawsuit from Brown & Williamson for breaking a confidentiality agreement (*Frontline*, "Inside the Tobacco Deal").
10. The anonymous caller, dubbed "Research," turned out to be the famed whistle-blower and former Brown & Williamson vice president for research Jeffrey Wigand.
11. For a detailed recounting of the Y-1 detective work by the FDA, see Mollenkamp et al., *The People vs. Big Tobacco*.
12. R. M. Davis and A. L. Holm, "Clearing the Airways: Advocacy and Regulation for Smoke-Free Airlines," *Tobacco Control* 13 (suppl., 2004): 130–136; Kessler, *A Question of Intent*, 119.
13. Mary H. Cooper, "Tobacco Industry: Do Ads and New Products Still Target Teen Smokers?" *CQ Researcher* 14, no. 13 (2004): 13.
14. PBS *Frontline*, "Inside the Tobacco Deal" (1998).
15. Kessler, *A Question of Intent*, 83–94.
16. PBS *Frontline*, "Inside the Tobacco Deal."
17. PBS *Frontline*, "Inside the Tobacco Deal."
18. Kessler, *A Question of Intent*, 93.
19. Kessler, *A Question of Intent*, 93.
20. Kessler, *A Question of Intent*, 94.
21. PBS *Frontline*, "Inside the Tobacco Deal."
22. PBS *Frontline*, "Inside the Tobacco Deal."
23. *Action on Smoking & Health v. Harris*, 655 F. 2d 236, 239 (1980).
24. Kessler, *A Question of Intent*, 301.
25. Kessler, *A Question of Intent*, 304.
26. Clinton carried two of the five tobacco states and lost one, Georgia, by only 1 percent.
27. Kessler, *A Question of Intent*, 267.
28. Kessler, *A Question of Intent*, 333.

29. Mollenkamp et al., *The People vs. Big Tobacco*, 115.
30. The FDA heard from Congress on this issue. According to one count, 124 members of the House sent a sharply worded letter to the FDA. Two weeks later, thirty-two senators signed a virtually identical letter. See Gene Borio, *Tobacco Timeline: The Twentieth Century, 1950–1999—The Battle Is Joined*, chap. 7, available at http://www.tobacco.org/resources/history/Tobacco_History21.html.
31. Kessler, *A Question of Intent*, 337.
32. Kenneth Jost, "Closing in on Tobacco," *CQ Researcher* 9, no. 43 (November 12, 1999): 11–12.
33. Cooper, "Tobacco Industry," 4, 15
34. The syllabus of *Food and Drug Administration et al. v. Brown and Williamson Tobacco Corp. et al.*, prepared by the Reporter of Decisions, explains, "The court concluded that construing the FDCA to include tobacco products would lead to several internal inconsistencies in the Act. It also found that evidence external to the FDCA—that the FDA consistently stated before 1995 that it lacked jurisdiction over tobacco, that Congress has enacted several tobacco-specific statutes fully cognizant of the FDA's position, and that Congress has considered and rejected many bills that would have given the agency such authority—confirms this conclusion." Hence, the Court did not overturn its position that agencies have the authority to act through implied delegation; instead, the case of tobacco is exceptional for the reasons stated here.
35. Cooper, "Tobacco Industry," 15.
36. Cooper, "Tobacco Industry," 15.
37. Cooper, "Tobacco Industry," 3.
38. P. A. McDaniel and R. E. Malone, "Understanding Philip Morris's Pursuit of US Government Regulation of Tobacco," *Tobacco Control* 14 (2005): 193–200.
39. The following is from Bario, *Tobacco Timeline: The Twenty-First Century: A New Millenium*, chap. 8, available at http://www.tobacco.org/resources/history/Tobacco_History21.html: "2003-10-01: Federal judge approves farmers' class-action settlement. About 500,000 tobacco growers had charged that tobacco companies conspired to rig bids at auctions. Philip Morris, B&W, Lorillard, Universal, Dimon and Standard agree to buy more than 400 million pounds of tobacco over the next 10 years and to pay farmers $200 million in cash. RJR did not participate in the settlement; its case will be heard in April, 2004."
40. For a demonstration of this observation as applied to banning smoking in aircraft, see Davis and Holm, "Clearing the Airways."
41. In the aggregate, half of all males in the world smoke. Eighty percent of the 1.1 billion people who smoke reside in developing countries, a rise from 72 percent in 1998 (Ron Scherer, "War against Smoking Goes Worldwide," *Christian Science Monitor*, October 16, 2000; *The Tobacco Epidemic: A Crisis of Startling Dimensions* [Geneva: World Health Organization, 1998) November 23, 2004 http://www.who.ch/ntday/ntday98/ad98e_3.htm.
42. An estimated 3.5 million people worldwide die each year from tobacco-related illness. Over the next 30 years tobacco will be implicated in more deaths than the combined impact of AIDS, tuberculosis, automobile accidents, maternal mortality, homicide and suicide. From Campaign for Tobacco-Free Kids at http://www.tobaccofreekids.org/campaign/global/ [cited June 30, 2005].
43. Between 1993 and 1996, global cigarette exports increased 42 percent, indicating the substantial rise in international trade in tobacco products. (Economic Research Service, U.S. Department of Agriculture, *Tobacco*, September 16, 1997). The Congressional Research Service suggests that the 1998 agreement may have had an independent impact on cigarette use in the United States: "Now actions taken as a result of the 1998 Master Settlement Agreement between cigarette manufacturers and states' attorneys general are further diminishing the consumption of tobacco products in the United States" (Jasper Womach, *U.S. Tobacco Production, Consumption, and Export Trends* [Washington, D.C.: Congressional Research Service, Library of Congress, June 3, 2003], Order Code RL 30947).
44. Campaign for Tobacco-Free Kids, *Overview Global Crisis*, Prepared for the International Policy Conference of Children & Tobacco, March, 1999, http://www.tobaccofreekids.org/campaign/global/prices.shtml [cited April 6, 2001].
45. World Bank, *Curbing the Epidemic: Governments and the Economics of Tobacco Control* (Washington D.C.: World Bank Group, 1999), 14.
46. Cooper, "Tobacco Industry," 16. While the dynamic of free trade has not affected the Chinese yet, their recent membership in the World Trade Organization should eventually pry open the government's monopoly on cigarettes.

47. Borio, *Tobacco Timeline: The Twentieth Century.*
48. Nancy J. Kaufman, "Pre-Hearing Submission to WHO Framework Convention on Tobacco Control, for October 12–13, 2000 Hearing," available at http://www3.who.int/whosis/fctc/Submissions/F6340627.doc.
49. Wolfgang H. Reinicke, "The Other World Wide Web: Global Public Policy Networks," *Foreign Policy*, no. 117 (Winter, 1999): 44–57.
50. See Margaret E. Keck and Kathryn Sikkink, *Activists beyond Borders: Advocacy Networks in International Politics* (Ithaca, N.Y.: Cornell University Press, 1998).
51. BBC News, "Ireland Stubs Out Smoking in Pubs," March 29, 2004, available at http://news.bbc.co.uk/1/hi/world/europe/3577001.htm.
52. From Campaign for Tobacco-Free Kids, available at http://www.tobaccofreekids.org/campaign/global.
53. Nivedita Mookerji, "I&B Ministry Cautious on Smoking Ban Issue," *The Financial Express* (New Delhi), June 3, 2004, available at http://www.financialexpress.com/fe_full_story.php?content_id=92803. This issue has not been resolved in the United States either. In the United States, the latest technique is to have actors pictured smoking in their private lives offscreen. According to *The New York Times* reporter Mireya Navarro, antismoking groups are alarmed at this development, given past evidence of the effect of onscreen smoking. "While overall smoking rates have been down since the mid-90's, existing research has shown a direct correlation between on-screen smoking and the onset of smoking in teenagers. . . . One study, by researchers at Dartmouth College, found that adolescents who viewed the most smoking in movies were almost three times more likely to take up smoking than those who viewed the least." She reported that Centers for Disease Control researchers assert that "the prevalence of cigarette smoking among middle- and high-school students has not changed much from 2002 to 2004 after previous dramatic drops—it stands at 8 percent for middle-school students and 22 percent for high schoolers—and they cite among the factors slowing the rate of decline the frequency of smoking in film" ("Where There's Smoke, There's a Star," *The New York Times*, September 18, 2005). Smoking in films made in the United States is pervasive and is perhaps one major cause of increased smoking among women and girls around the world. According to one study, more than half the top-grossing United States films released between 1991 and 1996 exhibited smoking. In these films, 80 percent of the male lead characters and 27 percent of the female characters smoked. For more information, see http://www.ceche.org/programs/tobacco/women/appeal.htm.
54. "Tobacco Ruling Expected," *Edmonton Sun*, September 29, 2005.
55. "Wild Health Claims by Huge China Tobacco Firm," *Toronto Globe and Mail*, June 14, 2005.
56. See Surgeon General, *Report on Reducing Tobacco Use* (2000), available at http://www.cdc.gov/tobacco/sgr/sgr_2000/index.htm.
57. World Health Organization, Framework Convention on Tobacco Control, World Health Organization (2003), available at http://www.who.int/gb/fctc.
58. Campaign for Tobacco-Free Kids (CTFK), available at http://tobaccofreekids.org/campaign/global/pdf/infiltration.pdf. According to CTFK, the tobacco companies have for many years worked to subvert the work of WHO and to prevent the spread of anti-tobacco policies and attitudes in the Third World. For a detailed description of the U.S. position in the second round and subsequent rounds of negotiations of the FCTC, see Action on Smoking and Health (a nonprofit, antismoking organization), available at http://nosmoking.ws/usposition/uschangesinb2.htm and http://nosmoking.ws/usposition/usinb5.htm. According to Action on Smoking and Health, by the fifth round, "[t]he US has taken the tobacco industry's side and is going against most of the rest of the countries, where there is an incredibly strong shift toward a public-health approach."
59. Keck and Sikkink, *Activists beyond Borders*, chap. 1.

10

BUREAUCRACY CENTERED POLICYMAKING IN A DEMOCRACY

[T]he three primary branches have necessarily supported the creation of a semiautonomous bureaucracy as an instrument to enable our government to meet the challenges it has faced.

—Peter Woll, *American Bureaucracy*

The ebb and flow of power experienced by the Federal Trade Commission (FTC), the Federal Communications Commission (FCC), and the Food and Drug Administration (FDA) over the years reflects well the ongoing tensions between agency activism and restraint that exist in the American policymaking process. At times, it seems as though the bureaucracies on the anti-smoking side of the debate enjoyed a great deal of leverage in shaping the cigarette regulation controversy. The political power and delegated authority possessed by bureaucratic agencies made both the initiation and the continuation of this controversy possible. Had the decision on cigarettes and health been left to Congress alone, it is safe to assume that the manufacturers would have triumphed and no regulations of any significance would have been promulgated. The cigarette labeling controversy is a clear example of an agency's power to influence and even formulate public policy. Similarly, though the FDA ultimately lost its battle to regulate cigarettes, it also succeeded. Many of the elements of the FDA's proposed rule are currently in place, and the extensive research reported and information uncovered by the agency has had a decisive effect on court cases and public opinion.

Regulatory agencies found themselves rebuked and rebuffed in the policymaking process repeatedly. Congress watered down the labeling restriction proposed by the FTC in its Cigarette Labeling Act of 1965 and imposed a four-year ban on FTC regulation of the industry. Congress extended the ban on FTC rule making for another year in 1970 with passage of the Public Health Cigarette Smoking Act, a law that also required the FTC to give six months' notice of any agency intentions to initiate rule-making procedures that would affect the tobacco industry. The FTC and its allied agencies forced the issue onto the government agenda, and that fact suggests that agencies enjoy a measure of policymaking power. But at the same time, it is true that Congress successfully blunted the most significant thrusts of antismoking bureaucracies by passing laws in 1965 and 1970 that were sympathetic to tobacco industry interests. Even when Congress could not muster the majorities necessary to rebuke an agency for activities inhospitable to the tobacco industry, as in the cases of the Environmental Protection Agency (EPA) and the FDA, their leaders were called to task in congressional hearings and, in the case of David Kessler, were pilloried by the cigarette companies.[1]

When Congress enacted statutes consistent with antismoking positions, such legislative acts were partial, as legislative compromises inevitably are. What Congress gave with one hand it took away with another. It would concede on a stronger warning on cigarette packages but then prohibit the states from imposing any regulations on tobacco corporations. Or it would enact legislation meant to curb smokeless tobacco use by kids but simultaneously proscribe any federal agency from regulating tobacco. The courts, in turn, were guided by law passed by Congress and signed by the president. This history suggests that agency power is limited, but neither critics nor champions of agency discretion would find anything absolute to write about in this history of events.

BUREAUCRATS HAVE TOO MUCH POWER

For those who argue that government agencies have too much power, the case is relatively straightforward. Criticisms of bureaucratic policymaking powers are made on the grounds that bureaucrats have the ability to act capriciously, unchecked by public opinion or other government institutions and undisciplined by the rigors of standing for election. As the tobacco industry argued in the congressional hearings of 1965, there should be little room for bureaucrats to play an important role in policymaking under traditional theories of representation. The cigarette manufacturers emphasized that the FTC does not have (or at least should not have) the power to make policy—a power that is rightly the prerogative of Congress alone. This argument was to reverberate three decades later when an aggressive FDA tried to regulate cigarettes as drug delivery mechanisms.

This position has attracted support from many quarters over the years. Individuals and groups who think their interests are threatened by agency action frequently adopt the narrow view that agencies, under the Constitution, are prohibited from making policy. Some argue that agencies are only the servants of Congress and that the lack of full congressional control over the bureaucracy is a serious obstacle to democratic governance.[2]

There is no question that the bureaucracy enjoys a measure of political power that was not anticipated or acknowledged by those who have written over the years about the supposedly clear dichotomy between politics and administration.[3] Information is a key source of that power. Bureaucrats control the flow of much information to other policymakers and the general public, and their expertise in collecting and interpreting this information provides these individuals with an important base of political power. Over the years, Americans have come to depend on these educated government professionals to help construct a shared social reality regarding a range of important questions associated with health and safety. The data are often technical, arcane, and hard to find and interpret, and this fact gives government bureaucrats their entrée. The process of selecting what information is to be collected and used to construct a social reality about the hazards of smoking has made it easier for bureaucrats to assume a policymaking role and has, in turn, made it easier for antismoking members of Congress to advance their cause.

In recent decades, the role of the media in the policymaking equation has only enhanced the savvy bureaucrat's ability to steer policy in one direction or another. Surgeon General Luther Terry's strategically orchestrated release of the report of the Advisory Committee on Smoking and Health in 1964 magnified the impact of that report well beyond what may have been expected had the report been quietly released on a typical, otherwise-busy weekday. An interest-piquing news blackout followed by a high-profile press conference led to splashy headlines in the Sunday papers and helped propel the smoking and health issue up on to the government agenda. The FTC began holding rule-making hearings within weeks of the report's release, and President Johnson was signing the Cigarette Labeling and Advertising Act of 1965 only eighteen months later. The final policy product might not have been everything the surgeon general had hoped for, but strategic use of the media as a conduit of information, interpretation, and evaluation made the passage of some policy almost inevitable.

The provision in that legislation requiring the surgeon general to issue regular reports on smoking and health provided the bureaucracy with a regular timetable for issuing what has turned out to be "a steady output of progressively grimmer official reports on the consequences of smoking."[4] These reports have made it possible for public health advocates—inside and outside of the bureaucracy—to keep the policy issue alive and coax the regulatory process along. Bureaucratic agencies that release newsworthy reports and make disturbing claims about the health hazards of cigarettes have reinforced efforts of the antismoking segments of the American government and paved the way to increased regulation of the tobacco industry. Good examples include Surgeons General Koop and Sullivan on the damage smoking causes, EPA Commissioners William Reilly and Carol Browner on secondhand smoke, FDA Commissioner David Kessler on the manipulation of nicotine levels and addiction of minors, and Surgeon General Joycelyn Elders on the impact of the tobacco industry's promotional activities in encouraging young Americans to take up smoking.[5]

Critics who worry about bureaucratic accountability might describe activist, freewheeling agency heads such as Sullivan, Koop, Elders, Reilly, Browner, and Kessler as minions run amuck. Yet it can reasonably be argued that the master–servant view of the relationship between legislators and bureaucrats advanced by Wilson, Goodnow, and others is no longer tenable from either a practical or a legal perspective. In practice, the demands of a complex society require the specialized skills of bureaucrats in policymaking. It is in large part this conflict between traditional democratic theories and the demands of the modern state that is at the heart of the debate over the policymaking powers of bureaucratic agencies. Professor Peter Woll has summarized the situation neatly:

> It is difficult to grasp the concept that the bureaucracy is not subordinate to one or more of the three initial branches of American government. But the fact is the three primary branches have necessarily supported the creation of a semiautonomous bureaucracy as an instrument to enable our government to meet the challenges it has faced. Given the needs of modern government for economic regulation, specialization, continuity, and speed in the dispatch of business, to mention only a few, it is the bureaucracy that has stepped in to fill the gap created by the inability of the other branches to fulfill all of these requirements. The other branches, particularly the Presidency and the Supreme Court, have also greatly expanded their ability and willingness to meet the challenges of the twentieth century, but they could not possibly solve by themselves the extraordinary problems that have confronted our government.[6]

At the same time, the political reality of the regulatory process is that multiple checks are imposed on presidential appointees and career bureaucrats who work for them, for Congress, and for the American public. The constitutional system of separated powers, statutory law that prescribes certain administrative procedures and proscribes others, and accessibility of the regulatory process to private individuals and groups are among the forces in American government ensuring that bureaucrats hardly have a clear course in policymaking.

Government bureaucracy has taken on a significant role in democratic representation that is supplementary to the legislature and provides another point of access for citizens. Demographically, the federal bureaucracy is more reflective of both the American public and relevant experts in a particular field than Congress is, a fact that serves to curb regulatory actions that are out of step with the country (both the citizenry and subject-matter professionals) and to accelerate action on an issue that has no chance of being addressed in Congress, as was the case with tobacco regulation of various sorts through the years. This form of representation is augmented by a bureaucratic norm that public servants are to represent the entire country and not simply the strongest interest. The representation practiced by the federal bureaucracy is not identical to that practiced by members of

Congress, who must get elected in specific congressional districts that are not reflective of the whole country and must raise money from sources with specific interests that may not correspond to a larger public interest. The founders of the nation recognized both the democratic necessity and the unfortunate consequences of empowering a body composed of people impelled by such forces. They devised a government structure intended to shape and contain personal motives so that the policy process would serve the interests of the country as a whole. Checks and balances, coupled with federalism, were to accomplish this purpose. In modern times, the bureaucracy provides an additional structure of policymaking that was undreamt of by the founders and that is itself hemmed in by rules and by the checks and balances throughout the federal system.

EXTERNAL CHECKS ON BUREAUCRATIC AUTONOMY

Criticisms of agency power often gloss over two important points. First, much of an agency's discretion in policymaking matters is specifically delegated to it by enabling legislation passed by Congress. Second, there are very real checks on administrative policymaking discretion that exist in the U.S. system of separated powers. Indeed, it may be easier to make the opposite case, that there are too many restrictions on the ability of agencies and commissions to advance policy in the public interest. Certainly, bureaucrats in other Western democracies—Canada, Great Britain, and France, for example—have more policymaking leverage than their counterparts in the United States. And in one of the cases presented here, it is clear that while commissioners at the FTC helped move the regulatory process along, they were restricted at each step of the way by a Congress that was more sensitive to the interests of the tobacco manufacturers than to bureaucrats who were aligned with the health lobby. Similarly, the courts provide additional checks on the bureaucracy, as the FTC and FDA cases demonstrate.

In fact, there are numerous examples of agency power being checked at the national level when the agency moves beyond the boundaries of what Congress had intended. The surgically precise limits placed on FTC authority in the congressional acts of 1965 and 1970 are good examples of just what Congress is capable of. Passage of the FTC Improvements Act in 1980 provides another example of effective congressional oversight. As one correspondent described the situation at the time, "With a fervor worthy of St. George, Congress has galloped off to tame the regulatory dragon" by limiting the FTC's jurisdiction and establishing a system to override rules proposed by the commission.[7] The various statutes under which the FTC operates are, like the laws governing most government agencies, general in nature. They express broadly defined goals, while the details are left to the bureaucracy to write. When the bureaucracy moves outside the boundaries of congressional intent, as the FTC did late in the 1970s, Congress has only to pass new laws that effectively rein in the offending agency. Sometimes, Congress cannot muster a sufficient number of votes in both houses simultaneously to pass such a law, as was the case with the FDA's attempt to regulate tobacco in the 1990s. Congressional opponents to the FDA's proposed rule could resort to other means of trying to influence the agency. A group of senators and one of representatives each signed a letter strongly objecting to the FDA action, and both agency allies and opponents vigorously questioned leading officials at the FDA in congressional hearings. According to David Kessler, tobacco-friendly members of Congress would interrogate him by using questions prepared by the industry, a prong in a coordinated attack against him and the FDA.[8]

In addition, it should be noted that an FTC run amuck, the prevailing view held by Congress in the late 1970s, is hardly representative of perceptions held by FTC watchers over time. Rather, the years leading up to passage of the FTC Improvements Act of 1980 were marked by criticisms that the agency was too timid rather than too powerful. Philip Elman, one-time commissioner at the FTC, argued before a Senate committee that FTC actions regarding cigarette advertising were an exception in an otherwise lethargic picture in which the commission fails to perform "effectually any of the roles given it by Congress."[9] The FDA, for its part, was actually sued in the 1970s (*ASH v. Harris*) for *not* regulating cigarettes. The agency won its case and did not reverse its position until 1995 with the aggressive Kessler at the helm.

Typically, career bureaucrats try to keep their activities "below the radar screen" of Congress and the Office of the President and, as a result, operate cautiously and even lethargically. No one wants to be publicly humiliated before a congressional panel or by a political appointee doing the bidding of the president and his party. Further, even those, like Kessler and EPA's Browner, willing and constitutionally able to take the heat from antagonists know that they must bide their time, build the groundwork, collect the evidence, and create a solid case for the position they are advocating. Kessler, for example, waited for a change in administration and spent three years preparing a three-page letter to announce the FDA's new initiative. And that was only the first step in a battle that lasted a decade.

Like Congress, the president exerts considerable influence over the activities of agencies in the executive branch. Political principals monitor bureaucratic officials and use both rewards and sanctions to bring agency behavior into line with presidential priorities when bureaucrats stray from the desired course. In the case of the FTC, presidential appointments have been instrumental in changing the agency's course at different times in history. Although Congress had been nudging the FTC in the direction of taking a more consumerist orientation through the early and mid-1970s, the agency was not as responsive as some would have hoped until President Carter appointed Michael Pertshuk to head up the commission in 1977. Shortly after Pertshuk's arrival, the FTC assumed a much more consumer-friendly orientation. Then, in 1981, with relatively conservative views about the role of government sweeping across the country, President Reagan appointed James Miller III to chair the commission. Miller ushered in an era during which the FTC took a much more sympathetic stance toward business.[10] Figuratively speaking, the FTC handed the baton over to the FDA and became much less active in the area of tobacco after this time. In 1987, it ceded testing of tar and nicotine to the Tobacco Institute Testing Laboratory, a private entity controlled by the cigarette industry. The only notable activity in the decade of the 1990s occurred in May 1997 in a three-to-two vote when the commission announced a complaint and a proposed order to ban most uses of Joe Camel, the cartoon character used in advertising Camel cigarettes, after having dismissed a similar complaint in 1994 for lack of evidence. (A complaint is the first step in a formal hearing process.) Within days, the maker of Camels, R.J. Reynolds, responded by suing the FTC, a move right out of the industry's playbook. In January 1999, the FTC dismissed the suit as unnecessary in light of the multistate tobacco settlement[11] and settled a second complaint against R.J. Reynolds concerning its potentially deceptive "no additives" claim for Winston cigarettes.[12] In the 2000s, no significant action on tobacco control has emanated from the FTC, the FDA, or any other federal agency, reflecting the preferences of President Bush.

Political appointment, a power of the president shared with Congress (under the requirement that more than 1,100 of the top appointments of the president must be confirmed by the Senate), is among the most effective and frequently used tools employed by political leaders to control the activities of bureaucrats, not only to constrain them but also to empower them to act in a particular direction.[13] For example, President George W. Bush's appointments to the FCC were intended to point telecommunications further toward deregulation, a position consistent with that of his congressional party. His secretary of Health and Human Services, Tommy Thompson, did the bidding for the administration (and that of the tobacco industry) at the World Health Organization Framework Convention for Tobacco Control, muffling the voices of health advocates in the bureaucracy.

The judiciary provides yet another important check on bureaucratic discretion in America's system of separated powers. Recourse to the courts is one of the protections provided an individual or business that believes that an agency action has interfered with one's fundamental rights and liberties or simply that the agency has injured someone by mistakenly applying the law. The FDA's sails were, for example, trimmed twice in its efforts to control tobacco use. First, Judge William L. Osteen Sr. in federal district court in North Carolina ruled that the FDA's proposed restrictions on marketing and advertising violated the First Amendment right to free speech of the tobacco corporations. Although Judge Osteen determined that the FDA could regulate tobacco under current law, that ruling was overturned in 2000 by the Supreme Court, which decided on the most narrow of votes that the agency had overstepped its bounds.

The right to appeal an administrative decision to the courts is well established, although the extent to which a court will consent to fully substitute its judgment for that of an administrative agency is one of the most tangled areas in American jurisprudence. One of the reasons for this lack of clarity is that legal experience in administrative law is not as great as in other areas, which benefit from centuries of common law experience. In some respects, the functions of administrative agencies fall outside the traditions of and are incompatible with the common law, making it unclear precisely on what grounds agency actions can be overruled by the courts and which actions, if any, are excluded from review.[14] Generally, the courts are most interested in seeing that agency procedures do not infringe on an individual's fundamental rights and that agency decisions are based on a proper understanding of relevant statutes and judicial precedents. Here, the courts seek to determine if the agency has acted fairly, without caprice, and in a manner that is not arbitrary.[15] Guidelines for these procedures are found in the constitutional guarantees of due process as well as in the statutory law that speaks directly to questions of administrative process.[16]

The federal courts have been active in overseeing state and local bureaucracies to the degree that they intrude on constitutionally guaranteed rights. Decisions in landmark cases such as *Miranda v. State of Arizona* and *Brown v. Board of Education* are just two of many instances where the courts have impinged directly and dramatically on the operations of subnational bureaucracies.[17] Federal court rulings have affected federal agency activities of all kinds at the federal level as well, including the regulatory activities of the FTC. The 1972 decision of a U.S. district court prohibiting the FTC from requiring the display of octane ratings on gasoline pumps and stripping the commission of the rule-making power it had carefully nurtured into existence provides one good example of judicial oversight.[18] A U.S. court of appeals eventually reversed the lower-court decision, but critics of bureaucratic overreaching were allowed their day in court. Although they lost in the end, the FTC's detractors were able to call on the federal judiciary in their attempt to postpone the development of rule-making procedures at the commission.

Ultimately, whether the judiciary is called on to decide matters of substance or procedure, there should be no question about the important check on administrative power supplied by the federal court system. As Bernard Rosen has suggested,

> Knowing that the courts are there, knowing that an increasingly litigious citizenry—individuals and organizations—is prepared to go to court . . . strongly encourages administrators to be mindful of the intent of the law and the rights of individuals as they make policy and manage programs.[19]

Clearly, the separation of powers provides a set of powerful external checks on the policymaking discretion of administrative agencies. But if the norms of democratic decision making are to be adhered to, it is important that the internal operations of administrative agencies adhere to democratic principles. Citizens must be provided with the opportunity to participate in the formulation of policies that are every bit as binding on their lives as acts of legislatures. Elections expose legislators and presidents to public pressures, while administrative agencies are several steps removed from the electoral process and perhaps from responding to the public. Citizen participation and responsiveness to public interests must be built into the regulatory process to enhance the system's conformity with theories of representative government.

Techniques have been developed over the years to achieve fairness in administrative proceedings. The Administrative Procedure Act is the main repository for democratic guidelines for agency decision making. The *Federal Register* is another tool that adds a measure of democracy to the process by keeping interested parties informed of actions (both taken and proposed) by administrative agencies. The use of both independent administrative law judges and independent advisory committees can add democratic dimensions to agency policymaking routines as well. Making the administrative agencies accessible to private individuals and groups can also make the process more responsive to the wishes of the attentive public. All these mechanisms, however, can be exploited by interested parties if a wider public, subject-matter experts with no ax to grind, and public interest groups are not involved. Finally, to the degree that bureaucracies demographically reflect the characteristics and attitudes of the public at large, such reflective representation helps round out the forces that work collectively to bring the process and outcomes of agency policymaking more closely into line with the tenets of representative, democratic governance.

ADMINISTRATIVE PROCEDURE ACT: LEGISLATIVE AND JUDICIAL AUTHORITY OF AGENCIES

Demands to adopt court-like procedures for administrative agencies came from such quarters as the American Bar Association as early as the 1930s. The expansion of government activity during the New Deal sounded the alarm for many who were genuinely concerned about the infringement of fundamental rights that individuals might suffer at the hands of irresponsible bureaucrats. Others sought simply to curb the regulatory powers of government over business and industry.

In 1946, Congress passed the Administrative Procedure Act (APA), Public Law (P.L.) 79-404, which sets out procedures to be followed by agencies when they engage in rule making and adjudicatory proceedings.[20] The procedures mirror those used by courts, although they are not quite as formal or as carefully stated. Certain elements of congressional hearing procedures are also incorporated in the act. There are several exemptions from the requirements of the act in recognition of the fact that there are large numbers of issues before agencies that could not be effectively handled under these formal procedures.

If every policymaking action of an agency were to be treated as a judicial proceeding or a legislative hearing, the decision-making process would grind to a halt. So the first difficulty faced by those who wrote the APA was to decide which agency actions the act should cover. All military and foreign affairs functions were exempted from its requirements. Also exempted were "any matters relating to agency management or personnel or public property, loans, grants, benefits, or contracts." Framers of the act then went on to differentiate between rule-making, or quasi-legislative, functions and the adjudicatory functions of agencies. The most formal procedures in the act apply to all adjudicatory functions but to only some agency rule-making functions. There also is a distinction made in the act between formal and informal rule making.

In informal rule making, only some of the required adjudicatory procedures are employed; for example, hearings are conducted, a public record is kept, and certain rules of evidence are followed. However, the most important difference between formal and informal processes is that in the former a public hearing is required, and in the latter the decision as to whether to hold a hearing is left up to the agency. How does an agency know when it must hold a public hearing? A hearing is required only when the legislation under which the agency operates requires it. There are only a few statutes that require formal hearings for all rule making; in fact, none of the eleven major acts that the FTC administers requires hearings in rule making. When agencies are not required by legislation to hold a hearing, the rule-making section of the APA is followed only if the agency decides it should be followed.[21]

In formal rule making, the APA requires that a public notice of rule making be given, including (1) a statement of time, place, and nature of the proceedings (also giving details of plans for a hearing if one is to be held); (2) reference to the authority under which the rule is proposed; and (3) the terms and substance of the proposed rule. The APA goes on to say that those affected by a proposed rule must be given time to respond in writing. Thirty days' notice has to be given before a rule becomes effective, and interested persons have the right to petition for amendment or repeal.

Frequently, agencies elect to use formal rule-making procedures even when they are not required to, particularly when the proposed rule will affect large numbers of groups or individuals. There are several reasons for favoring the formal process, not the least of which is the practical matter of enlisting support for the rule. If those affected by a rule participate in its formulation, chances are they will better understand its provisions and the rationale behind it. This is no guarantee of support for the measure, but the rule that emerges from the more formal process should be easier to enforce than one made behind the closed doors of a bureau chief's office.

The FTC, the FCC, and the FDA all followed procedures to ensure public participation in their rule making regarding the tobacco industry. The FTC commissioners, for example, never seriously considered adopting cigarette labeling and advertising regulations without holding formal hearings because they sensed how controversial the issue would be. They knew that if they adopted the rule without hearings, the cigarette manufacturers could seize on the secretiveness of their action to argue that the FTC was undemocratic, arbitrary, and dangerous. To protect itself from such accusations—and with genuine interest in determining if anyone had sound arguments for rejecting their proposed rule—the commission set in motion the procedural machinery described in the APA for formal rule making, thereby making both the regulatory process and the end result of those deliberations more democratic.

ADMINISTRATIVE LAW JUDGES

The use of quasi-judicial agents—administrative law judges—is another internal dimension of the bureaucratic policy process that was established under the APA and that has the potential for enhancing the democratic character of that process.[22] All the regulatory commissions and several other agencies have assigned to them contingents of highly specialized individuals to serve in this capacity.

To ensure the more detached, judicial demeanor of these examiners, the APA requires that they behave according to the canons of judicial behavior. They cannot, for example, consult any party to the case outside the hearings over which they preside (*ex parte* communication) unless all parties participate in the consultation. And like their counterparts in the courts, administrative law judges are expected to refrain from discussing their cases with anyone outside the hearing room. The APA also requires that all communications with the judge during a hearing be made part of the public record. Furthermore, the judge is prohibited from participating in any of the agency's investigatory activities related to the development of a case he or she might hear. A judge first learns of a case and its details when the public hearing is scheduled. To prevent administrative law judges from being too dependent on the agency in which they serve, the Office of Personnel Management supervises the corps of examiners and is responsible for the hiring, setting rates of pay, removal, and discipline of the growing cadre of examiners.

In their role of hearing adjudicatory cases, administrative law judges play an important, counterbalancing role in checking agency power. The 1986 decision of an administrative law judge in the MR FIT (Multiple Risk Factor Intervention Trial) case brought by the FTC against R.J. Reynolds is a good example. The FTC argued that R.J. Reynolds had twisted and exaggerated the results of the MR FIT study in an advertising campaign designed to cast doubt on the scientific evidence about the hazards of smoking. But the administrative law judge hearing the case ruled that the advertisement was an editorial statement fully protected by the free speech guarantees of the First Amendment. The FTC appealed for another hearing (to no immediate avail) but later backed off when, in October 1989, it convinced R.J. Reynolds to sign a consent order that forbade further references to MR FIT in its advertising. In the end, the FTC got its way, but not for two years and only after negotiating a settlement with R.J. Reynolds. The FTC was prohibited, on First Amendment grounds, from acting capriciously by one of many administrative law judges who play an important role in a system of internal checks and balances on agency power.[23]

WRITTEN RECORDS

One other significant addition to the APA is the Freedom of Information Act (FOIA) signed by President Lyndon Johnson in 1966 and amended and incorporated into the legal code as part of the APA in 1974. The FOIA gives all persons the right to ask for and receive government documents that they describe in writing unless there is a specific exemption that permits the agency to refuse (e.g., for reasons of individual privacy or national security). In announcing its guidelines for enforcing the act, the attorney general said, "If government is to be truly of, by, and for the people, the people must know in detail the activities of government. Nothing so diminishes democracy as secrecy."[24] With the increasing practice of contracting out government activities to private entities and of shifting toward classifying documents as secret, however, the scope of the FOIA is more constricted than in the past.

The idea that democratic principles could be advanced by openness in government was not a new one in the 1960s. Rather, the creation of written, publicly accessible records of agency activities has been a central democratic component of agency decision making in the United States at least since 1936, when the *Federal Register* came into existence. This publication brought some order to administrative chaos that existed before its conception. Prior to that, there was no single published document containing the official actions of agencies and no effective way for the government to communicate with its constituents about the actions taken by administrators. Nor was there any way for various segments of the public and private sectors to know what decisions agencies were making or how those decisions changed the law. As the quantity of administrative decisions grew, it became literally impossible for the left hand of the bureaucracy to know what the right hand was doing. The resultant disorder was bad not only for administrative effectiveness but also for citizens, who had little access to information about what their government was up to.

The need for an official publication containing administrative actions came forcefully to the attention of the public in 1935 in an important and critical Supreme Court decision.[25] The Court, in striking down the National Recovery Act, noted that enforcement officials of the administration, industrialists, and the lower courts had not been informed that certain administrative regulations promulgated under the act had been revoked. Some of the worst fears of the legal community were confirmed in this case of ill use of administrative policymaking powers. This failure of administration prompted

Congress to pass the Federal Register Act in 1935, the same year the Court handed down its decision.

The Federal Register Act requires that all documents having general applicability and legal effect must be published in the *Federal Register*.[26] This requirement includes such items as general statements of agency powers and procedures and copies of the forms it uses for applications and other purposes. The APA spells out in detail those actions of agencies that must be published. It states, for example, that notice of proposed rule making shall be published in the *Register*. Accordingly, the FTC published in the *Register* a notice of rule-making proceedings in 1964 indicating its intention to establish trade regulation rules for the advertising and labeling of cigarettes. The notice contained a draft of the proposed rule, an explanation of the legal authority on which the action was to be taken, and the dates for hearings before the commission. The public was also informed in the notice that they could file written data, views, or arguments concerning the rule or the subject of the proceeding in general.

Most agencies make it a practice not to rely exclusively on the *Federal Register* for dissemination of information concerning its rule-making proposals. Common practices are to solicit opinions directly from interested parties and to issue press releases. With the advent of the widespread use of the Web, announcements are made online and responses easily sent to agencies electronically. Even before Internet use, by the time the hearings began for the FTC labeling rules on cigarette packages, the draft of the rule had been at least as widely circulated and commented as if Congress itself had proposed legislation. Similarly, the FDA rule and supporting documentation on regulating tobacco was publicized not only by the agency but also by those groups heartily opposed to it. The FDA materials were incorporated in court cases being brought by private litigants and by the state attorneys general. So successful was the dissemination that the FDA elicited literally hundreds of thousands of responses to the rule that were then reviewed by the agency before a final rule was issued.[27]

Clearly, the two-way flow of information generated in these cases opened up the political process and possibly helped allay what some have described as the "deep-seated suspicions that now surrounds non-elective bureaucracies in a representative U.S. system."[28] The wide circulation of draft rules and gathering of information added a democratic flavor to a decision-making process that otherwise could easily be viewed as elitist and maybe even autocratic, a charge frequently heard from the tobacco industry.[29]

ADVISORY COMMITTEES

With the increasing participation of the bureaucracy in policymaking, advisory committees (or advisory councils as they are sometimes called) provide one way of keeping bureaucrats in tune with public opinion and with experts in the field. This, in turn, has the potential of making the regulatory process more democratic than it might otherwise be. In theory, the thousand or so advisory committees made up of private citizens now active in federal government make it possible for individuals outside the bureaucracy to have an impact on the direction and substance of agency policymaking. Advisory committees are guided by Federal Advisory Committee Act (P.L. 92-463) of 1972, a law that speaks to the conduct and membership issues that have been raised over the years.[30] In 1987, the General Services Administration, the agency charged with responsibility for implementing the provisions of the 1972 act, published new proposed regulations to tighten even further committee management at the agency level.

In reality, the quality and usefulness of advisory committees has varied greatly over the years. Because of the particularized activities of agencies, membership on advisory committees tends to be limited to those who have some specialized knowledge, experience, or expertise. Often, those who find their way to an advisory committee owe allegiance to—or are somehow beholden to—the very groups the host agency is supposed to be regulating in the public interest. The rush to select individuals who have special knowledge or an industry bias makes it difficult for true outsiders (e.g., those who might represent a nonspecialized, broader perspective) to gain an appointment to an advisory committee so that they may be in a position to have an influence on policymaking. This leaves many observers of the administrative process skeptical of the value of advisory committees as vehicles for public interest representation.[31]

The Advisory Committee on Smoking and Health, appointed by Surgeon General Luther Terry in 1962 to report on the health effects of cigarette smoking, is an example of an advisory committee being used constructively to check the power of economic and bureaucratic elites in the tobacco subsystem who conspired to rig or derail the regulatory process for their own private interest. As such, this advisory committee played a significant role in the policy process. This group had a significant impact largely because its members, all of whom had impressive academic and scientific credentials, were highly regarded and also because its final report was neatly packaged and presented. Clearly, dissemination of this report proved to be a turning point in the debate about whether the sale and advertising of tobacco products should be regulated.

A similarly constructed and respected advisory committee, operating under the aegis of the EPA, was created in the late 1980s to assess the data on the health hazards of environmental (secondhand) tobacco smoke. The credibility and ultimately the impact of the final report issued by this group were bolstered by the perceived neutrality of the group's members. (Some even criticized EPA Director William Reilly for selecting members who were too closely aligned with the tobacco industry.) The findings of this committee in 1986 provided ammunition to the seven flight attendants who shortly thereafter filed a class-action suit against six major tobacco companies for the increased risk of disease the attendants claimed to have suffered from years of exposure to secondhand smoke. The report also helped set the stage for the Occupational Safety and Health Administration to begin considering secondhand smoke as a workplace safety hazard. The report of the EPA's advisory committee also added impetus in the Congress to consider regulations proposed under Carol Browner's leadership in 1994 that would effectively ban smoking in nearly every building in the country that is regularly entered by the public.

The power and propriety of advisory groups still depends on the degree of enthusiasm bureaucrats and their superiors have for creating balanced, impartial groups (to the degree that is possible) and following their advice. Meanwhile, where the departmental ethos is one of close cooperation with the groups that the department supposedly regulates, abuses will continue. Ultimately, advisory committees will succeed in checking the power of economic and bureaucratic elites in favor of larger public interests only when agencies make a determined effort to include within their structure individuals who have had, currently have, or will have no personal stake in the outcome of the regulatory process.

A sometimes ignored oversight activity has been established by law in most federal and many state agencies. The Office of the Inspector General was formalized in most federal agencies in 1978. The bureaucrats who occupy these government positions are independent of agency personnel and report directly to agency heads and Congress. The 1978 act spells out these among related functions for the inspectors general:

- Conduct and supervise independent and objective audits and investigations relating to agency programs and operations.
- Promote economy, effectiveness, and efficiency within the agency.
- Prevent and detect fraud, waste, and abuse in agency programs and operations.
- Keep the agency head and Congress fully and currently informed of problems in agency programs and operations.[32]

As agency policymaking powers have grown, so has the influence and importance of the inspectors general. Their activities provide a check on bureaucratic power that is not included in the Constitution.

ACCESSIBILITY

Responsiveness to complaints of individual citizens is another measure of democratic governance on which the bureaucracy has the potential (and, in some cases, the track record) for scoring well.[33] To be sure, members of Congress have become increasingly attentive to the pleas of individual citizens and have worked hard to respond to the personal complaints of their constituents, such as by setting up district offices and hiring staff members. Casework responsiveness is not the same as policy responsiveness, however. When it comes to policymaking, Congress is notoriously sensitive to the will of groups who are well organized, well connected, and well financed even when the interests of those groups run counter to the opinions of a wide, enduring majority of the general public. A premier example is that of gun control. Another is health care. The fact that the United States is the only Western democracy in the world without a national health care plan— despite strong and enduring support for the rudiments of such a plan—is often attributed to the strength of the insurance industry and various provider interest groups who oppose national health care provision because they would stand to suffer financially under such reforms. Members of Congress may be elected by majorities of voters, but time and again members have demonstrated sympathy for minority policy positions advanced by relatively small groups who have the financial resources to make their voices count in the legislative policymaking process.

Likewise, while many citizens might prefer tough controls on tobacco, they are not organized enough to counterbalance the influence of tobacco interests in the halls of Congress. For those private individuals and groups who are interested in having an impact on the policymaking process here and on other issues, the bureaucracy provides an alternative route to influence. John Banzhaf, a policy entrepreneur of the first order, is one individual whose experience serves as testament to the responsiveness of bureaucracies. Banzhaf, a New York City lawyer in private practice, filed a petition with the FCC, a move analogous to filing a complaint in the court system, in that the adjudicating body is more insulated from interest group pressures than is Congress. Ultimately, Banzhaf's complaint led to the FCC ruling in 1967 that applied the fairness doctrine to cigarette advertising.[34] The cigarette manufacturers appealed the decision of the FCC to the U.S. Court of Appeals for the District of Columbia, but despite the political and economic advantages enjoyed by the industry, Banzhaf prevailed, and the political weight of economically powerful groups was neutralized.[35]

Thereafter, Banzhaf and his nonprofit organization, Action on Smoking and Health (ASH), were directly involved in three other antismoking decisions made by various federal agencies: the Federal Aviation Administration's (FAA's) decision to limit smoking on domestic airline flights (1973) and the Interstate Commerce Commission's (ICC's) rules to limit smoking on buses (1974) and on trains (1976). Banzhaf's efforts were also instrumental in the FDA decision to include antismoking health warnings on all birth control devices.[36] According to Banzhaf, ASH focused its energies on regulatory agencies like the FCC, the ICC, the FAA, and the FDA precisely because they were more democratic in the classical sense; that is, they were more responsive to the will of individuals. In Banzhaf's words, "We pick very carefully areas where they [the tobacco interests] cannot use their muscle, more precisely where the outcome doesn't depend solely on muscle."[37]

Even groups with no resources at all can find a way to make their cases before regulatory agencies thanks to the advent of "intervener funding." During the 1970s, a number of federal agencies, including the FTC, began providing resources to cash-poor citizens' groups so that those groups could meet the expenses of participating in the regulatory process.[38] Intervener funding is designed to redress somewhat the advocacy and information imbalance in public hearings previously dominated by regulated industries. In addition, many other agencies that do not contribute funds directly to private organizations have, according to the U.S. comptroller general, "inherent authority to use appropriated funds to pay reasonable fees of attorneys and expert witnesses and other costs of needy interveners . . . provided their participation could 'reasonably be expected to contribute substantially to a fair and full determination.'"[39]

It has been said that the court serves as the "great equalizer": the counterbalance to the power of economically powerful factions in the democracy. Maybe the same could be said for the bureaucracy, at least in the case of smoking and politics, where economically strong and politically well-connected supporters of the status quo, members of the tobacco subsystem, have seen their clout erode substantially over time, thanks in part to the participation of private, public interest–minded interveners in the regulatory process.

THE POLICYMAKING ROLE OF BUREAUCRACIES RECONSIDERED

There are numerous ways to check agency power at the national level of government. Individually, each of the checks on bureaucratic power is inadequate in one way or another. But bureaucrats typically face many of these checks simultaneously; the degree of freedom to make policy enjoyed by an agency is always limited to one degree or another. Autonomy may ebb and flow with time, but it is rarely if ever absolute or uncontrolled.

As a result, capricious or arbitrary action is not as serious a problem in national government as it may be in state or local governments, where political institutions are often too weak or disorganized to challenge the bureaucracy.[40] The problem in Washington is more often one of persuading the bureaucracy to act when its members know from experience that doing as little as possible is the safest and easiest course. Hardening of administrative arteries can be more serious in the long run than agency aggressiveness. Ironically, an abundance of safeguards does not guarantee responsive government because their ready availability can make it easier for small, special interest groups to stop proposed changes in policy.

It is important to put the role played by American bureaucracies into comparative context. The situation in France is illustrative. As Robert A. Kagan and David Vogel point out, "French political culture and tradition endorses strong control of government over business, with policy making by elite educated bureaucrats who are relatively insulated from political pressure groups."[41] Indeed, bureaucrats play a lead role in formulating policy in France and many other Western democracies where parliamentary systems operate and where, once the executive branch endorses the proposed course of action, legislative approval is essentially pro forma. Such countries have well-developed traditions of public authority and political structures that are less sensitive to the interests of the business community.

In the United States, the political culture is more classically liberal and individualistic, less statist and communalistic. As a result, government in America is, *de facto*, more sensitive to the interests of economically powerful groups. All this is to suggest that whatever the bureaucracy has accomplished in the United States, its clout is relatively limited when compared to what bureaucracies in other Western countries have accomplished and are capable of accomplishing.[42] Certainly, bureaucratic accomplishments in America in the area of regulating tobacco seem puny when compared to the magnitude of the problem, with related health care and lost productivity costs totaling $150 billion annually and with 1,200 Americans dying each day as a result of smoking-related diseases. The public knows these facts not because the industry reports them but because the bureaucracy does, in this case the Centers for Disease Prevention and Control, which maintains an active, authoritative office on smoking and health. Its up-to-date Web site distributes new research findings instantaneously, thus influencing policy not only in the United States but throughout the world regardless of the desires of a particular administration.

At times, agencies may fail to make positive contributions to larger public interests because they respond only to the small, powerful interest groups on which they may depend for their political strength. At the same time, the existence of discretionary authority in the bureaucracy does make it possible for agencies—working together with sympathetic members of Congress and with advocates outside of government—to break the grip of economically and politically powerful interests on the policymaking process. The time, money, and energy required to gain government acceptance of the cigarette health warning and the ultimate failure of the FDA to regulate tobacco illustrate well, however, a reality that will be reassuring for some and sobering for others: those who would challenge the status quo in American government make advances slowly, even with the assistance of agencies that enjoy a fair measure of policymaking authority.

NOTES

1. Davis A. Kessler, *A Question of Intent: A Great American Battle with a Deadly Industry* (New York: Public Affairs, 2001).
2. The political science literature is replete with examples of this argument. For the classic—and still one of the best—expositions on this theme, see Theodore J. Lowi, *The End of Liberalism: The Second Republic of the United States*, 2nd ed. (New York: Norton, 1979).

3. The classic argument about the supposed dichotomy between politics and administration was made by former president and political scientist Woodrow Wilson late in the nineteenth century and early in the twentieth by Frank J. Goodnow, one of the founders and the first president of the American Political Science Association. The position advanced by Wilson and Goodnow—that politics (policymaking) and administration (the neutral implementation of policy) could be and were separate—became the public administration orthodoxy in the twentieth century as a stream of scholars reiterated this normative claim and attempted to support it empirically. See Woodrow Wilson, "The Study of Administration" (1887), and Frank J. Goodnow, "Politics and Administration," both reprinted in Jay M. Shafritz and Albert C. Hyde, eds., *Classics of Public Administration*, 2nd ed. (Chicago: Dorsey Press, 1987).

4. Elizabeth B. Drew, quoted in Kenneth Michael Friedman, *Public Policy and the Smoking-Health Controversy* (Lexington, Mass.: Lexington Books, 1975), 59.

5. Kenneth Michael Friedman, *Public Policy and the Smoking Health Controversy: A Comparative Study* (Lexington, Mass.: Lexington Books, 1975), 154–55.

6. Peter Woll, *American Bureaucracy*, 2nd ed. (New York: Norton, 1977), 248–49.

7. Helen Dewar, "Congress Doing Battle with a Monster of Its Own Creation," *Washington Post*, October 21, 1979, A6.

8. Kessler, *A Question of Intent.*

9. Quoted in Friedman, *Public Policy and the Smoking Health Controversy*, 43.

10. Dan B. Wood and Richard W. Waterman, "The Dynamics of Political Control of the Bureaucracy," *American Political Science Review* 85 (September 1991): 808–9.

11. "Federal Trade Commission Dismisses Joe Camel Complaint," FTC press release (January 27, 1999), available at http://www.ftc.gov/opa/1999/01/joeorder.htm.

12. R.J. Reynolds Tobacco Company agreed to settle FTC charges that its ads for Winston "no additives" cigarettes are deceptive. The agency alleged that Reynolds implied in its advertisements, without a reasonable basis, that Winston cigarettes are safer to smoke because they contain no additives. Under the settlement, which the FTC has accepted for public comment, Reynolds agreed to make the following prominent disclosure in future Winston ads: "No additives in our tobacco does NOT mean a safer cigarette" (FTC press release [March 3, 1999], available at http://www.ftc.gov/opa/1999/03/winston.htm).

13. James P. Pfiffner, *The Modern Presidency*, 4th ed. (Belmont, Calif.: Wadsworth, 2005), 133–27; Wood and Waterman, "The Dynamics of Political Control of the Bureaucracy," 822.

14. In some agency actions, statutes prohibit or limit court review. The Federal Trade Commission Act, for example, contains one of the common statutory limits on judicial review of administrative actions: "The findings of the Commission as to the facts, if supported by the evidence, shall be conclusive." This section of the commission's act indicates one area of law where agencies and the courts have come to some agreement on the subject of review, at least at a high level of generalization.

15. For this reason, adjudicatory proceedings of agencies are subject to closer judicial scrutiny than rule making. Agency rule-making procedures can be as lax as those of congressional committees; as such, there are far fewer grounds on which an agency rule might be appealed to the courts.

16. The Administrative Procedure Act of 1946 is an example of a general statute that guides the regulatory process, while the Public Health Cigarette Smoking Act of 1969 represents a statute that specifically prescribes certain agency procedures. The 1969 act requires that the FTC give six months' warning of any intentions to initiate rule-making procedures that would affect the tobacco industry.

17. In *Miranda*—a decision binding on local, state, and federal law enforcement officials—the Supreme Court held that confessions of an individual charged with a crime were not admissible if the charged individual was not first advised of his or her rights to remain silent. See 87 S. Ct. 11(1968). In *Brown*, the Supreme Court ruled that separate schooling for children of different races was inherently unequal and mandated that public schools at all levels of government be integrated with "all deliberate speed." See 347 U.S. 483 (1954).

18. *National Petroleum Refiners Association v. Federal Trade Commission*, 482 F. 2d 672 (D.C. Cir. 1973), reversing 340 F. Supp. 1343 (D D.C. 1972). cert. denied 415 U.S. 951 (1974).

19. Bernard Rosen, *Holding Government Bureaucracies Accountable*, 3rd ed. (New York: Praeger, 1998), 133–134.

20. 60 Stat. 237 (1946). In 1966, the act was incorporated in Title 5 of the *United States Code*. The *Code* is supplemented annually and revised every six years.

21. The rule-making section of the APA states that requirements for notice and hearing need not be followed "in any situation in which the agency for good cause finds . . . that notice and public procedure . . . are impracticable, unnecessary, or contrary to the public interest." The courts may declare invalid any rule made if an agency acted arbitrarily or capriciously in failing to give notice of rule making and/or failing to hold hearings.

22. On August 19, 1972, an executive order eliminated the title "hearing examiner" and created the title "administrative law judge" (37 *Federal Register* 162 [August 19, 1972]). The change had been sought for many years by the hearing examiners' association, the Federal Trial Examiners Conference (now called the Administrative Law Judges Conference).

23. Judges are also subject to their own internal set of checks. The qualifications for appointment are quite rigorous. In addition to being a member of the bar, one must have had at least seven years of experience in preparation and presentation of cases in courts or before administrative agencies. A board of examiners within the Office of Personnel Management evaluates the written materials and recommendations of applicants and administers oral examinations. As such, administrative law judges are considered to be a select, prestigious group fully capable of playing the role assigned them in the regulatory process.

24. Bernard Rosen, *Holding Government Bureaucracies Accountable*, 112.

25. *Panama Refining Company v. Ryan*, 293 U.S. 388 (1935).

26. The Office of the Federal Register, a part of the National Archives, publishes the *Register* daily, Monday through Friday. Thousands of copies are distributed to courts, executive agencies, and members of Congress. Copies are available by subscription or can be found on the Web.

27. Kessler, *A Question of Intent*, 353.

28. Wood and Waterman, "The Dynamics of Political Control of the Bureaucracy," 824.

29. In addition to the requirements of the FOIA and the *Federal Register*, regulatory commissions such as the FTC also are guided by a sunshine law, approved by Congress in 1976. This law prohibits private communications between commission members and parties affected by commission decisions. It also requires that top officials open their meetings to the public unless agency officials vote to close a particular meeting for a reason (e.g., individual right to privacy or national security) permitted by law. Even when meetings are closed, agencies are required to keep a verbatim transcript so that the decision to close the meeting can be challenged in court on its merits. The burden of proof in these cases falls on the agency, and any parts of the transcript found by a federal court not to meet the exemption standards set out by the sunshine law are then released to the public.

30. The law stipulates, generally, that all committees should be strictly advisory. More specifically, the following rules of committee operations are also charted: (1) any committee whose duration is not fixed by law must terminate its activities no more than two years after it is established, (2) all meetings have to be called by a government employee, (3) the agency retains the right to draft the agenda, (4) all meetings are open to the public, and (5) meetings must be conducted by an agency employee who is empowered to adjourn the meeting whenever he or she determines that adjournment would be in the public interest.

31. Avery Leiserson, in *Administrative Regulation: A Study in Representation of Interests* (Chicago: University of Chicago Press, 1942), discusses the history and early use of advisory councils in bureaucracies. For a more recent discussion of the role played by advisory committees in participative decision making, see James W. Fesler and Donald F. Kettl, *The Politics of the Administrative Process* (Chatham, N.J.: Chatham House, 1991), 192–93.

32. *U.S. Code*, Title 5, 1978, Inspector General Act.

33. See Charles T. Goodsell, *The Case for Bureaucracy: A Public Administration Polemic*, 3rd ed. (Chatham, N.J.: Chatham House, 1994), chap. 2.

34. In the FCC's words, "The licensee . . . is presenting commercials using the consumption of a product whose normal use has been found by the Congress and the Government to represent a serious potential hazard to public health. . . . This obligation to inform the public of the other side of the matter stems not from any esoteric requirements of a particular doctrine but from the simple fact that the public interest means nothing if it does not include such a responsibility" (U.S. Federal Communications Commission, Memorandum Opinion and Order in the Matter of Television Station WCBS-TV, New York, N.Y.: Applicability of the Fairness Doctrine to Cigarette Advertising, Washington, D.C., 1967, 42, 43; quoted in Friedman, *Public Policy and the Smoking Health Controversy*, 50).

35. *John H. Banzhaf III v. Federal Communications Commission*, 405 F. 2d 1082 (1968).

36. Ronald J. Troyer and Gerald E. Markle, *Cigarettes: The Battle over Smoking* (New Brunswick, N.J.: Rutgers University Press, 1983), 85.
37. Banzhaf estimates that the Tobacco Institute alone spent $4.5 million in 1978, compared to ASH revenues in that year, which totaled less than $300,000, one-fifteenth the Tobacco Institute total (Troyer and Markle, *Cigarettes*, 83, 100, 105). This helps explain why ASH activities were directed almost exclusively toward influencing regulatory agencies. From its inception in 1967 through 1979, ASH had filed over 150 complaints with regulatory agencies and provided input (testimony, briefs, petitions and soon) in forty-five other cases. Meanwhile, less than a dozen contacts between ASH and the legislative branch could be documented (Troyer and Markle, *Cigarettes*, 85).
38. Other agencies involved in the provision of intervener funding include the EPA, the National Highway Transportation Safety Administration, and the Department of Energy (Rosen, *Holding Government Bureaucracies Accountable*, 93).
39. Comptroller General of the United States, B-139703, December 1976, quoted in Rosen, *Holding Government Bureaucracies Accountable*, 93. This decision has an effect similar in type to the Equal Access to Justice Act, which requires federal agencies to pay the legal expenses of needy individuals (net worth under $1 million), businesses (net worth under $5 million), and nonprofit organizations (regardless of financial status) bringing suit against agencies in federal court (Rosen, *Holding Government Bureaucracies Accountable*, 118).
40. For example, some state legislatures are poorly organized, relatively weak institutions whose members serve for little compensation and with almost no staff support only a few months every other year. These kinds of institutions can hardly be expected to provide the sort of check on bureaucratic policymaking at the state level that the U.S. Congress exerts on the federal agencies.
41. Robert A. Kagan and David Vogel, "The Politics of Smoking Regulation: Canada, France, and the United States," in *Smoking Policy: Law, Politics, and Culture*, ed. Robert L. Rabin and Stephen D. Sugarman (New York: Oxford University Press, 1993), 34.
42. This is certainly true at least with regard to levels of tobacco taxes and control of cigarette advertising, both of which are minimal compared to taxes and controls in Canada and France, for example (Kagan and Vogel, "The Politics of Smoking Regulation," 44–45).

INDEX